A CULTURAL HISTORY OF FAIRY TALES

VOLUME 6

A Cultural History of Fairy Tales
General Editor: Anne E. Duggan

Volume 1
A Cultural History of Fairy Tales in Antiquity
Edited by Debbie Felton

Volume 2
A Cultural History of Fairy Tales in the Middle Ages
Edited by Susan Aronstein

Volume 3
A Cultural History of Fairy Tales in the Age of the Marvelous
Edited by Suzanne Magnanini

Volume 4
A Cultural History of Fairy Tales in the Long Eighteenth Century
Edited by Anne E. Duggan

Volume 5
A Cultural History of Fairy Tales in the Long Nineteenth Century
Edited by Naomi J. Wood

Volume 6
A Cultural History of Fairy Tales in the Modern Age
Edited by Andrew Teverson

A CULTURAL HISTORY OF FAIRY TALES

IN THE MODERN AGE

VOLUME 6

Edited by Andrew Teverson

BLOOMSBURY ACADEMIC
LONDON • NEW YORK • OXFORD • NEW DELHI • SYDNEY

BLOOMSBURY ACADEMIC
Bloomsbury Publishing Plc, 50 Bedford Square, London, WC1B 3DP, UK
Bloomsbury Publishing Inc, 1359 Broadway, New York, NY 10018, USA
Bloomsbury Publishing Ireland, 29 Earlsfort Terrace, Dublin 2, D02 AY28, Ireland

BLOOMSBURY, BLOOMSBURY ACADEMIC and the Diana logo
are trademarks of Bloomsbury Publishing Plc

First published in Great Britain 2021
Paperback edition published 2025

Copyright © Andrew Teverson, 2021

Andrew Teverson and Contributors have asserted their right under the Copyright, Designs and Patents Act, 1988, to be identified as Author of this work.

Series design by Raven Design
Cover image: Enchanted Forest © oversnap/ Getty Images

All rights reserved. No part of this publication may be: i) reproduced or transmitted in any form, electronic or mechanical, including photocopying, recording or by means of any information storage or retrieval system without prior permission in writing from the publishers; or ii) used or reproduced in any way for the training, development or operation of artificial intelligence (AI) technologies, including generative AI technologies. The rights holders expressly reserve this publication from the text and data mining exception as per Article 4(3) of the Digital Single Market Directive (EU) 2019/790.

Bloomsbury Publishing Plc does not have any control over, or responsibility for, any third-party websites referred to or in this book. All internet addresses given in this book were correct at the time of going to press. The author and publisher regret any inconvenience caused if addresses have changed or sites have ceased to exist, but can accept no responsibility for any such changes.

A catalogue record for this book is available from the British Library.

A catalog record for this book is available from the Library of Congress.

ISBN:	HB:	978-1-3500-9571-7
	PB:	978-1-3505-9415-9
	ePDF:	978-1-3502-8760-0
	eBook:	978-1-3502-8759-4
	Set:	978-1-3505-9409-8

Series: A Cultural History of Fairy Tales

Typeset by Integra Software Services Pvt. Ltd.
Printed and bound in Great Britain

For product safety related questions contact productsafety@bloomsbury.com.

To find out more about our authors and books visit www.bloomsbury.com and sign up for our newsletters.

CONTENTS

LIST OF ILLUSTRATIONS	vii
SERIES PREFACE	ix
Introduction: Fairy Tale in the Modern Age *Andrew Teverson*	1
1 Forms of the Marvelous *Sara Cleto and Brittany Warman*	27
2 Adaptation *Mayako Murai*	43
3 Gender and Sexuality *Jeana Jorgensen*	69
4 Humans and Non-Humans: Nature, Anima, Matter *Amy Greenhough*	91
5 Monsters and the Monstrous *Christa Jones and Claudia Schwabe*	113
6 Space: The Magically Real Spaces of Twentieth- and Twenty-First-Century Fairy Tale *Sara Upstone*	137
7 Socialization: Traditional Wonder Tales and Other Guides for Growing Up *Jill Terry Rudy*	159

8 Power: The Archaeology of a Genre 181
    Kimberly J. Lau

NOTES 197
REFERENCES 200
NOTES ON CONTRIBUTORS 226
INDEX 229

ILLUSTRATIONS

0.1	Dina Goldstein, *Snowy*, 2008. Photograph, *Fallen Princesses* Series	8
0.2	Dina Goldstein, *Princess Pea*, 2009. Photograph, *Fallen Princesses* Series	8
0.3	Leonora Carrington, *Self-Portrait (Inn of the Dawn Horse)*, 1937–8	9
0.4	Dorothea Tanning, *Birthday*, 1942	10
0.5	Dorothea Tanning, *Pour Gustave l'adoré*, 1974	11
0.6	Gustave Doré, *Les Océanides (Naiades de la Mer)*, c. 1860	12
1.1	Illustration by W. W. Denslow for Frank L. Baum's *The Wonderful Wizard of Oz*	31
1.2	Film still, *Princess Tutu* (2002–3)	36
1.3	"Ashenputtel goes to the ball," illustration by Arthur Rackham from *The Fairy Tales of the Brothers Grimm* (1909)	40
2.1	Illustration by Leslie Brooke for *The House in the Wood and Other Fairy Stories* (1909)	56
2.2	Statue of the Bremen Town Musicians by Gerhard Marcks (1953)	57
2.3	Maurizio Cattelan, *Love Saves Life*, 1995. Taxidermied donkey, dog, cat, and rooster	59
2.4	Maurizio Cattelan, *Love Lasts Forever*, 1997. Donkey, dog, cat, and rooster skeletons	60

2.5	Art by Durga Bai for *The Old Animals' Forest Band*	64
2.6	Art by Durga Bai for *The Old Animals' Forest Band*	65
4.1	Tomoko Kōnoike, mixed media sculpture, *The Planet is Covered by Silvery Sleep*, 2006	92
4.2	Tomoko Kōnoike, mixed media sculpture, *Donning Animal Skins and Braided Grass*, 2013	92
5.1	Film still from Catherine Breillat's *Barbe bleue* (2009)	116
5.2	Film still from Guillermo del Toro's *The Shape of Water* (2017)	120
5.3	Film still from Guillermo del Toro's *Pan's Labyrinth* (2006)	121
5.4	Film still from *A Monster Calls* (2016), directed by J. A. Bayona	123
5.5	Film still from Bong Joon-ho's *Okja* (2017)	127
6.1	Map of Neverness by Isobel Simonds (2018), from *Folk* by Zoe Gilbert	149
7.1	Still from "Fearnot" (1987), an episode of Jim Henson's television series *The StoryTeller*	163
7.2	Still from "Little Red Riding Hood" (2011), television episode, Cartoonito's *Fairy Tales for Kids*	176
7.3	Still from television series *Raven Tales* (2006–)	179

SERIES PREFACE

Taking a transnational approach, *A Cultural History of Fairy Tales* seeks to deepen our appreciation for and knowledge about a type of *text* (understood in the broadest sense of the term) that is often taken for granted due to its association with children's literature, old wives' tales, and oral peasant culture. Whether we think of the Brothers Grimm or films by Walt Disney Studios, fairy tales are often viewed as naïve and timeless stories with universal appeal, which suggests they are ahistorical, innocent narratives. This series brings together scholars from a diversity of disciplines to challenge many of these preconceptions about the fairy tale, shedding light on its very complex cultural history.

The chapters included in these six volumes foreground how the fairy tale was deployed in different historical periods and geographical locations for all kinds of cultural, social, and political ends that cross categories of class, age, gender, and ethnicity. "Fairy tale" here serves as a broad umbrella term for what more generally could be referred to as "wonder tale," which encompasses but is not limited to texts that feature fairies, witches, enchanters, djinn, and other beings endowed with magical or supernatural powers; anthropomorphized animals; metamorphosis (humans transformed into animals or other objects and vice versa); magical objects; and otherworlds and liminal spaces. "Fairy tale" also refers to texts that may not include any of these qualities but have been received as—that is, read or categorized as or are generally considered to be—a fairy tale.

By moving from antiquity to the present and transnationally, chapters crossing the six volumes foreground, for instance, how ancient animal fables present both continuities and discontinuities with the representation of animals in later wonder tales; how conceptions of fairies, djinn, and other magical characters change across historical periods and geographical locations;

and how the very notion of what is marvelous, natural, or supernatural is understood differently across space and time. Chapters showcase the range of different types of characters and themes one can find in wonder tales as well as the multiple forms and functions tales can take. Together these volumes paint a broad picture of the ways in which different national tale traditions interact with and mutually influence each other, giving us a transnational and transhistorical understanding of the fairy tale. Indeed, readers will discover the rich, complex, and often ideologically charged cultural history of texts that can seem so familiar to us, which helps us understand them in new and exciting ways.

All six volumes cover the same eight themes for the reader to gain a sense of continuities and discontinuities between types of characters, narratives, and traditions over time. Readers will move from *forms* of the fairy tale and the ancillary genres that fed into it to the history of *adaptations*, revealing the ways in which tales are always already a blend of multiple local, regional, and national traditions. A genre often focusing on questions related to development and initiation into adulthood and sometimes (less than we might think) concluding with marriage, tales often feature the norms of *gender and sexuality* grounded in a particular culture. Through the prevalence of non-human characters and problematic human figures, the fairy tale allows for the exploration of the boundaries between *the human and the non-human*, as well as between what is considered normal and *monsters or the monstrous*. As a nonmimetic genre, generally speaking, the fairy tale also plays with the delimitations between real and imaginary *spaces*, opening up both utopic and dystopic possibilities. Tales have often been used in the processes of *socialization*, for both children and adults, men and women, articulating class, gender, and ethnic differences. As such, tales cannot be separated from questions of *power* and ideology.

This cultural history of the fairy tale is divided into the following historical periods:

> Volume 1: A Cultural History of Fairy Tales in Antiquity (500 BCE–800 CE)
>
> Volume 2: A Cultural History of Fairy Tales in the Middle Ages (800–1450)
>
> Volume 3: A Cultural History of Fairy Tales in the Age of the Marvelous (1450–1650)
>
> Volume 4: A Cultural History of Fairy Tales in the Long Eighteenth Century (1650–1800)
>
> Volume 5: A Cultural History of Fairy Tales in the Long Nineteenth Century (1800–1920)
>
> Volume 6: A Cultural History of Fairy Tales in the Modern Age (1920–2000+)

Readers will come away with a new and fresh understanding of the fairy tale, which indeed enhances our appreciation for a genre that has touched many of us since childhood. Far from being naïve, innocent, timeless texts, *A Cultural History of Fairy Tales* foregrounds the ways wonder tales are embedded in sophisticated social, cultural, political, and artistic practices across history, anchored in specific cultural contexts that shape their meaning as tales are adapted from one cultural and historical context to another.

Anne E. Duggan, *General Editor*

Introduction

Fairy Tale in the Modern Age

ANDREW TEVERSON

This volume begins in the 1920s—the period between the First and Second World War, associated, in the field of culture, with modernism, and with the imperative, in artistic and literary circles, to innovate and experiment with established genres and forms. In the genre of fairy tale, this modernity may be seen to assert itself in at least two dominant ways in the opening decades of the twentieth century. In the newly emergent field of film, pioneers of the medium, following the lead of the illusionist and cinematic innovator George Méliès (1861–1938), were seeking to make use of the new visual potentialities of cinema to retell and reformulate the magical narratives of earlier eras. The German cinematographer Lotte Reiniger's first experiments with silhouette animation fairy tales appeared during this period (*Cinderella* 1922, *Sleeping Beauty* 1922, *The Adventures of Prince Achmed* 1926), as did the early fairy tale adaptations of the American animator Walt Disney—notably, the seven short animated fairy tales that were made in 1922 by the "Laugh-O-Gram" studio. Simultaneously, in the field of literature, experimental young writers were turning increasingly to the narratives of tradition—primarily myths, but also folk and fairy tales—in T. S. Eliot's words, to find "a way of controlling, of ordering, of giving a shape and a significance to the immense panorama of futility and anarchy which is contemporary history" (1923: 483). James Joyce, in *Ulysses* ([1922] 1993), finds in the fairy-tale narratives of wandering and return, rise and fall, loss and recovery, paradigms for quotidian human experience, and in *Finnegans Wake* ([1939] 1992) he has recourse, repeatedly, to the nursery rhymes, folk and fairy tales that conjure the impression of multiple voices, speaking, whispering, exchanging stories, at dusk, evening, and in the novel's dreamlike nighttime settings. In the same period, as Ann

Martin (2006) has shown, Virginia Woolf and Djuna Barnes were making use of fairy-tale allusions and narrative patterns in their work, both as a means of negotiating an inherited Victorian tradition and of appropriating for their own uses an unstable narrative form concerned with themes of transformation, change, gender instability, and sexual desire. In Barnes's novel *Nightwood*, the image of the wolf as grandmother with Little Red Riding Hood in bed disrupts conventional gender roles and offers a powerful traditional precedent for the transvestitism of Barnes's gender fluid, cross-dressing character Doctor Matthew O'Connor ([1936] 2007: 71). Likewise, in *Mrs Dalloway* ([1925] 2019), Woolf's protagonist Clarissa Dalloway makes a subtle and highly personalized use of the story of "Sleeping Beauty," drawing upon it as a fiction that is concerned with patriarchal authority over women, but one that also allows her to position herself in more enabling ways. Clarissa, Martin observes, "is alternately the Princess who is asleep in her attic room, the Princess who awakens herself, the Princess who is awakened to her lesbian desire by another Prince-Princess, and the Queen who fights off the Prince" (2006: 88). In these modernist resituatings of fairy tales, Martin writes, modernist writers recognize "the layers of history" in the stories, but even as they invoke the influence of the past they simultaneously demonstrate "the potential of fairy tales as texts through which legacies—both social and literary—can be drawn upon and opened up to further uses" (79). This dual attitude is captured expressively in one of Matthew O'Connor's extraordinarily inventive monologues in *Nightwood*, in which he reflects upon the role played by fairy tales in conditioning gender identities:

> What is this love we have for the invert, boy or girl? It was they who were spoken of in every romance that we ever read. The girl lost, what is she but the Prince found? The Prince on the white horse that we have always been seeking. And the pretty lad who is a girl …. We were impaled in our childhood upon them as they rode through our primers, the sweetest lie of all, now come to be in boy or girl …. They go far back in our lost distance where what we never had stands waiting; it was inevitable that we should come upon them, for our miscalculated longing has created them. They are our answer to what our grandmothers were told love was, and what it never came to be; they, the living lie of our centuries.
>
> (Barnes [1936] 2007: 123–4)

Fairy tales, in O'Connor's account, are at once the "primers" of the past that convey to the children of the present a previous generation's conception of love, but they are simultaneously fictions that offer a durable image of gender instability that holds out the promise of reinvention of the self. "Matthew reads the tales twice," Martin writes, first by focusing on what his Victorian grandmothers were told love was, and second, by presenting a "miscalculated longing" for the "Prince on a white horse" that serves as a riposte and a response to nineteenth-century visions of gender and marriage (2006: 116).

The pervasive interest in the fairy tale, in evidence in the literature and visual culture of the period covered by this volume, is attributable in part to the massive expansion in availability of fairy-tale texts at the turn of the century. Joyce, Woolf, and Barnes had grown up with popular, curated collections of fairy tales such as Andrew Lang's enormously successful *Colored Fairy Books* (1889–1910)—collections which Ruth Bottigheimer has argued "codified fairy-tale narrative in the English language" for the twentieth century, and in the process provided "a mother lode" of the imagination "for many twentieth-century 'authors' of fairy tales for children" (2004: 159). Early twentieth-century readers also had access to an extensive and growing body of fairy-tale influenced literature, including Lang's own novels *The Gold of Fairnilee* (1888) and *Prince Prigio* (1889), Oscar Wilde's *The Happy Prince and Other Stories* (1888), the works of E. Nesbit, George MacDonald's reworked fairy tales, L. Frank Baum's *The Wonderful Wizard of Oz* (1900), and Rudyard Kipling's *Puck of Pook's Hill* (1907) and *Rewards and Fairies* (1910). At the same time, this generation of writers and artists was also encountering the fairy tale at a point when the genre was being extensively reconceptualized in the intellectual cultures of Europe and America. Lang's lifelong endeavor, in his journalism and scholarship, to demonstrate that fairy tales should not be regarded as frivolous and immoral but as fictions that "unobtrusively teach the true lessons of our wayfaring in a world of perplexities and obstructions" (1893: 714) had begun to gain widespread traction at the start of the twentieth century, and was being reinforced by simultaneous explorations of the significance of fairy tales in various fields. In psychoanalysis, Sigmund Freud and Carl Jung were stimulating speculation about the significance of fairy tales for our understanding of the human unconscious—arguments that would have a profound impact upon the thinking of scholars such as Joseph Campbell (1904–87), Bruno Bettelheim (1903–90), and Marie von Franz (1915–98). Simultaneously, fairy tales were also gaining increased significance as narratives associated with cultural identity and cultural revival—a phenomenon in evidence in the Celtic revival of the late nineteenth and early twentieth centuries, and in emerging anti-colonial movements in Asia, Africa, and the Americas. In a different vein, fairy tales were also being evaluated afresh by formalist and structuralist critics of the early twentieth century who saw in these common and oft-told stories a means of understanding and explicating the fundamental patterns of narrative. The fairy tale, for all these reasons, was not only widespread in the early decades of the twentieth century but also newly valued as a form of expression that could speak to readers in profound ways, about identity, politics, society, and art.

This new valuation of fairy tales is widely in evidence in critical writing on fairy tale by the mid-twentieth century. In a 1944 review of a revised edition of

Margaret Hunt's translation of the tales of the Brothers Grimm, for instance, the British poet and essayist W. H. Auden makes the striking assertion that the stories of Grimm are "among the few indispensable, common-property books upon which Western culture can be founded" and "rank next to the Bible in importance" (Auden 1944). For Auden, as a Marxist intellectual, this evaluation of fairy tales has an important social and political dimension. Reading fairy tales to children, he notes in a 1952 review of a new edition of the fairy tales of Grimm and Andersen, is a means by which parents can counteract "the encroachment of the power of the state" enacted through instrumentalized and constraining forms of education (Auden 1973: 199). "It is to be hoped," Auden writes, "that the publication of the tales of Grimm and Andersen in one inexpensive volume will be a step in the campaign to restore to parents the right and the duty to educate their children which, partly through their own fault, and partly through extraneous circumstances, they are in danger of losing for good" (199).

Another position from the political left is expressed by Walter Benjamin (1892–1940) in his influential essay of 1936, "The Storyteller: Reflections on the Work of Nikolai Leskov." For Benjamin, the value of fairy tales lies in their capacity to mediate traditional wisdom, and to express the cunning and high spirits of the oppressed and powerless—a mode of creative resistance that is in danger of being lost as storytelling is appropriated for the purposes of commercialized mass-reproduction. Likewise, Benjamin's contemporary, Ernst Bloch (1885–1977) in his essays "The Fairy Tale Moves on Its Own Time" (1930) and "Better Castles in the Sky at the Country Fair and Circus, in Fairy Tales and Colportage" (1954), presents fairy tales as fictions that are a product of a rebellious and resistant popular culture that "does not allow itself to be fooled by the present owners of paradise" (Bloch 1988: 169) and so is capable of arousing hopes for change that may become politically mobilizing. These important twentieth-century essays on fairy tales articulate and defend the value and continuing significance of storytelling in an age of urbanization, industrialization, the dissolution of communities, incipient globalization, the rise of fascism and war—in particular the Spanish Civil War (1936) and the Second World War (1939–45). In such turbulent contexts one might expect storytelling to fade into an afterthought. But Bloch, Benjamin, and Auden argue, on the contrary, for its continuing—and ever more pressing—relevance in a period of struggle. For Benjamin, storytelling mediates the ancestrally communicated "counsel" of the common people, and can therefore assist humankind in its imaginative struggle against dehumanizing systems of power imposed from above (1999: 101). For Bloch, the peasant protagonists of popular tales—figures such as "smart Hans"—provide instruction in the art of resisting intimidation by power. In the fairy tale, in Bloch's view, "the power of the giant is painted as a power with a hole in it through which the weak individual can crawl ... triumphantly" (1988: 170).

At the same time as these affirmative evaluations of the value of storytelling were being articulated, however, the fairy tale was simultaneously being exploited as a propaganda tool by authoritarian regimes. In Germany in the 1930s, Nazi folklorists co-opted the fairy tales of the Grimms as expressions of a pure Germanic heritage that connected Germany to an assumed Nordic, Aryan past, transforming the stories into propaganda tools that could assist in the process of developing a "new racial consciousness and a positive attitude towards life under National Socialism" (Kamenetsky 1984: 71). Suitably edited and expurgated, the stories became a tool for embedding attitudes seen as desirable in Hitler's Germany—the notion that (as one Nazi approved anthology has it) "The Stronger One Always Wins," that the weak are to be overcome, that forceful leadership is to be celebrated, and that racial others are a threat to family, community, and nation (72).

Following the war, these Fascist applications of fairy tales led some scholars to conclude that Grimms' tales bore some of the responsibility for the susceptibility of German youth to Nazi policies. The German Jewish scholar, Louis Snyder, in his 1951 article "Nationalistic Aspects of the Grimm Brothers' Fairy Tales," argued that the pervasive depictions of cruelty in the tales, their frequent expressions of anti-Semitism and their apparent endorsement of hierarchical social structures and hero cults identified them as protofascist fictions that had helped prepare the cultural ground for the rise of Nazism in Germany. In Snyder's words, the Grimms' concern to "glorify German traditions and ... stimulate German national sentiment" together with the tendency of their stories to emphasize "such social characteristics as respect for order, belief in the desirability of obedience, subservience to authority [and] ... acceptance without protest of cruelty, violence, and atrocity" place the tales in the vanguard of extreme right-wing nationalism (Snyder 1951: 222).

Responding to Snyder, however, a number of scholars have contended that Nazi interpretations and applications of the tales misrepresent the intentions of the Grimms and the significance of the stories. In *Children's Literature in Hitler's Germany*, Christa Kamenetsky argues that the Fascists approached Grimms' tales in a highly selective way, emphasizing "their collections of *national* folklore" but ignoring "their contributions to comparative folklore and literature as well as to international understanding" (1984: 5; emphasis in the original). The German American scholar Jack Zipes has, in addition, conducted detailed work on applications of Grimms' fairy tales in East and West Germany after the war that show how the stories were swiftly reclaimed and resituated to fulfill very different functions to those exploited by the Nazis. In postwar West Germany, for instance, Zipes points to the extensive creative endeavor to "reclaim ... German classics" such as Grimms' tales "in the name of democratic humanism" (Zipes 2002: 233). Such diversity of applications of the tales in different contexts tend to make arguments for the innate authoritarianism of the stories unsustainable. Indeed, for Zipes, the fairy tales of the Grimms, in common with all popular storytelling, have an inborn orientation toward articulations of hopefulness and freedom because they access the imagination and an enduring spirit of popular resistance, and because they embody forms of conditional and situated thinking that are resistant to the absolutes and certainties of totalitarian polemic. This view represents a strain of thought that runs through intellectual approaches to fairy tale in the twentieth century, from Bloch and Benjamin, to the philosophical work of Hannah Arendt (see Disch 1993), and the fiction and nonfiction of Salman Rushdie (see Teverson 2001, 2008). In these debates and discussions we may find a microcosmic reflection of a form of engagement with the fairy tale that has characterized twentieth- and twenty-first-century approaches to the genre.

* * *

Amongst the most extensive and influential early uses of fairy tales in the twentieth century is that made by the writers, filmmakers, and artists of the surrealist movement, who saw in the fairy tale a vehicle for their creative endeavor to bypass the constraints of reason and access the imaginatively liberating realm of the unconscious. In his first *Manifesto of Surrealism* of 1924, the founder of the movement André Breton had identified "the marvelous" as a principal aesthetic attitude of surrealism, and argued that all forms of creative expression in which the marvelous is cultivated should become sources for surrealist art and literature (Breton 1972: 14). In particular, fairy tales have the vital function of cultivating sensitivity to the marvelous during childhood. Breton, however, also sees fairy tales as having been "tainted by puerility" (15) because of their relegation to the nursery by a rationalist bourgeoisie intent on suppressing access to the marvelous in all spheres of human experience. He therefore calls for art forms that permit the continuation of the marvels of fairy tales into adulthood:

> At an early age children are weaned on the marvelous, and later on they fail to retain a sufficient virginity of mind to thoroughly enjoy fairy tales. No matter how charming they may be, a grown man would think he were reverting to childhood by nourishing himself on fairy tales, and I am the first to admit that all such tales are not suitable for him. The fabric of adorable improbabilities must be made a trifle more subtle the older we grow …. But the faculties do not change radically. Fear, the attraction of the unusual, chance, the taste for things extravagant are all devices which we can always call upon without fear of deception. There are fairy tales to be written for adults, fairy tales still almost blue.
>
> (Breton 1972: 15–16)

Several surrealist writers and artists took Breton up on this invitation to create adult fairy tales, amongst them the English painter and writer, Leonora Carrington, whose short stories and novels draw liberally upon the imagery of fairy tales—in particular, Beauty and the Beast narratives that destabilize the boundary between humans and animals. Carrington's story "La Débutante" ("The Debutant"), for instance, features a young woman who persuades a hyena that she befriends in the zoo to take her place at a debutant ball. The hyena successfully disguises itself for the ball by killing a maid and wearing her face, but the imposture is finally revealed when the hyena's intense stench gives it away, and like an inverted Goldilocks it must escape through a window. The story is at once a parody of the fairy-tale romance in which the ball is the location of the young heroine's transfiguration and apotheosis, and simultaneously a homage to the fairy tale, as a form of fiction that blurs the lines between wild animal and civilized beauty whilst lending to Carrington images of grotesque, disturbing violence. Carrington, in this dual approach to the fairy tale, displays the equivocation that Ann Martin finds in the work of other modernist writers: on the one hand, the fairy tale is a narrative that is seen as reflective of Victorian social inheritances that must be debunked and resisted; on the other, it can be re-owned as a form that allows for a personalized interrogation of those inheritances.

The influence of surrealist aesthetics upon the fairy tale has endured throughout the twentieth century and into the twenty-first. The surrealist influence is, for instance, evident in the dreamlike narratives and bizarre visual conjunctions of the Czech animator Jan Švankmajer in films such as Alice (1988) and *Little Otik* (2000), and in the irruptions of magic that take place in the work of Guillermo del Toro, notably the films *Pan's Labyrinth* (2006) and *The Shape of the Water* (2017). In photography too, surrealist use of the striking image has persisted in disruptive restagings of fairy tales. In the Canadian photographer Dina Goldstein's *Fallen Princesses* series (2007–9) conventional fairy-tale characters are shown in surprising modern contexts that expose and undermine the romantic illusions of the traditional fairy tale. In *Snowy* (2008; Figure 0.1), Snow White in disheveled Disney regalia, juggles children, whilst the Prince, unemployed and depressed, reclines in a chair with a beer, watching TV. In *Princess Pea* (2009; Figure 0.2), the protagonist of the Hans Christian Andersen story, now an environmental activist, sits on a pile of mattresses on a landfill dumping site having felt the weight of responsibility of humanity's ecological destruction.

In the field of literature too, surrealist narrative effects have become a common feature of the tale retold. This is exemplified in the work of Kate Bernheimer who, in collections such as *Horse, Flower, Bird* (2010) and in her novel trilogy beginning with *The Complete Tales of Ketzia Gold* (2001) makes familiar tales strange by the use of disorientating narrative shifts, sudden inexplicable developments, undefined character relationships, and mysterious doublings. The surrealist and gothic short story "Whitework," for instance, in

FIGURE 0.1: Dina Goldstein, *Snowy*, 2008. Photograph, *Fallen Princesses* Series.

FIGURE 0.2: Dina Goldstein, *Princess Pea*, 2009. Photograph, *Fallen Princesses* Series.

Horse, Flower, Bird, offers a disorientating version of "Hansel and Gretel," in which it is unclear whether the opaque and decontextualized events of the story are accounts of real occurrences, or the fractured fantasies of a madwoman who has immersed herself in the romance of fairy tales.

Whilst the aesthetic philosophy of surrealism has continued to influence treatment of the fairy tale in the later twentieth and early twenty-first century, a number of the writers and artists who make use of its aesthetic strategies have also worked to challenge some of its initial assumptions. In particular, artists who draw upon the surreal have sought to acknowledge and adjust what Manuel Borja-Villel calls its "predominantly European and male discourse" (2018: 9). This challenge is already implicit in the work of some early adherents of the movement, such as Carrington and her close contemporary Dorothea Tanning, both of whom interrogate and resist the image of woman in surrealist painting as "a kind of talisman, powerful but mute, with a petrified gaze" (9). In their respective self-portraits, *Self-Portrait (Inn of the Dawn Horse)* (1937–8) and *Birthday* (1942) (see Figures 0.3 and 0.4), Carrington and Tanning present a profound challenge to this convention—projecting themselves as artists and

FIGURE 0.3: Leonora Carrington, *Self-Portrait (Inn of the Dawn Horse)*, 1937–8. © Estate of Leonora Carrington/ARS, NY and DACS, London 2020.

FIGURE 0.4: Dorothea Tanning, *Birthday*, 1942. © ADAGP, Paris and DACS, London 2020.

makers in their own right, with beast familiars that are expressive of their connection to a natural and magical world that lies outside of conventional patriarchal control and authority.

Challenges to the surrealist presentation of gender roles have also become emphatic in later works that draw upon the movement's disruptive aesthetic strategies whilst simultaneously resisting its gendered assumptions. Writing of surrealism in her 1978 essay, "The Alchemy of the Word," Angela Carter records the impact of the movement upon her own work, and testifies to the ongoing attractions of its aesthetic philosophy: "the old juices can still run," she writes, "when I hear the old incendiary slogans, when I hear that most important of all surrealist principles: 'The marvelous alone is beautiful'" (1998: 512). Simultaneously, however, Carter also recognizes that "the surrealists were not good with women .... They were, with a few patronised exceptions, all men and they told me that I was the source of all mystery, beauty and otherness, because I was a woman" (1998: 512). This complicated relationship with surrealism is reflected in Carter's 1979 story "The Courtship of Mr Lyon" in *The Bloody Chamber*, which operates both as a homage to Jean Cocteau's surrealist-inspired film *La Belle et la Bête* (1946) and a simultaneous parody of the wide-eyed innocence and dreamy passivity of his surreal muse who, in the film, is "une drôle enfant" (a strange/amusing child) who likes to be afraid of her lover. "J'aime avoir peur ... avec vous" Beauty tells the transformed beast.

The later work of Dorothea Tanning also sustains her early challenges to surrealism—in particular, by recognizing the dangers, for women of an uncritical and ahistorical celebration of the marvelous. Her 1974 painting *Pour Gustave l'adoré* (For Gustave the Beloved) (Figure 0.5), for instance, engages

FIGURE 0.5: Dorothea Tanning, *Pour Gustave l'adoré*, 1974. © ADAGP, Paris and DACS, London 2020.

critically with the cultural representation of the woman as mermaid, particularly as presented in the nineteenth-century work *Les Océanides (Naiades de la Mer)* by Gustave Doré (Figure 0.6). Here Tanning expresses her admiration for Doré as a curator of the marvelous in fairy tale and myth—an admiration that many of the surrealists shared. As her title implies with a pun, she adores Gustave Doré. At the same time, however, Tanning refuses the representation of women enacted in Doré's work by transforming the scenario radically. Where Doré's

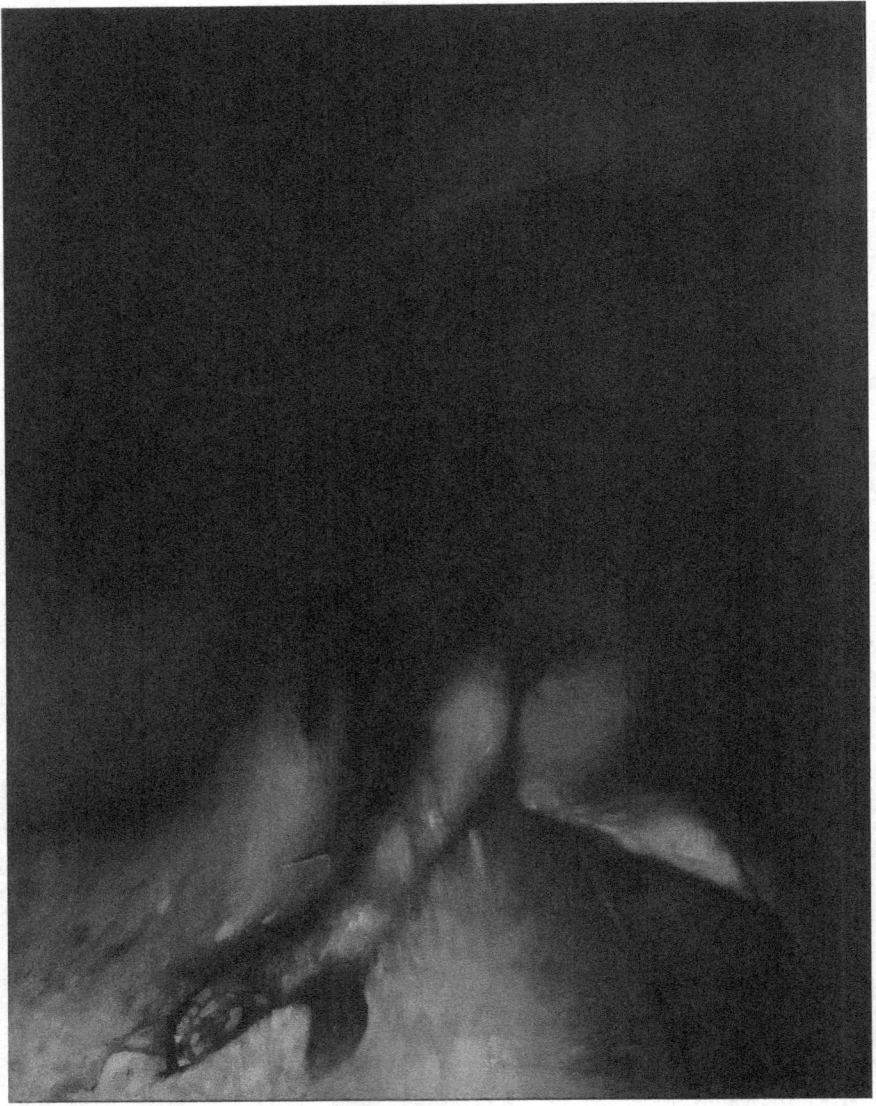

FIGURE 0.6: Gustave Doré, *Les Océanides (Naiades de la Mer)*, c. 1860.

naiads are on display for the viewer—passive creatures to be observed and admired—Tanning's mermaid flits from sight, with only a tail and what is perhaps the hazy image of a human limb visible. The mermaid as Tanning sees her (or refuses to see her) is in the process of escaping a legacy in which she is a passive object of male scrutiny whose destiny is, like Andersen's Little Mermaid as described by Simone de Beauvoir, to take on "the yoke of love and suffering that is her lot" (de Beauvoir [1949] 2011: 314). Surrealism, and its passion for the disruptive potential of the marvelous, we conclude, is useful to women because of its capacity to produce forms of representation that destabilize settled assumptions about gender and identity; at the same time, however, women artists have also had to use surrealist techniques to unsettle and destabilize the unequal relationship between the male surrealist artist and the female muse that is fostered in early surrealist writings—an act that is powerfully symbolized in Tanning's disappearing mermaid.

* * *

The potential and the limits of surrealism have also been explored by writers working outside the European and North American cultural context, amongst them the writers, artists, and intellectuals who have come to be associated with the Afro-surrealist movement. A key figure in the emergence of this movement is the Martiniquan poet and political activist Aimé Césaire, who became identified with surrealism in 1941 after Breton, escaping occupied France, stayed briefly on the island of Martinique whilst awaiting a crossing to America. Breton recognized in Césaire's writing, and in particular his long poem *Cahier d'un retour au pays natal* (*Notebook of a Return to My Native Land*, first published in the journal *Volontés* in 1939 and reworked as an extended edition in 1947) parallels with the literary activities of the surrealists, and encouraged his identification with the movement. Yet whilst Césaire's work makes use of surrealist techniques of defamiliarization, surprising juxtaposition, dramatic image, and manifesto-like statement, it is also apparent that these aesthetic strategies challenge the European surrealist movement, with its dominant focus on European culture, and its tendency to exoticize African art and culture. It is notable, for instance, that when Césaire and his fellow poet Rene Ménil collected instances of the folk and fairy tale in Martinique and published them in their journal *Tropiques*, they collected these fictions not as evidence of a timeless impulse for the "marvelous" in the human creative imagination, but as a set of narratives that have specific cultural significance and value in the context of Martinique's struggle against a history of slavery and European cultural imperialism. The stories, for Césaire and Ménil, were not collected because they presented visions of a wondrous alterity, as measured against an implicit idea of European normativity, but because they rooted the Martiniquan creative imagination in a cultural history, reaching back before European colonization, which could be used to disrupt and challenge a European cultural consensus. Simultaneously, these stories also provide a record of struggle against palpable historical injustice and suffering. "Ne sourions pas, à ces "naïvetés'" ("do not smile at these 'naiveties'"), Césaire and Ménil instruct the reader in their "Introduction au folklore martiniquais" ("Introduction to Martiniquan Folklore"):

> Sous une forme de prime abord puérile, mais, en tout cas, directe, document historique d'une valeur inestimable. Quand on aura dépouillé toutes les archives, compulsé tous les dossiers, fouillé tous les papiers des abolitionnistes, c'est à ces contes que reviendra celui qui voudra saisir, éloquente et pathétique, la grande misère de nos pères esclaves.
>
> Et voilà qui révèle le mécanisme secret du merveilleux. Quand l'homme écrasé par une société inique cherche en vain autour de lui le grand secours, découragé, impuissant, il projette sa misère et sa révolte dans un ciel de promesse et de dynamite.
>
> (At first glance childish, they are in fact direct, historical documents of inestimable value. When we have emptied all the archives, examined all the files, searched all the papers of the abolitionists, it is these tales that will give us again what we want to grasp, eloquent and pathetic, the great misery of our slave fathers.
>
> And here is revealed the secret mechanism of the marvelous. When man, crushed by an iniquitous society, searches in vain for the great succour, discouraged, impotent, he projects his misery and his revolt into a sky of promise and dynamite.)
>
> (Césaire and Ménil 1942: 8; my translation)

Equivalent applications of surrealist principles are apparent in the essays published in *Tropiques* by its cofounder and editor, Suzanne Césaire, who in a 1943 essay pointedly titled "Surrealism and Us," connects the liberating capacity of the marvelous directly to anti-colonial struggle:

> Far from contradicting, diluting, or diverting our revolutionary attitude toward life, surrealism strengthens it. It nourishes an impatient strength within us, endlessly reinforcing the massive army of refusals.
> And I am also thinking of tomorrow.
> Millions of black hands will hoist their terror across the furious skies of world war. Freed from a long benumbing slumber, the most disinherited of all peoples will rise up from plains of ashes.
> Our surrealism will supply this rising people with a punch from its very depths. Our surrealism will enable us to finally transcend the sordid

antinomies of the present: whites/Blacks, Europeans/Africans, civilized/ savages—at last rediscovering the magic power of the mahoulis, drawn directly from living sources. Colonial idiocy will be purified in the welder's blue flame. We shall recover our value as metal, our cutting edge of steel, our unprecedented communions.

(Rosemont 1998: 136–7)

In such statements, Suzanne Césaire acknowledges the continuing importance of the marvelous in the literature and art of anti-colonial resistance, but also insists that the marvelous must be, in the words of D. Scott Miller, "re-contextualized with regard to contemporary black arts and interventions" (Miller 2016; see also Kelley 1999).

In the realm of the folk and fairy tale, one such recontextualization has been enacted by the later Martiniquan writer Patrick Chamoiseau, himself profoundly influenced by the work of the Césaires. In his collection, *Au temps de l'antan: Contes du pays Martinique* (1988, translated into English as *Strange Words* in 1994), Chamoiseau reworks twelve Martiniquan folktales, each of which deals with themes of dispossession, oppression, and the possibility of revenge and resistance. The story of "Glan-Glan the Spat-Out Bird," for instance, which opens with an epigraph from Aimé Césaire, uses a folktale about a greedy couple who devour a marvelous bird and are subsequently forced to reconstruct it piece by piece, as an implicit metaphor for the dismemberment of the Caribbean by greedy Europeans and a utopian performance of reconstruction and reconstitution. "The bird with plumes once more lovely than the past / demands an accounting for its scattered finery," the book's suggestive epigraph from Césaire reads (Chamoiseau [1988] 1994: ix). The function of these stories is made explicit by Chamoiseau in his introduction to the tales. "Our stories and our Storytellers," Chamoiseau writes:

date from the period of slavery and colonialism. Their deepest meanings can be understood only in relation to this fundamental period in the history of the West Indies. Our Storyteller speaks for a people enchained: starving, terrorized, living in the cramped postures of survival. Their voice is heard in the Creole tale, where the symbolic bestiary of Africa—whale, elephant, tortoise, tiger, brother rabbit—is introduced by the Storyteller to human or supernatural characters of a more distinctly European influence: the Devil, the Goodlord, Cétoute, Ti-Jean Horizon …

While their ludic function is undeniable (for surely laughter is the greatest wellspring of hope for those forced to live in a kind of hell), when taken as a whole, these tales provide a practical education, an apprenticeship in life—a life of survival in a colonized land.

(Chamoiseau [1988] 1994: xii)

* * *

One of the distinguishing characteristics of the approach to fairy tales taken by the writers and artists considered in the last few pages, is a concern with the ideological functions of fairy tales. The fairy tale, in the hands of Tanning, Goldstein, Carter, the Césaires, Chamoiseau, and Bernheimer is not conceived in its Romantic guise as a spontaneous irruption of the creative imagination that takes place outside of time, history, and cultural context; but rather as a form of fiction that emerges in history, and reflects the cultural and ideological orientations of the societies and cultures that reshape and retell it. It is, arguably, this aspect of the fairy tale that has proved most energizing in creative uses of the genre in the later twentieth century and early twenty-first. Increasingly, writers and artists are recognizing that the fairy tale is a carrier of ideas and belief systems—and this in turn has given rise to the creative revelation that there is art to be made from both the contestation of the belief systems that fairy tales have reflected in their dominant canonical forms, and from the transformation of fairy tales to reflect new belief systems—or belief systems that may be recovered from non-canonical conceptions of the historic tale.

There are a number of ways in which we might trace the emergence of this orientation in the treatment of popular narrative tradition. On the broadest canvas, we would sketch a trajectory that starts with the revolution in our understanding of the political functioning of culture brought about by Marxist-influenced intellectuals such as Antonio Gramsci (1891–1937), Walter Benjamin (1892–1940), Mikhail Bakhtin (1895–1975), Frantz Fanon (1925–61), and Edward Said (1935–2003). For the purposes of this introduction, however, I want to propose two texts as key origin points of the ideological approach to the fairy tale specifically. The first of these is Simone de Beauvoir's pioneering work of feminist thought *Le deuxième sexe* (*The Second Sex*, 1949), in which the fairy tale, amongst other dominant narratives of Western culture, is presented as a narrative form that has played a critical role in the prescription of limiting gender roles for women. Two passages in *The Second Sex* are critical in this regard. In the first, which appears in the section on "Myths," de Beauvoir examines the function of the poverty and passivity of the fairy-tale princess in canonical fairy tales such as "Cinderella" and "Sleeping Beauty" and concludes that these mythologized representations of women work to reaffirm male authority and power within a patriarchal order. "Clearly man wants woman's enslavement when fantasising himself as a benefactor, liberator or redeemer," de Beauvoir writes: "If Sleeping Beauty is to be awakened she must be sleeping; to have a captive princess, there must be ogres and dragons .... Sleeping Beauty's smile [thus] fulfils Prince Charming: the captive princesses' tears of happiness and gratitude give meaning to the knight's prowess" ([1949] 2011: 207–8).

In the second key passage relating to fairy tale in *The Second Sex*, which appears in the section on "Childhood," de Beauvoir examines the impact of the romance script upon the developing identity of young girls. The passage represents a vital contribution to the contemporary understanding of the shaping role played by the canonical fairy tale in the sedimentation of gender roles:

> Everything [in cultural representation] encourages [the child] to abandon herself in dreams to the arms of men to be transported to a sky of glory. She learns that to be happy she has to be loved; to be loved, she has to await love. Woman is Sleeping Beauty, Donkey Skin, Cinderella, Snow White, the one who receives and endures. In songs and tales, the young man sets off to seek the woman; he fights against dragons, he combats giants; she is locked up in a tower, a garden, a cave, chained to a rock, captive, put to sleep: she is waiting. *One day my prince will come … Someday he'll come along, the man I love …* the popular refrains breathe dreams of patience and hope in her. The supreme necessity for woman is to charm a masculine heart; this is the recompense all heroines aspire to, even if they are intrepid, adventuresome; and only their beauty is asked of them in most cases … [W]hether it be a question of God or a man, the little girl learns that by consenting to the most serious renunciations, she will become all-powerful: she takes pleasure in a masochism that promises her supreme conquests. St Blandine, white and bloody in the paws of lions, Snow White lying as if dead in a glass coffin, Sleeping Beauty, Atala fainting, a whole cohort of tender heroines beaten, passive, wounded, on their knees, humiliated, teach their younger sisters the fascinating prestige of martyred, abandoned and resigned beauty. It is not surprising that, while her brother plays at the hero, the little girl plays so easily at the martyr: the pagans throw her to the lions, Bluebeard drags her by the hair, the king, her husband, exiles her to the depth of the forests; she resigns herself, she suffers, she dies and her brow is haloed with glory.
>
> ([1949] 2011: 316; emphasis in the original)

In so writing, de Beauvoir establishes a critical premise of the feminist interrogation of fairy tale that has resonated through fairy-tale criticism since the 1950s and that has influenced the approach to fairy tales taken by several major twentieth- and twenty-first-century fairy-tale theorists, including Andrea Dworkin (1974), Sandra Gilbert and Susan Gubar (1979), Maria Tatar (1987, 1992), Marina Warner (1994a), and Cristina Bacchilega (1997, 2013).

Also vitally important as a twentieth-century text that stands at the inception of a self-conscious recognition of the ways in which ideology functions in the genre, is Roland Barthes *Mythologies* (1957), a collection of twenty-nine essays, in which Barthes sets out to show how the seemingly innocent materials of popular culture mediate in disguise a set of social beliefs and assumptions that support the interests of those with social and economic power. Thus, in his essay on "Wine and Milk," he argues that the marketing of wine as "unalloyedly blissful" and natural serves to obscure the fact that "its production is deeply involved in French capitalism" and depends upon expropriation of land in the then French colony of Algeria where the "big settlers ... impose on the Muslims, on the very land of which they have been dispossessed, a crop of which they have no need, while they lack even bread" (Barthes [1957] 1972: 61). Likewise, in his final essay on "Myth Today" Barthes shows how a photograph on the cover of the magazine *Paris-Match* presenting a man of African origin in French military uniform saluting a flag operates as a covert—but suitably transparent— argument in support of French imperialism (116). In these essays, Barthes shows little if any interest in mythology in the sense that a folklorist would understand the term; rather he borrows and repurposes the concept to describe a process whereby ideological discourses are made to seem natural and inevitable by being inscribed repeatedly in powerful and persuasive popular representations. But though Barthes may not have traditional storytelling in mind when he writes of myths, many subsequent scholars have worked to apply Barthes's concept of myth back to the literary and cultural materials after which it was named. That is, they have sought to show how popular, traditional stories such as myths, fairy tales, folktales, themselves work to naturalize and render invisible powerful ideological discourses about gender, race, class, age, disability, and sexuality. Barthes's essays therefore stand at the inception of a systematic understanding of popular stories as fictions that can be read semiologically to reveal the ways in which they reflect and perpetuate the ideological discourses of a given era or class.

Amongst the writers most heavily influenced by Barthes is Angela Carter, whose stories in *The Bloody Chamber* (1979) bring to the fore, and creatively interrogate, the ideological subtexts of traditional narratives. In the story "The Tiger's Bride," for instance, the status of the female protagonist as an object of exchange between male protagonists, concealed but implicit in fairy tales such as Madame Leprince de Beaumont's "Beauty and the Beast" (1756), is rendered explicit and parodied. "My father lost me to The Beast at cards," the story begins (Carter [1979] 2006: 56). Likewise, Carter's titular story, "The Bloody Chamber," self-consciously exposes and interrogates the ideologically loaded narrative of Charles Perrault's story "Bluebeard" (1697), in which the victimized heroine must be rescued from a murderous husband by her military brothers. In Carter's story, the heroine must still be rescued, but in this instance it is by her intrepid gun-toting mother. Writing in her essay "Notes from the Front Line" Carter identifies this practice of engaging with the concealed ideological orientations of traditional narratives, which she calls "the social fictions that regulate our lives," as one of the principle motivations of her work (1998: 38). "I believe that all myths are products of the human mind," she writes, "and reflect only aspects of material human practice. I'm in the demythologising business. I'm interested in myths ... just because they *are* extraordinary lies designed to make people unfree" (38; emphasis in the original). Importantly, however, Carter also recognizes that different kinds of narratives impose themselves upon us in different ways. Myths are "extraordinary lies designed to make people unfree," she writes, but folklore offers "a much more straightforward set of devices for making real life more exciting and is much easier to infiltrate with different kinds of consciousness" (38). Thus where Carter sees the myth, in its Barthesian sense, as a narrative about authorized power that imposes itself upon us, she sees the fairy tale, like Walter Benjamin, as a form of narrative that also permits an escape from the constraints mythological world. As she recalls: "I wrote one anti-mythic novel in 1977, *The Passion of New Eve* [1977b]—and I conceived it as a feminist tract about the social creation of femininity, amongst other things" but in 1979 "relaxed into folklore with a book of stories about fairy stories, *The Bloody Chamber*" (38).

Barthes *Mythologies* also became a model for the British writer and mythologist Marina Warner in her 1994 Reith Lectures for the BBC, in which she seeks to explore how fairy tales, legends, and myths "interpenetrate and influence our lives" (1994b: xii). In the preface to the published version of these lectures, Warner notes that she is "indebted" to Barthes's essay collection and to his "analysis of French contemporary culture," but she also notes that she is "less pessimistic" than Barthes about the functions of myths, and so has sought to depart from and develop his "fundamental principle" (xiii). In the first place, she does not see mythologies only as a form of speech that conceals and obscures history, but also, more affirmatively, as an enabling form of human creative activity, that helps humankind to "make sense" of its world and its experiences (xiii). "Myths are not always delusions," Warner writes, and "deconstructing them does not necessarily mean wiping them" (xiii). Connectedly, Warner also argues that "the process of understanding [myths] ... to which Barthes contributed so brilliantly can give rise to newly told stories, can sew and weave and knit different patterns into the social fabric" (xiii).

Warner's own short stories, many of which reformulate traditional tales, are illustrative of this process of interrogating and investigating established versions of stories to reveal them to be narratives that have ongoing significance for ordinary, daily life. The collection *Fly Away Home: Stories* (2015), for instance, incorporates several fictions in which myths, legends, and fairy tales are made more everyday, even domesticated, as Warner seeks to show that these enduring narrative patterns need not be remote and mythical, but can continue to play themselves out in ordinary lives. This treatment is thematized explicitly, for instance, in the story "Forget My Fate," which, as the titular snatch of lyric suggests, alludes to the mythic tale of Dido and Aeneas. In this story an Italian-Jewish music teacher from Egypt named Nino, with a complicated past, offers a classics teacher, Barbara May, an alternative to the epic myth of Dido and Aeneas as it was imagined by the "dreadful Roman collaborator" Virgil

(Warner 2015: 137). In this alternative story, Dido, reimagined as Elissa, the exiled queen of Tyre, is "NOT a woman who gives up in despair and shame" (142), but instead ends her days happily married to the king of Mauritania. This altered trajectory for Dido illustrates a thesis that Nino articulates for Barbara May, that "you can push a story in other directions—ones that are less frenzied. Towards ordinary moments of love and satisfaction and happiness" (138). It also reveals to Barbara May, once she has recognized references to Nino's own love affair in the tale of Dido and Aeneas, that behind epic tragedy is:

> an alternative story—one that isn't so compelling, but one that fits closely, if not obviously, to another kind of experience, a little more commonplace, with a happy ending. That story also invites us to enter but it is harder to notice. The voice is fainter when it says, "I think you'll recognise this."
>
> (Warner 2015: 146)

Such narratives exemplify a practice that Warner identifies as a distinctive feature of contemporary storytelling: the strategy of telling different versions of a story to challenge and expose the assumptions of the versions we have come to accept as normal and inevitable. "Replying to one story with another which unravels the former," as Warner writes, "has become central to contemporary thought and art" (1994b: 4).

Warner's response to Barthes is a testament to his profound influence upon thinking about fairy tale in the twentieth century, but it also reveals the extent to which creative practice and scholarship in this field has evolved in new directions. Barthes's *Mythologies* provided a language and a methodology through which modern writers and intellectuals could seek to understand how fairy tales as semiotic systems have worked to mediate powerful ideological discourses about race, gender, sexuality, physical ability, the environment, and class. Simultaneously, however, contemporary writers and scholars such as Carter and Warner have also sought to show how fairy tales can be fictions that provide us with tools for comprehending, constructing, and reconstructing the stuff of human experience in more enabling ways.

* * *

What is modern about the fairy tale in the modern age? This introduction has begun to propose some responses to this question—some tentative and sketchy, others more fully realized. One of these answers depends upon technology. The modern age has been a period in which the numbers of platforms available to the fairy tale have grown exponentially: the fairy tale in the twentieth and twenty-first centuries has become a genre that flourishes on film, on TV, in digital media—as well as in the older technologies of print, performance, and the visual arts. There are a number of implications of this development. First, it has enabled the mass circulation of fairy tales, on a scale not previously possible—a phenomenon that has, paradoxically, served both to globalize the fairy tale as a genre, whilst shrinking international conceptions of it to a narrow selection of canonical works recognized in mass media. Second, the arrival of the fairy tale in mass media has, in some fundamental ways, changed our understanding of what the fairy tale is. It has, for instance, transformed the genre into a predominantly visual form of storytelling; it has also emphasized the association of the fairy tale, in the mainstream, with commodified romances, such as those produced by Disney.

If the mechanical and technological developments in our capacity to tell and disseminate stories have proved decisive in shaping the twentieth- and twenty-first-century fairy tale, however, so too have developments in intellectual and cultural history in the period, which have been characterized by the imperative to reexamine, rework, and renew conventional genres. This imperative, as the present introduction has tried to show, was to the fore in modernist—and particularly surrealist approaches to fairy tales—and these approaches have continued to shape creative responses to fairy tales throughout the period covered by this volume. Foremost in creative responses to fairy tale, in this respect, is a desire to use the marvelous component of fairy tales to disrupt and challenge rationalist epistemologies, and a willingness to renew the genre of fairy tale by making use of it in surprising and innovative ways. The disruptive and renewing approach to fairy tales pioneered by modernists and surrealists has, however, continued to evolve and transform in the later twentieth and early twenty-first centuries—in particular as concerns our appreciation of the relationship between fairy tales and ideology. Both feminist and anti-colonial writers have, from different perspectives, seen the importance of approaching the marvelous, not as a timeless and universal eruption of human creative expression but as a product of creative activity that has taken place in history, and been shaped and determined by specific social and historical contexts. For the marvelous to retain the disruptive functions attributed to it by surrealism in the feminist fairy tale or the anti-imperial fairy tale, therefore, it must be rehistoricized and recontextualized.

In part as a result of these processes there has been an increasing determination, in evidence throughout the period, to destabilize the canon of fairy tales that emerged in the nineteenth century and was broadcast globally at the start of the twentieth, by examining what stories and collections the canon ignores, and, in a potent alliance of creativity and scholarship, to return the marginalized stories and traditions to public attention. This process, broadly speaking, has challenged the centrality of the Euro-American canon, and worked to reveal the popular tale of magic as a transnational and intercultural phenomenon. The fairy tale of the twentieth and twenty-first centuries, therefore, has also been subject to a contest over ownership—characterized by, on the one hand, unprecedented global presence of the Euro-American canon and, on the other hand, a simultaneous movement in scholarship and the creative arts to destabilize, reposition, and expand the canon.

The eight chapters in this collection will continue to explore the distinctive characteristics of fairy tales in the twentieth and twenty-first centuries. In Chapter 1, Brittany Warman and Sara Cleto survey the wide variety of "forms" that fairy tales have taken in the modern age, focusing primarily upon forms that are unique to the period, including graphic novels, films, television shows, Broadway and West End musicals, and iterations of fairy tales in digital media. The fairy tale, they conclude, has "attained a new order of prominence in the twentieth and twenty-first centuries" in part because the adaptability and versatility of the form has enabled it to flourish in a period of proliferating media platforms.

Chapter 2, by Mayako Murai, explores the phenomenon of fairy-tale adaptation in the twentieth and twenty-first centuries further, focusing upon the ways in which the intertextuality of the contemporary fairy tale is a product of numerous iterations of popular stories across diverse media, but without stable or fixed "original" texts. Using adaptations of the story "The Bremen Town Musicians" as a case study, Murai shows how modern creative responses to the story in a variety of media—from text to taxidermy—and in diverse national contexts—from Germany to India—have employed the narrative intertextually to address contemporary concerns about social exclusion, human animal relations, and the possibilities of multispecies coexistence.

In Chapter 3, Jeana Jorgensen examines the use of fairy tales to mediate ideas about gender and sexuality, arguing that in the twentieth and twenty-first centuries "there has been more explicit dialogue around gender and sexuality in fairy tales than in previous time periods, and with more nuance as well." This dialogue, Jorgensen shows, is driven by both "the desire to uphold current normative regimes," as is the case with mid-twentieth-century Disney films that emphasize "stereotypical gender roles," and the imperative to "restructure" normative conceptions of gender and sexuality by, for instance, the creation of narratives that validate "explicitly queer or non-heterosexual" identities.

In Chapter 4, Amy Greenhough turns to consider the modern fairy tale's mediation of the interrelationship between humans and non-humans, arguing that "changes to the contemporary fairy tale and its depiction of human/non-human relations reflect changing cultural and theoretical approaches to anthropocentrism." In the early to mid-twentieth century, Greenhough notes, Walt Disney "solidified, at least in the Western cultural consciousness, a specific and pervasive image of anthropomorphic non-humanity that still echoes through our fiction, film, and cultural engagements with fairy tale today." Increasingly, however, contemporary writers have come to challenge the assumptions that lie behind the anthropomorphic creations of Disney, using the genre's "animist engagement with objects, nature and transformation" to offer more complex and subtle accounts of the intersections between the human and non-human. "Alongside the new and ever-expanding theories of the twenty-first century—of posthumanism, new materialism, and ecocriticism," Greenhough proposes, "the fairy-tale genre has seen the beginnings of a more contemporary model of writing about non-humanity in which humanity is not the center or the leader, but simply one part of an interconnecting web of experience."

Greenhough's analysis of depictions of the non-human in fairy tales is complemented in Chapter 5 by Christa Jones and Claudia Schwabe's exploration of constructions and reconstructions of the notion of monstrosity in the modern fairy tale. In the twentieth and twenty-first centuries, Schwabe and Jones argue, representations of monstrosity associated with the conventional fairy tale have changed significantly in meaning and application. Fairy-tale figures such as the witch, the ogre, and the giant "traditionally epitomize human fears that are exteriorized … so they can be safely contemplated from a distance"; but increasingly, in twentieth- and twenty-first-century narratives, the social and ideological functions of the demonization of monstrous others has been exposed, questioned, and dismantled. Monsters, in modern works, are more likely to be reimagined in ways that "elicit human compassion," and their monstrosity to become a consequence of social alienation that a reader or viewer is asked to comprehend and sympathize with. "Today's fairy-tale adaptations," Jones and Schwabe write, "oftentimes unsettle the simplistic dichotomy of good versus evil and present us with complex characters that destabilize our traditional understanding of monstrosity." One of the reasons for this change in approaches to monstrosity, they argue, is a growing inclination to recognize that representations of monstrosity often function as a way of demonizing difference and of sedimenting forms of social, political, and physical exclusion.

In Chapter 6, Sara Upstone explores a wide range of constructions of space in modern fairy tales, including fairy-tale spatial locations that involve a move away from the abstraction of traditional fairy tales into spaces presented as "real." In these relocations of fairy-tale magic, Upstone argues, the departure from traditional fairy-tale spaces entails both "a reconstructed relationship to the notion of the 'real'" and "a rethinking of the nature of enchantment."

Chapter 7, by Jill Terry Rudy, considers twentieth- and twenty-first-century analysis of the ways in which folk and fairy tales have functioned to socialize readers, listeners, and viewers—especially children. In the main, Rudy observes, recent critical approaches to fairy tales have tended to "register concern" about the tendency of stories to "portray limiting social roles" to younger audiences, with leading scholars such as Jack Zipes concentrating primarily upon the capacity of fairy tales to operate ideologically to "indoctrinate children so that they will conform to dominant social standards." Whilst acknowledging these dimensions of the commodified European literary fairy tale, however, Rudy also looks to forms of storytelling that take place as a result of "intergenerational, participatory relationships," and argues that in such contexts the socialization enacted through storytelling must be understood as socially and culturally affirming. "Considered as a European narrative form, especially in popularized versions," Rudy writes:

> the fairy tale has participated in authoritarian processes. But, considered as traditional narratives developed and shared in distinctive cultures over time and space, these stories have more to contribute to the growth of human beings and the perpetuation of relationships extending from humans to other creatures, nature, and spirituality. Attentive scholarship adds communalist views to earlier discourses on fairy-tale socialization and places fairy tales in context with other wonder tale traditions and cultures.

This is especially the case, Rudy affirms, where "storytelling and other traditional expressive performances" are "components of indigenous knowledge systems (IKS), which stem from and support given cultures and societies." A complex and complete reading of the twentieth- and twenty-first-century fairy tale, Rudy suggests, must acknowledge these more culturally constructive and inclusive forms of socialization through storytelling, whilst simultaneously forging a critique of authoritarian modes of socialization that seek to constrain children to conform to narrow social codes.

The final chapter in this volume, by Kimberly J. Lau, focuses upon the representation of power in fairy tales, and the operation of power through popular traditional storytelling and the discourses that surround it. Drawing upon the work of Michel Foucault, Lau conducts an analysis of fairy-tale studies as a scholarly discipline that reveals "the troubling and almost complete absence of race as a topic." More than simply a "bias" or a "blindspot" in the critical scholarship in the field, Lau proposes, this elision of the discussion of race in discourses concerning fairy tale is a consequence of the systematic production of fairy tale as a "universal" genre that occludes attention to "the discourses—both historical and contemporary—of imperialism, colonialism, ethnic chauvinism, and racialized thinking." To support this discussion, Lau offers a critical case study of Helen Oyeyemi's fairy-tale novels, which, she argues, may function as "examples of how racially inflected contemporary fairy tales might highlight, as well as attend to, such critical absences." "If the fairy tale's universality is a European illusion propped up by patriarchal and Eurocentric structures of power," Lau avers, then contemporary fairy-tale fiction such as Oyeyemi's "might very well be its undoing, its decentering and deconstruction."

Coming at the end of this volume, Lau's chapter also functions as a conclusion to the key arguments of the book as a whole. In the twentieth and twenty-first centuries, writers, filmmakers, artists, and scholars have increasingly come to understand the fairy tale as a genre through which power operates—whether it is the power to enforce conformity to dominant norms, or the power to articulate emergent ideologies that resist and challenge dominant discourses—and it is this understanding that has, intentionally or otherwise, informed some of the most influential and enduring works of the period. It is this recognition of the capacity of fairy tale to mediate power, moreover, that helps to explain the importance granted to storytelling in this period by writers and thinkers such as Auden and Tolkien, Bloch and Benjamin, de Beauvoir and Barthes, Carter and Zipes. In each case, and in different ways, they recognize that, as another great advocate of the power and value of storytelling Salman Rushdie puts it, "stories tell us who we are" (1998), and that the telling and retelling of these stories is, therefore, a profound investment in our efforts to grapple with ideas of what it is to be human within society and within the wider intersectional environment in which we live.

CHAPTER ONE

Forms of the Marvelous

SARA CLETO AND BRITTANY WARMAN

INTRODUCTION

Any relatively short chapter with the aim of being a comprehensive overview of fairy-tale forms in the modern age faces a difficult, if not impossible, task. The explosion of fairy-tale media in the twentieth and twenty-first centuries, its seemingly everlasting popularity, and its uncanny ability to reinvent itself anew over and over again ensures that, no matter the form, the fairy tale will find a way to thrive. With countless texts to choose from, and only a short space within which to tackle all the innovative new forms of the modern age, the only hope we can have is that this chapter provides a glimpse at the insightful, ridiculous, unexpected, traditional, subversive, conventional, and magical ways that the fairy tale lives today.

To use our space in the most effective way possible, we have chosen to follow a few guidelines. First, this overview is, by necessity of our own familiarity and language capabilities, focused chiefly on North American and Western European media. That said, we have included discussion of several Japanese animations and video games as well, as their international popularity dictates that they be treated as part of the cultural landscape of the global fairy tale as well as that of their native culture.[1] Second, we have chosen to spend the majority of our space discussing particularly modern media, namely, graphic novels, film, video games, born-digital content, and so on. While we have not by any means ignored literature, this chapter emphasizes forms unique to the twentieth and twenty-first centuries. In making this move, we aim to ground our assertion that the fairy tale remains an important part of our ever-changing and increasingly digital world.

TWENTIETH- AND TWENTY-FIRST-CENTURY THINKING ABOUT FORM

In writing a chapter specifically on the twentieth and twenty-first centuries with the title "Forms of the Marvelous," we recognize the need to acknowledge the fact that this is a period in which the concept of "form" itself has been most discussed and debated in both academic circles broadly and with the fairy tale specifically in mind. This said, the fairy-tale form has always been difficult to pin down precisely. Though the fairy tale may indeed "persist" largely "because of a flexible, resilient form that requires attention and allows compelling personal and collective affordances" (Rudy 2018a: 32), this fact has not stopped scholars from attempting to define what, exactly, the fairy-tale form is. The argument is, of course, "how else does one recognize a fairy tale in general, or in a specific story, unless one attends to its form" (32)? In what follows we briefly note a few of the key thinkers who have shaped fairy-tale scholarship's discourse of form.

Most notable early on is the ubiquitous presence of the work of Vladimir Propp. Though Alan Dundes rightly considers Propp as only "a starting point for analysis" because his work "does not attend to context" and "form must ultimately be related to the culture or cultures in which it is found" (Rudy 2018a: 34, referencing and quoting Dundes 1968: 2), Propp's *Morphology of the Folktale* (1928) has contributed immeasurably to fairy-tale studies and remains a particularly popular introductory text "for identifying and describing fairy tale's component parts" (Rudy 2018a: 34). Arguing that the stories we call "fairy tales" are unique in that they consist of thirty-one specific functions—including such events as the "interdiction" or warning, the "violation of the interdiction," "villainy," and the "wedding" (Propp [1928] 1968: 26–63)—all of which may or may not appear in a single tale but must regardless be accomplished in a particular order (21–2), Propp set the stage for scholars to begin thinking about what "distinguish[es these] tales from other expressive forms while also relating or juxtaposing them to each other and to changes in literary history and other sociocultural forms" (Rudy 2018a: 33). Following Propp, Max Lüthi's *The European Folktale: Form and Nature*, written in 1947 but not translated into English until 1982, is another highly influential text on the fairy-tale form. Focusing on style as opposed to structure, as Propp did (Niles 1982: xix), Lüthi draws attention to the fairy tale's "one-dimensionality," its "abstract style," its "pure colors," its "sharply defined and distinct" storyline (28), its "lack of realism" (24), and its "liking for all extremes," among other things (Lüthi [1947] 1982: 4–34). Though Lüthi maintains that the elements of the fairy tale he outlines are "present invisibly behind every folktale," he also allows that his "basic form is hardly ever perfectly realized" (101). Thus, despite both Propp and Lüthi's work, the perfect definition of the fairy-tale form remains elusive—it is, more often than not, a victim of the assumption that everyone simply "knows it when they see it."

The later twentieth century brought the advent of postmodernism, a "critical keyword" and "fashionable buzzword" that can mean many things, but for our purposes here in discussing form speaks to the style of contemporary work that specifically *plays* with form, "privileg[ing] flatness, pastiche, parody, and self-reflexivity" (Bacchilega 2018b: 74). In postmodern fairy-tale texts, the standards of fairy-tale form outlined by Propp, Lüthi, and others are deliberately turned inside out, destabilized, twisted, and transformed. Cristina Bacchilega notes that "typical to postmodern poetics is also a rejection of the hierarchical opposition of high/low culture," a fact that has made the fairy tale a popular form to engage with creatively (75). Postmodern writers tend to eschew the typical features of the traditional fairy tale to produce fragmented parodies of the form, as in the film *Shrek* (2001); retell stories from different perspectives, often revealing far deeper and more complex inner worlds for familiar characters, as in Disney's reimagining of their version of the evil fairy of "Sleeping Beauty" in *Maleficent* (2014); or remix the tales in unexpected ways so that, perhaps, the beast of "Beauty and the Beast" is also Snow White in the tale of the same name, as in Emma Donoghue's *Kissing the Witch: Old Tales in New Skins* ([1993] 1997). Indeed, postmodernism's reimagining of form has impacted the cultural understanding of the fairy tale in ways far too numerous to count.

That said, the recent and influential essay "Fairy Tale is Form, Form is Fairy Tale" by Kate Bernheimer deserves mention as well. Speaking from the perspective of an artist and writer who draws heavily on the fairy tale, Bernheimer points again to such elements as "flatness, abstraction, intuitive logic, and normalized magic" (2009: 64). Her focus is on contemporary literary fairy tales (66), but these elements, of course, continue to apply more broadly. As Bernheimer's essay shows, the form of the fairy tale has—despite postmodern experimentation and "many centuries of manipulation to its discrete techniques"—"survive[d] mutation" and retains, at least to a certain extent, some kind of recognizable form that continues to be "adaptable to a diverse range of narrative styles and shapes" (62–3). This is important to keep in mind, particularly as we move to our discussion of the many broad forms that have called upon fairy tales in the twentieth and twenty-first centuries: literature, film, television, stage, music, visual arts and material culture, and digital media.

LITERATURE

Though certainly not a twentieth- or twenty-first-century invention, the novel remains a popular and prolific form and one through which the fairy tale continues to evolve. The fairy tale appears in novels shelved as both genre and literary fiction, and the role it plays in the creation of new novels can vary widely.

The simplest and most straightforward manifestation of the fairy tale in the novel is as the kernel of a retelling. In these novels, the initial fairy tale provides the plot, characters, and other key features of the story. Because the novel is much longer than a classic fairy tale, the author expands considerably upon the material within the fairy tale, wildly upending the source text. Robin McKinley's *Beauty: A Retelling of the Story of Beauty and the Beast* (1978) is a useful example of this kind of novel. McKinley fleshes out Jeanne-Marie Leprince de Beaumont's "Beauty and the Beast" but does not stray far from her source material; McKinley's protagonist, Beauty, is an avid reader who goes to the Beast to save her father, and her love transforms her captor from a monster into a man whom she happily marries.

Other novelistic retellings drastically change one or multiple elements of the fairy tale that inspire them. Gregory Maguire's *Wicked: The Life and Times of the Wicked Witch of the West* (1995) reimagines L. Frank Baum's influential literary fairy tale *The Wonderful Wizard of Oz* (1900) (see Figure 1.1), providing a backstory for Baum's antagonist and reframing her as a kind of folk hero. Maguire's Cinderella novel, *Confessions of an Ugly Stepsister* (1999), once more centers upon a traditional antagonist and imagines a happy ending for Cinderella's stepsister, a plain but talented artist. In *Beast* (2000), Donna Jo Napoli shifts the emphasis from Beauty to the Beast, and her hero is a Persian prince cursed by a peri to take the shape of a lion. Jane Yolen's *Briar Rose* (1992) retells the tale of Sleeping Beauty as her heroine's personal narrative that provides identity and history in the face of the Holocaust.

Other authors use the fairy tale as a narrative touchstone in novels that otherwise diverge from a traditional plot. Helen Oyeyemi's *Boy, Snow, Bird* (2014) and *Gingerbread* (2019) take Snow White and Hansel and Gretel, respectively, as points of inspiration rather than as blueprints or maps. Each novel explores themes central to each fairy tale—the nature of beauty and acceptance in *Boy, Snow, Bird* and hunger and being lost in *Gingerbread*—but they are only lightly tethered to the fairy tales that anchor them. Other authors whose novels are dependent upon but diverge from traditional fairy tales include Catherynne M. Valente, whose novel *Deathless* (2011), for example, explores Russian fairy tales in a modern setting.

Finally, there are novels that tell original literary fairy tales, though they have roots in tradition and often draw upon multiple preexisting tales to create a new plot. It is here that the boundaries between the genres of fairy tale and fantasy can become intensely blurry and even begin to break down. *The Wonderful Wizard of Oz*, for example, is frequently regarded as a fairy tale, though it could also be considered alongside fantasy novels such as C. S. Lewis's *The Lion, the Witch, and the Wardrobe* (1950). A discussion of the differences between

"*Dorothy gazed thoughtfully at the Scarecrow.*"

FIGURE 1.1: Illustration by W. W. Denslow for Frank L. Baum's *The Wonderful Wizard of Oz* (Chicago: George M. Hill Company, 1900).

fairy-tale novels and fantasy novels lies beyond the scope of this chapter, and so here we merely acknowledge this genre-bending and point readers toward the excellent work of Farah Mendlesohn (2013). The aforementioned *The Wonderful Wizard of Oz* is arguably the first significant literary fairy-tale novel of the twentieth century, but many others have followed. Others in this vein include *Weirdstone of Brisingamen* ([1960] 2017) by Alan Garner, *The Princess*

Bride ([1973] 2007) by William Goldman, *Nights at the Circus* ([1984] 2006) by Angela Carter, *Stardust* (1997) and *Coraline* (2002) by Neil Gaiman, *Ombria in Shadow* (2002) by Patricia McKillip, and *Uprooted* (2015) by Naomi Novik.

Like the novel, short stories are hardly a contemporary invention, but they continue to offer a common, easily digestible shape for the fairy tale. Part of this persistence is surely due to form itself—though fairy tales can influence or exist in any media imaginable, they are historically bound up with the broader form of the short story.

Individual fairy-tale themed short stories by a multitude of authors have been published in a wide spectrum of books, journals, and magazines. For the sake of brevity, however, we will focus here on some of the many fairy-tale anthologies and single-authored collections that have proliferated over the last several decades. Angela Carter's groundbreaking book *The Bloody Chamber* ([1979] 2006) transformed the fairy-tale landscape with her carnivalesque, unapologetically feminist revisions of stories such as "Little Red Riding Hood," "Sleeping Beauty," and "Beauty and the Beast." Likewise, the fairy-tale anthology series edited by Ellen Datlow and Terri Windling reignited interest in adult retellings and remixes of traditional stories. Their first anthology, *Snow White, Blood Red* (1995), was the first of six books that have been recognized as a significant contribution to modern fairy tales. Emma Donoghue's landmark collection of interconnected tales, *Kissing the Witch: Old Tales in New Skins* ([1993] 1997) explores queer themes and ideas of kinship, and Francesca Lia Block's otherworldly yet distinctly LA-flavored book *The Rose and the Beast* (2000) offers lyrical, edgy fairy-tale retellings for a young adult audience.

More recently, editors have begun to seek out explicitly diverse short stories for their fairy-tale collections. Notable anthologies in this vein include *Beyond the Woods: Fairy Tales Retold* (2016) edited by Paula Guran, *The Starlit Wood: New Fairy Tales* (2016) edited by Dominik Parisien and Navah Wolfe, and *A Thousand Beginnings and Endings* (2018) edited by Ellen Oh and Elsie Chapman.

Fairy-tale poetry has proliferated throughout the twentieth and twenty-first centuries and continues to enjoy popularity in magazines and journals, both on and off the web. In Anne Sexton's collection *Transformations* ([1971] 2016), sixteen Grimm fairy tales are retooled as feminist critiques, recontextualized with contemporary references and slang, and infused with dark humor. Olga Broumas's poems in *Beginning with O* (1977) explore a lesbian take on traditional tales. Roald Dahl, the wildly popular author of children's books such as *Charlie and the Chocolate Factory* ([1964] 1995) and *Matilda* (1988), wrote a number of fairy-tale themed poems in his book *Revolting Rhymes* ([1982] 2009), including the memorable "Little Red Riding

Hood and the Wolf" in which Little Red shoots the wolf with a pistol she is concealing in her knickers.

A distinctly twentieth- and twenty-first-century form in which the fairy tale has thrived is the graphic novel, a book-length narrative in comics form. An umbrella term that encompasses fiction, nonfiction, and anthologized content, graphic novels have proved particularly fertile ground for the fairy tale, potentially due at least in part to the fact that the combination of text and image presents continuities with another form many fairy tales took throughout the twentieth century: picture books for children, as discussed later in this chapter. Perhaps the most famous example of a fairy-tale graphic novel is *Fables*, a series written by Bill Willingham and published in installments from 2002 to 2015. *Fables* follows various characters drawn from fairy tales and folklore more broadly as they navigate life in contemporary New York City after their fairy-tale homeland was conquered by a shadowy figure called The Adversary. Darker fare includes Emily Carroll's horror-tinged *Through the Woods* (2014) and Carroll's collaboration with author Marika McCoola, *Baga Yaga's Assistant* (2015). *Damsels* (2017) by Leah Moore and John Reppion remixes several familiar tales as characters such as Little Red Riding Hood, the Frog Prince, and the Little Mermaid team up to save their kingdoms from the outbreak of a war. Siblings Kit and Cat Seaton explore a folk version of Beauty and the Beast in *Norroway Book 1: The Black Bull of Norroway* (2018), and Allison O'Toole's *Wayward Sisters: An Anthology of Monstrous Women* (2018) celebrates female and nonbinary monstrosity drawn from fairy tales and folklore. Kate Ashwin and Kel McDonald curate the *Cautionary Fables and Fairytales Series* (2016–), which presents tales from Europe, Africa, and Asia. Still other graphic novels, for instance Katie O'Neill's *The Tea Dragon Society* (2017), present original fairy tales.

FILM

Any thorough discussion of fairy-tale film requires an acknowledgment of the behemoth that is Disney, or The Walt Disney Company: "a highly diversified, multinational mass media and entertainment conglomerate, considered one of the most influential brands in the world and valued by Forbes (2015) at approximately $180 billion" (Haas and Trapedo 2018: 178). The studio released its first full-length animated feature film, *Snow White and the Seven Dwarfs*, in 1937, and it has dominated fairy tales in the box office ever since. "Walt Disney," as Jack Zipes puts it, "cast a spell on the fairy tale" using "the most up-to-date technological means" and "his own 'American' grit and ingenuity" (Zipes 2017: 414). Over the last eight decades, the Walt Disney Company has produced dozens of live-action and animated fairy-tale (and fairy-tale adjacent) films, and its reach extends into television shows, toys, clothes, theme parks, and more. Some of Disney's most significant fairy-tale films include *Cinderella* ([1950] 1997), *Sleeping Beauty* (1959), *The Little Mermaid* (1989), *Beauty and the Beast* (1991), *Aladdin* (1992), *Enchanted* (2007), and *Frozen* (2013). The 2010s have seen a slew of live-action remakes of many of their most popular animated features, including *Cinderella* (2015), *Beauty and the Beast* (2017), and *Aladdin* (2019), each of which attempted to recapture and expand upon the success of their originals. Disney films, and related Disney media, are often the vehicles through which US audiences first encounter fairy tales. Because "the empire began by appropriating fairy tales that speak to both children and parents, Disney learned early how to attract this dual audience: children and parents alike have come to equate all fairy tales with Disney" (Haas and Trapedo 2018: 179). There is simply no denying Disney's colossal impact on the fairy-tale landscape, but though Disney has long dominated the arena, particularly in the US, "they by no means encompass, delimit, or prescribe criteria for fairy-tale films" (Greenhill 2018: 357). Many other studios have produced noteworthy fairy-tale films with very different perspectives and agendas. Jean Cocteau's stunning black-and-white French film *La Belle et la Bête* (*Beauty and the Beast*) (1946) had a dramatic impact not only on Disney's animated and live-action films of the same name but numerous other adaptations of the fairy tale. *Ever After* (1998), directed by Andy Tennant, is a bold, feminist retelling of Cinderella, while Mark Palansky's *Penelope* (2006) offers a gender-swapped version of Beauty and the Beast. DreamWorks' *Shrek* (2001) is yet another reworking of the Beauty and the Beast theme, a parody that pokes fun at such fairy-tale staples as beauty, chivalry, etiquette, and transformation. Less familiar, foreign, and/or independent films that have, nevertheless, inspired critical attention—such as director Jacques Demy's *Donkeyskin* (1970), Neil Jordan's *The Company of Wolves* (1984), based on the Angela Carter short story of the same name, Nietzchka Keene's *The Juniper Tree* (1990), and the David Kaplan 1997 short *Little Red Riding Hood*—should also be mentioned. More recently, we saw a spike in Snow White films in 2012 with the release of Tarsem Singh's *Mirror Mirror* and Rupert Sanders's *Snow White and the Huntsman*.

Fairy-tale films that flirt with, or entirely embrace, horror have also experienced immense popularity. As Sue Short observes, "horror's kinship with fairy tales is especially apparent in providing a host of monsters (both supernatural and ostensibly human) to jangle our nerves and chill our blood" (2018: 532). Notable fairy-tale horror, or horror-adjacent, films include Catherine Breillat's *Barbe bleue* (Bluebeard) (2009), Tommy Wirkola's *Hansel and Gretel: Witch Hunters* (2013), and Matteo Garrone's *Tale of Tales* (2015). Perhaps most significant are the masterful fairy-tale films of Guillermo del Toro: *Pan's Labyrinth* (2006) and *The Shape of Water* (2017), which won Academy Awards for best director and best picture.

TELEVISION

Since television first aired, fairy tales have graced its screens. In 1957 Rodger and Hammerstein's musical *Cinderella*, starring Julie Andrews as the title character, was broadcast, and 100 million people tuned in. The only Rodger and Hammerstein musical written specifically for television, the show's incredible popularity led it to be remade for TV in 1965 (starring Leslie Ann Warren) and again in 1997 (starring Brandy Norwood). While *Cinderella* is perhaps the most famous example of a made-for-TV fairy-tale special, as well as the subject of Patricia Sawin's delightful book chapter "Things Walt Disney Didn't Tell Us (But at Which Rodgers and Hammerstein at Least Hinted): The 1965 Made-for-TV Musical of Cinderella" (2014), it is not an isolated phenomenon. Other notable examples include the made-for-TV movie *Snow White: A Tale of Terror* (1997), featuring Sigourney Weaver; the mini-series *The 10th Kingdom* (2000); and the Broadway musical adapted for TV *Peter Pan* (1955, 1960, and 2014).

Dozens of television series engage with fairy tales, from retellings to postmodern remixes, from Netflix original productions to K-dramas. Some of these shows are aimed at a child audience while others are geared toward adults. "Fractured Fairy Tales," a segment on the animated variety show *The Adventures of Rocky and Bullwinkle and Friends* (1959–64), retold traditional fairy tales with modern twists. The short sketches employed copious puns and often presented a satirical perspective on the tale at hand, bridging both child and adult audiences.

The 1980s saw an explosion of fairy-tale content on the small screen. From 1982 to 1987, Shelley Duvall's *Faerie Tale Theatre* retold stories drawn largely from the collections of the Grimm brothers and Hans Christian Andersen. This live-action anthology series was aimed at children but featured stars such as Robin Williams, Susan Serandon, Mick Jagger, and Liza Minnelli. Jim Henson's *The Storyteller* (dir. Steve Barron 1987) starred John Hurt in the title role and mingled live-action actors and puppetry to retell chiefly German folk and fairy tales. Yet another landmark series from the 1980s is *Beauty and the Beast* (1987–90), a fantasy-drama series that reimagines the titular fairy tale in contemporary Manhattan. In this series, Beauty is Catherine, an assistant district attorney, to the leonine Vincent, the series' Beast. A grittier show than *Faerie Tale Theatre* or *The Storyteller*, *Beauty and the Beast* catered to an adult audience, and eventually spawned a reboot series of the same name that aired from 2012 to 2016.

Fairy-tale television only seems to be rising in popularity in recent years. *Once Upon a Time* (2011–18) placed Disney characters into the fictional town of Storybrooke, where they have been exiled and stripped of their memories and true identities. *Grimm* (2011–17) embedded creatures from fairy tales,

FIGURE 1.2: Still from the anime series *Princess Tutu* (2002–3), created by Ikuko Itoh (Hal Film Maker Studio, Japan).

folklore, and pure invention into the form of a procedural drama. Most recently, *Disenchantment* (2018–), an animated fantasy series, offers a comical send-up of fairy-tale tropes. Created by Matt Groening of *The Simpsons* and *Futurama* fame, *Disenchantment* follows the adventures of a rebellious, alcoholic princess named Bean and her companions Elfo (her lovesick, elven sidekick) and Luci (a demon tasked with Bean's destruction).

Beyond American and European productions, fairy tales play a significant role in the Japanese genre of anime (and the related form of manga). Bill Ellis has written extensively about the roles fairy tales play in anime such as *Princess Tutu* (2002–3) (see Figure 1.2), *Cardcaptor Sakura* (1998–2000), and *Sasami: Magical Girls Club* (2006–7) (see Ellis 2016). Other notable shows include *Gurimu meisaku gekijou* (Grimm's Fairy Tale Classics) (1987–9), which offers fairly straightforward but subtly feminist retellings (see Jorgensen and Warman 2014), and *Snow White with the Red Hair* (2015–16), which takes Snow White as an initial inspiration but veers into a fantasy slice-of-life format. Still other anime, such as *Revolutionary Girl Utena* (1997) and *Puella Magi Madoka Magica* (2011), fragment and remix the fairy-tale to create alternate narratives of femininity (see Cleto and Bahl 2016; Lezubski 2014).

STAGE

The stage productions in which the fairy tale has undoubtedly shone the brightest in the twentieth and twenty-first centuries are the full-scale musicals of Broadway. Marketed to both adults and children, these extravagant productions are both "thriving" and, perhaps unexpectedly, even "using latent potentialities of the fairy-tale genre to subvert dominant ideologies" (Schacker 2018: 343).

Perhaps the first fairy-tale musical most people think of is Stephen Sondheim and James Lapine's well-loved mash-up of tales, *Into the Woods* (1987). With its complex intertwined narratives, the show "challenges the audience to be constantly aware of the contrast between [its] plot and [those] of the traditional tales it draws from" (Hallett and Karasek 2014: 113). Featuring a large cast of fairy-tale characters, from Little Red Riding Hood and the Wolf to Cinderella, and questioning nearly everything about the fairy-tale form, this funny and thought-provoking show remains popular even years later. It was, in fact, recently made into a big-budget Disney fairy-tale film (*Into the Woods* 2014). Even before that, however, was another fairy-tale parody *Once Upon a Mattress* (1959), an unconventional retelling and expanding of Hans Christian Andersen's story of "The Princess and the Pea," which also enjoyed considerable popularity and launched the career of theatre and television superstar Carol Burnett. Here too we see the fairy-tale musical used to question societal stereotypes about beauty, marriage, family, and more. In addition to these original productions, Disney has branched out into Broadway musicals as well. Fairy-tale musicals such as *Beauty and the Beast* (1994) and *The Little Mermaid* (2008)—both based on the popular Disney films of the same names—have proven to be massive successes in the musical theatre world. In recent years, shows such as *Wicked* (2003), which purports to tell the true story of Oz's Wicked Witch of the West, and *Shrek: The Musical* (2008), based on the parodic fairy-tale film of the same name, have drawn on the fairy tale as well. Even the very recent *Hadestown* (2016), a retelling of the Greek myth of Orpheus and Eurydice, taps into fairy-tale themes.

In focusing on the musical, we do not mean to ignore the other incredible stage work that has been done with the fairy tale in recent years. For example, the innovative productions of Matthew Bourne's British dance-theatre company, New Adventures, have achieved worldwide success with fascinating new takes on *Cinderella* (1997), *Sleeping Beauty: A Gothic Romance* (2012), *The Red Shoes* (2016), among other familiar tales. There is also Zach Morris, Tom Pearson, and Jennine Willett's intense immersive theatre experience *Then She Fell* (2012), based on the writings of Lewis Carroll, and James Ortiz' play *The Woodsman* (2012), which, like *Wicked*, draws from the works of L. Frank Baum to challenge what we think we know about the beloved characters of Oz.

MUSIC

Music has long been entwined with the fairy tale, from traditional songs to symphony scores to operas. While these connections remain, we have chosen to focus our attention on recent pop and rock music and the related genre of the music video. These contemporary forms borrow voraciously from the fairy tale. While some songs' lyrics are constructed around a single tale, others remix characters and motifs from multiple tales to create an intertextual web. Still other songs embed scattered references to fairy tales within the lyrics, and these kernels recontexualize the song as part of the fairy-tale realm. Music videos created to complement these songs often adopt a distinctive fairy-tale atmosphere, particularly through costuming and the strategic use of props and setting.

Some of the songs that predominantly interact with or retell a single tale include "Beauty and the Beast" (1997) by Nightwish, "Snow-White" (2003–4) by Xandria, and "Rapunzel" (2003a) and "Rose Red" (2003b) by Emilie Autumn. Perhaps the most famous example of a "retelling" fairy-tale song is "Li'l Red Riding Hood" (1966) by Sam the Sham and the Pharaohs. Based on the iconic fairy-tale popularized by Charles Perrault and, later, Jacob and Wilhelm Grimm, the lyrics are written from the perspective of the Big Bad Wolf as he encounters Little Red Riding Hood in the woods. The famous lines detailing the size of the wolf's eyes and teeth are revised ("What big eyes you have / The kind of eyes that drive wolves mad ... What full lips you have / They're sure to lure someone bad") to describe Little Red's irresistible allure, explicitly framing the fairy tale in terms of desire and sex appeal.

Fairy-tale remix songs include "Jack's Place" (2011a) and "Wicked Girls" (2011b) by fantasy and science-fiction writer Seanan McGuire. "Jack's Place" imagines such popular fairy-tale characters as Cinderella, "Goldie" (or Goldilocks), the Little Mermaid, and Prince Charming as the employees at a bar, owned by Jack himself. "Wicked Girls," a tour-de-force that imagines the fates of the girls who were expelled from their magical worlds, proved so resonate that it has inspired McGuire's *Wayward Children* series, the first of which (2016's *Every Heart a Doorway*) swept the Hugo, Nebula, and Locus awards. "Fairytale" (2004) by Sara Bareilles and "Wonderland" (2011) by Natalia Kill offer feminist critiques of the expected fairy-tale plot, giving voice to disillusioned fairy-tale heroines who "can't take no more of your fairytale love" (Bareilles) and "don't believe in fairy tales" (Kills).

Other songs interact more subtly with the fairy tale. Florence + the Machine's oeuvre provides a wealth of examples of this kind of music. Her song "Rabbit Heart" (2009b) is woven through with references to the King Midas myth, but the accompanying music video is a tribute to the Mad Hatter's tea party in *Alice's Adventures in Wonderland* (1865). By contrast, "Blinding" (2009a) draws on sleeping maiden stories, troubling the boundaries between sleeping, death, and knowledge.

VISUAL ARTS AND MATERIAL CULTURE

The fairy tale has always been a deep wellspring of material for the fine arts and illustration—the descriptions of far-off castles, evil witches, enchanted dresses, and talking animals provide endless inspiration. Indeed, "as our culture has become so visually oriented, the illustration has come to dominate the word to the extent that certain climatic episodes in the classic fairy tales have achieved instant recognizability" via central images, such as red cloaks and glass slippers (Hallett and Karasek 2014: 104). Particularly popular throughout the nineteenth and early twentieth centuries were fairy-tale illustrations, with such significant artists as Arthur Rackham (Figure 1.3), Edmund Dulac, Kay Nielsen, and Walter Crane leading the way. This medium has remained popular into the later twentieth and twenty-first centuries, and notable more recent fairy-tale illustration artists include Charles Vess, Kuniko Craft, and Mercer Mayer. While picture-book illustration has been the dominant visual medium for working with the fairy tale, the fine arts have of course played with the form as well, "engag[ing] mindfully with fairy-tale elements with the intent to provoke conversation surrounding the issues inherent in both the work and the tale" (Slack-Smith 2018: 497). Recent artists of particular note include Paula Rego, Kiki Smith, David Hockney, Dina Goldstein, Nicoletta Ceccoli, José Rodolfo Loaiza Ontiveros, and Shaun Tan. There have also been numerous popular exhibitions focused around fairy-tale themes, including the very recent exhibitions "Fantasies and Fairy Tales" by the Los Angeles County Museum of Art in Los Angeles, California (2018–19) and "Dread and Delight: Fairy Tales in an Anxious World," a traveling exhibition that began at the Weatherspoon Art Museum of the University of North Carolina at Greensboro in Greensboro, North Carolina (2018). This is, of course, to say nothing of the influence fairy tales have had on the visual media of advertising. As Martin Hallett and Barbara Karasek put it, "central to the fairy-tale vision is the achievement of the *ultimate*, generally in the form of happiness, wealth, and beauty, so it isn't difficult to see the appeal for a retailer" (2014: 129; emphasis in the original).

Fairy tales have also served to inspire various pieces of material culture, including figurines, home decor, toys, and board games such as Magpie Games' role-playing Bluebeard's Bride (2017) and Atlas Games' card-based games Fairytale Gloom (2015) and Once Upon a Time (1994). Perhaps the most unexpected combination of fairy tale and material culture, however, occurs in the relatively recent proliferation of fairy-tale-inspired clothing.

FIGURE 1.3: "Ashenputtel goes to the ball," illustration by Arthur Rackham from *The Fairy Tales of the Brothers Grimm* (New York: Doubleday, Page and Co., 1909).

The retail chain store Hot Topic, for example, is a staple of many malls in America and often features inexpensive clothing and accessories inspired by famous fairy tales. On the opposite end of the spectrum, the recent "Fairy Tale Fashion" exhibition by the Fashion Institute of Technology in New York City (2016) showcased high fashion designers who frequently turn to the fairy tale, including such masters as Alexander McQueen, Dolce and Gabbana,

Prada, and Marchesa. High fashion also uses the fairy tale for photography inspiration, as evidenced by the hugely popular fairy-tale fashion photography of Tom Walker for *Vogue* magazine.

DIGITAL MEDIA

The forms that perhaps necessitate the most attention as we progress through the twenty-first century are those of our always-evolving digital culture. Innovative, unconventional, and frequently quite wonderful, digital projects—from video games to web comics to YouTube videos—provide new and exciting places for the fairy tale to grow.

The earliest of these new digital forms, the video game has repeatedly been and continues to be inspired by the fairy tale. Early games such as *The Legend of Zelda* (1986) and even *Super Mario Bros* (1985), with its insistence on the player repeatedly rescuing a princess (Whatman and Tedeschi 2018: 640), tended to simply take fairy-tale tropes as starting places, but more recent games engage with the form more directly. Examples include Disney's *Kingdom Hearts* series (2002–19), which takes the Disney versions of fairy-tale characters on new adventures; *American McGee's Alice* (2000), a horror game based on Lewis Carroll's *Alice's Adventures in Wonderland*; *The Path* (2009), a game that invites the player to interact as different versions of Little Red Riding Hood; *Cinders* (2012), a choose-your-own-adventure game based on "Cinderella"; and *The Wolf Among Us* (2013), a noir mystery game starring the Big Bad Wolf as he appears in Bill Willingham's comic series *Fables*. Though the video game has proven to be a fruitful site for fairy-tale exploration of all kinds, many of these games do, as Emma Whatman and Victoria Tedeschi point out, "demonstrat[e] a move to the darker traditions of earlier fairy tales and oral folktales" by engaging specifically with themes such as violence and death (Whatman and Tedeschi 2018: 635). The later evolution of the video game—the mobile games and apps that entertain us on our smartphones and tablets—also deserve a mention, as they frequently find inspiration in the fairy tale as well. Consider, for example, *Tasty Tales* (2014), a cooking puzzle game featuring fairy-tale characters, the picture book app *The King's Ears* by Cynthia Nugent (see Nugent 2018), and the very recent strategy game *Revolve8* (2019), which features heroes from fairy tales and folklore from around the world.

Meanwhile, since the inception of the internet, the fairy-tale form has thrived online as well. Largely a participatory space, one that encourages "individuals to produce content themselves" and "shift away from producer hegemony to audience or consumer power" (Miller 2011: 87), much of the fairy-tale content on the internet is created by enthusiastic fans eager to engage with the material they love. Audiences become "active, critically engaged, and creative" (Jenkins 2006: i). This results in fairy-tale databases such as the *SurLaLune Fairy Tales* site by Heidi Anne Heiner (1998) and D. L. Ashliman's *Folktexts* (1996–2020);

blogs, such as Gypsy Thornton's *Once Upon a Blog* (2009–) and fairy-tale author and editor Terri Windling's *Myth and Moor* (2008–); web comics, including the deeply intertextual *No Rest for the Wicked* (2003) by Andrea L. Peterson and Sfé R. Monster's queer tale *Eth's Skin* (2014); and online videos, such as the queer fairy-tale parodies of Todrick Hall, including "Cinderfella" (2014) and "Disney Dudez" (2013); and the more straightforward adaptations aimed at children like those by Smart Kids TV (2014–) and Cool School (2014–).

The proliferation of the fairy tale in participatory digital media on the web has allowed for other forms of fan culture to thrive (and be documented) as well. Fan events such as Disney's D23 Expo, costuming and cosplay, and the fairy-tale fanfiction posted on websites like Fanfiction (1998–) or An Archive of Our Own (2007–) are new forms that have expanded the concept of what the fairy tale can be in recent years. Even more subtle forms of fan participation such as "bounding" (in which a person dresses up in a way that slyly evokes a specific character) have expanded to include the fairy tale, with fans dressing in everyday items like red hoodies to reference Little Red Riding Hood, pale foundation and red lipstick to recall Snow White, and see-through shoes to conjure Cinderella.

CONCLUSION

Though fairy tales have long been a significant cultural force, they have attained a new order of prominence in the twentieth and twenty-first centuries. While much of their increasing presence is surely due to the ever-expanding influence of Disney, fairy tales remain a force to be considered well beyond the corporation's domain. Fairy tales flourish in literature and art, online and in games, in fashion and fan culture, and they will undoubtedly continue to do so in whatever media and cultural forms arise in the future. They help shape the narratives we consume, the way we play, and the identities we create. In their book *Marvelous Transformations: An Anthology of Fairy Tales and Contemporary Critical Perspectives*, Christine Jones and Jennifer Schacker argue that "the idea of the fairy tale might be better understood as an open-ended, playful way of engaging social and political issues in a form that defies the constraints of realist fiction rather than as a *fixed* discursive form that corresponds to a set of narrative rules" (2012: 488; emphasis in the original). We suspect that the ease with which the fairy tale can adapt to new media and remain relevant to ever-changing landscapes has much to do with this versatility of form.

CHAPTER TWO

Adaptation

MAYAKO MURAI

INTRODUCTION

The modern age has seen a global circulation of fairy-tale adaptations on a scale never experienced before. Technological developments since the early twentieth century have enhanced the traditional multimediality and intermediality of the fairy tale, especially its visual dimension. New critical perspectives developed in this period have also inspired writers, artists, filmmakers, and creators in various other fields to adapt the fairy tale to address contemporary social, cultural, and aesthetic concerns relating to gender, sexuality, class, race, ethnicity, and species. While new media forms such as film, TV, and digital media, combined with older media of print, performance, and visual images, have often commodified certain features of canonical—mainly European—fairy tales, such as the heteronormative romance plot that ends happily ever after with a royal marriage, they have also served to inspire and disseminate innovative adaptations of hitherto marginalized and indigenous fairy tales globally.

This chapter considers adaptation as intertextuality, that is, dialogic relations among texts, rather than as a one-way process of adapting the original into a secondary text. In "Adaptation and the Fairy-Tale Web," Cristina Bacchilega points out the fundamentally decentered aspect of fairy-tale adaptations as follows:

> Grappling, as we must for most fairy tales, with the absence of an original text calls for a sharp turn away from adaptation as the result of a one-way transfer from its given source (e.g. tale to film) and an approach to fairy-tale adaptations as fluid texts that are produced and processed, in this

century perhaps even more than before, in a web of connections that are "hypertextual," in that they do not refer back to one center.

(2018a: 150)

To examine what characterizes fairy-tale adaptations in the modern age, I use Linda Hutcheon's oft-quoted definition of adaptation as "an announced and extensive transposition of a particular work or works" (2013: 7). For Hutcheon "this 'transcoding' can involve a shift of medium (a poem to a film), or genre (an epic to a novel), or a change of frame and therefore context: telling the same story from a different point of view, for instance, can create a manifestly different interpretation" (7–8). In what follows, I first give an overview of fairy-tale adaptations from these three perspectives, that is, medium, genre, and frame, which are closely intertwined. I then analyze the Grimms' "The Bremen Town Musicians" as a case study to illustrate some of the ways in which remediation, translation, and diffusion are interrelated in global and local contexts today. This chapter concludes by pointing toward the possibility of creating a cross-disciplinary adaptation of this animal tale for multispecies coexistence.

INTERMEDIA TRANSFORMATIONS

Throughout its history, the fairy tale has always involved a wide variety of media beyond oral and print forms and has evolved through various multimedia and intermedia transformations. I use the term media to mean different forms of communicating information, including oral storytelling, writing, dance, theatre, visual arts, music, film, radio, television, fashion, digital media, the internet, and any combination of these forms. More recently, interactive adaptations in such forms as video gaming, social media, online apps, and fandom have become increasingly popular, as the new media platforms covered by *The Routledge Companion to Media and Fairy-Tale Cultures* (2018), edited by Pauline Greenhill, Jill Terry Rudy, Naomi Hamer, and Lauren Bosc, indicate. Intermediality refers to the interconnectedness and interactions between different media forms, and I use this term to stress the ways in which fairy tales have been transmitted not only through the combinations of multiple media forms, an aspect that overlaps with the concept of multimediality, but also through the interactions—and, in some cases, in the interstices—between different sensory modalities of communication. For example, the powerful visual appeal inherent in such canonical tales as "Little Red Riding Hood," "Cinderella," and "Sleeping Beauty" is evident from numerous visual adaptations in traditional print media such as illustrations and picture books (these two media are distinguished from each other in that the latter treats both words and visual images as essential narrative components). These visual adaptations, in turn, have played a crucial role not only in disseminating but also in shaping and reshaping certain tales and images of characters especially after the massive expansion of print culture in the nineteenth century. As Bacchilega argues, to approach fairy-tale adaptations in various modern media

> demands some attention to how their story power draws upon their "mediality" ... and their circulation in a broader cultural economy. So in contrast to "retelling," which emphasizes narrative reoccurrence, and "revision," which points to interpretation, (fairy-tale) "adaptation" invites a consideration of transformative interpretation as grounded in the materiality, codes, experience, and promotion of a (fairy) story's move across media—and thus into new contexts, audiences, markets, and potential for further adaptation.
>
> (2018a: 147)

Since the early twentieth century, film has become one of the most influential media in disseminating the fairy tale and has also helped expand the possibilities of fairy-tale adaptations.[1] The earliest film adaptations of fairy tales by two pioneering filmmakers, Walt Disney and Lotte Reiniger, appeared in 1922. Disney adapted seven fairy tales including "Little Red Riding Hood," "Cinderella," and "The Bremen Town Musicians" into short animation films at the Laugh-O-Gram studio, while Reiniger made experimental silhouette animation films based on "Cinderella" and "Sleeping Beauty." From this point onward, animated pictures on the screen have been incorporated into the traditional multimediality of the fairy tale, breathing new life into familiar tales and characters to enhance the genre's ability to enchant audiences, especially children.

Disney then went on to make the first feature-length animated film *Snow White and the Seven Dwarfs* in 1937. It is significant that this film stylistically models itself on another increasingly popular medium at the time, musical theatre,[2] by making use of singing, music, and choreography for character and plot development. The widespread and long-standing popularity of the songs from the film such as "Heigh-Ho" and "Some Day My Prince Will Come," written by Frank Churchill (music) and Larry Morey (lyrics), indicates the importance of music in this cinematic storytelling. Regarded as the first feature film to have a soundtrack album released commercially, Disney's *Snow White* can be said to have pioneered the multimedia franchises widely in evidence today. The film's commercial and critical success has resulted in its further transmedia adaptations by Disney, including theme park attractions (e.g., Snow White's Scary Adventures at Disneyland), a variety of Snow White-themed merchandise, video games, live-action films, and television series (e.g., ABC's *Once Upon a Time* [2011–18]). Other fairy-tale films by Disney that followed have also adopted and developed this transmedia strategy. For example, Disney's "Dream Big, Princess" campaign (2016–) uses social media platforms such as Instagram and Facebook to create online communities among young girls around the world. Such strategies have had a significant impact on the diffusion and the refashioning of certain fairy tales on a global scale.

At the same time, as Bacchilega points out, the image of fairy tales has become "more fragmented and more expansive" since the 1970s due to more diversified approaches to them in both creative and critical practices and to wider and more interactive accessibility for audiences (2018a: 150). This tendency can be also found even among fairy-tale animation films, a medium that has been largely dominated by Disney's works in many parts of the world. For example, DreamWorks' *Shrek* (2001), a computer-animated film adaptation of the 1990 picture book of the same title by William Steig, and its sequels are parodies of Disney's adaptations of "Beauty and the Beast" and other tales, questioning the various social and cultural assumptions on which Disney's fairy-tale films are based. *Shrek*'s playful subversion of Disneyfied fairy-tale narratives and characters and its incorporation of pop culture have helped fragment the genre in a way that appeals to both adult and child audiences. On the other hand, Studio Ghibli's animation films such as *Ponyo* (2008), an adaptation of Hans Christian Andersen's "The Little Mermaid," and *The Tale of the Princess Kaguya* (2013), an adaptation of a traditional Japanese literary fairy tale "The Tale of the Bamboo Cutter," have helped expand awareness of the cultural diversity of fairy tales. Many of Ghibli's films draw on fairy-tale intertexts from both Western and Japanese traditions and combine them to address social, cultural, and aesthetic issues that are both specific to a localized culture and shared among rapidly globalizing cultures.

Fairy tales have been adapted into films not only for children but also for adults. Fairy-tale films such as Jean Cocteau's *La Belle et la Bête* (*Beauty and the Beast*) (1946), Jacques Demy's *Donkeyskin* (1970), and Catherine Breillat's *Bluebeard* (2009) have subversive intentions both aesthetically and politically, since they use the fairy tale to explore alternative forms of art, enchantment, and pleasure. Live-action Hollywood films such as *Snow White and the Huntsman* (2012) and *Maleficent* (2014), on the other hand, focus on adult-oriented themes such as sexual jealousy and betrayal (see Szugajew 2020). As I will argue below, these adult-oriented film adaptations are largely influenced by psychoanalytic interpretations of fairy tales popularized in the late twentieth century.

The fairy tale has also been a source of inspiration for visual art in the modern age. In the early twentieth century, surrealist artists used motifs and images from fairy tales to evoke dreamlike, disturbing visions. René Magritte's painting *The Collective Invention* (1934), for example, subverts the conventional image of the alluring bare-breasted mermaid by inverting the configuration of her hybrid body. British artist and writer Leonora Carrington's (1917–2011) works often adapt motifs, themes, and images from both European and Mexican fairy tales to express female-oriented aesthetics (see McAra 2017).

In the late twentieth century, artworks that adapt fairy tales from a feminist perspective began to appear. As is the case with feminist literary adaptations of fairy tales (as I will discuss below), "Little Red Riding Hood" has been one of the most frequently adapted fairy tales in contemporary feminist art. Kiki Smith (1954–) has adapted motifs, themes, and images in traditional fairy tales using multiple media to explore the themes of sexuality, animality, and the body. For example, Smith visualized "Little Red Riding Hood" in the form of twelve glass sheets with fired paint in *Gang of Girls and Pack of Wolves* (1999), a mixed-media installation originally exhibited with recorded sound *Daughter* (1999), the bronze sculpture *Rapture* (2001), and the lithographs *Companions* (2001) and *Born* (2002b). In these works, images of women and wolves are melted together, remolded, and reborn in various substances that keep changing their form and nature. Paula Rego's (1935–) *Little Red Riding Hood Suite* (2003), consisting of six pastel paintings, is a visual retelling of the tale from the viewpoints of three generations of women in a contemporary society. Tomoko Kōnoike (1960–), as Amy Greenhough discusses in Chapter 4 of this volume and I have discussed elsewhere (Murai 2015), has adapted fairy tales, most notably "Little Red Riding Hood," using multiple media and materials such as painting and embroidering on animal skins and video installations of the artist singing folk songs and howling with real wolves in the snow. In these ways, her works expand the boundaries of our sensory perception and narrative imagination.

Fairy-tale adaptations have also been adapted into photographic works. As a medium that starts with real-world objects, people, and animals, photography draws the viewer's attention to the staged and performed aspect of the fairy tale, a genre engaged with the imaginary, as well as to the racial, sexual, social, and cultural biases that many canonical European fairy tales such as "Snow White" and "Cinderella" presuppose and reproduce (Murai 2018: 348).[3] Carrie Mae Weems's (1953–) *Mirror, Mirror* (1987–8), for example, challenges the supposed universality of the equation of beauty with whiteness in "Snow White" by restaging the famous mirror scene as a scene in which a white figure in the mirror racially assaults a black woman standing in front of the mirror. Miwa Yanagi's (1967–) *Fairy Tale* series (2004–6), on the other hand, juxtaposes Asian and Caucasian models in the same scene to defamiliarize the racial assumptions inherent in such canonical tales as "Cinderella" and "Sleeping Beauty" while at the same time destabilizing the well-established binary opposition between the young beautiful princess and the old ugly witch by presenting such stereotypical images as arbitrary and therefore open to revision. In his *Existing in Costume* series of photographs (2006–), Chan-Hyo Bae (1975–) exposes the Eurocentric colonizing norm still dominant in today's globalizing fairy-tale culture by casting himself in the role of fairy-tale princesses such as Cinderella and Beauty in carefully staged photographs that reference traditional European oil paintings portraying powerful rulers. Dina Goldstein's (1969–) *Fallen Princesses* series (2007–9) parodically recasts Disney's fairy-tale princesses such as Snow White and Cinderella in present-day realistic—and often conflictual—settings to question the sexual, cultural, and racial stereotypes endorsed by the Disneyfied adaptations of fairy tales.

Photography has also added another dimension to picture-book adaptations of fairy tales. Fashion photographer Sarah Moon's (1941–) *Little Red Riding Hood* ([1983] 2002) transposes Perrault's cautionary tale into a modern urban setting. Moon's stylish black-and-white photographs make visible the way contemporary visual culture commodifies little girls as passive objects of male gaze and make viewers recognize their own potential complicity in normalizing the narrative of their victimization. In contrast to Moon's *Little Red Riding Hood*, which portrays a flesh-and-blood girl, Cindy Sherman's (1954–) photographic picture book *Fitcher's Bird* (1992) undermines the kind of realism usually expected of photography by using wax dolls and other artificial objects whose artificiality is emphasized with intense lighting and vividly saturated colors. While closely following the Grimms' tale, Sherman's photographic adaptation brings to light the morbid and excessive desires underpinning the fairy-tale romance. By applying the photographic grammar such as focus, camera angle, framing, composition, light, and color to visual storytelling, these photographic picture-book adaptations invite viewers to reframe familiar fairy tales from another angle.

Various writers have also experimented with the multimediality of fairy tales to address newly emerging social and cultural issues. For example, Angela Carter (1940–92) adapted traditional fairy tales into different media forms to critique dominant assumptions about gender and sexuality in a patriarchal society and to explore alternative modes of being and desiring. Carter's adaptation of fairy tales first appeared in the form of translation in *The Fairy Tales of Charles Perrault* (1977a). Her English translation updated the worldly morals of Perrault's tales for late twentieth-century readers, adapting them to the sociosexual politics of her own time. As Martine Hennard Dutheil de la Rochère argues in *Reading, Translating, Rewriting: Angela Carter's Translational Poetics* (2013: 75), Carter's translation of Perrault's "Little Red Riding Hood" for this book is related to her multiple retellings of the tale in *The Bloody Chamber and Other Stories* ([1979] 2006).

The Bloody Chamber, an anthology of ten short stories based on traditional European tales, is threaded through with the theme of a pubescent girl's encounter with a beast. "The Company of Wolves," one of Carter's adaptations of "Little Red Riding Hood," addresses this theme by foregrounding the sexual subtext of the tale and repurposing it for contemporary adult readers. Carter also adapted "The Company of Wolves" into a radio play bearing the same title (1980). In the preface to her radio play anthology, *Come Unto These Yellow*

Sands: Four Radio Plays (1985), she describes her interest in the particular mediality of radio as follows: "It is the necessary open-endedness of the medium, the way the listener is invited into the narrative to contribute to it his or her own way of 'seeing' the voices and the sounds, the invisible beings and events, that gives radio story-telling its real third dimension, which is the space that, above all, interests and enchants me" (Carter 1985: 7). Radio is here perceived as an expanded form of oral storytelling that can provoke the listener's visual imagination through sounds alone, a medium that enhances the enchantment of the fairy tale in a different way from other types of media. In *"Anagrams of Desire": Angela Carter's Writing for Radio, Film and Television* (2003), Charlotte Crofts makes a formal comparison between the radio play and the short story for their "elliptical" style: "Both forms paradoxically contain more imaginative space precisely because of their 'lack'" (Crofts 2003: 23). Carter then went on to explore the visual dimension of "The Company of Wolves" in cinematic form and coscripted the screenplay bearing the same title (1984) with the director Neil Jordan. The film's emphasis on werewolves' corporeal transformations using various graphic effects intertextually refers to the horror film genre, while each sequence is loaded with ambiguous visual symbolism that intermedially evokes Carter's other textual retellings of wolf stories in *The Bloody Chamber*. Bacchilega argues that "while intertextually and intermedially linked, *The Company of Wolves* print, audio, and filmic adaptations have no center of origin or fixed message; rather as they each exploit the singularity of medium and genre, they powerfully reenact the traditional multimediality of fairy tales, and they put it to work toward transformative performances of sexuality and gender" (2018a: 148–9).

In her final intermedia project on fairy tales, Carter returned to print form, this time, as the editor of tale collections from around the world, titled *The Virago Book of Fairy Tales* (1990) and *The Second Virago Book of Fairy Tales* (1992). Carter's *Virago Books*, as I have argued elsewhere (Murai 2012), can be regarded as a feminist and postcolonial adaptation of Andrew Lang's rainbow-colored series of fairy-tale collections. Carter's own translation of Perrault's "Little Red Riding Hood" without his "Moral" appears in a chapter titled "Moral Tales." These fairy-tale collections published by Virago, one of the leading publishers of women's writing, recontextualize "Little Red Riding Hood" within a female-centered storytelling tradition that can be found across cultures through various editorial strategies. Importantly, in a footnote to this tale, she recollects her childhood memory of listening to her maternal grandmother's oral retelling of the tale accompanied by the gesture of gobbling the girl up at the conclusion, which gave her "excited pleasure" (Carter 1990: 240n). This autobiographical episode told in the footnote seems to complete the sequence of Carter's intermedia adaptations of "Little Red Riding Hood" by foregrounding the power of oral storytelling and the presence of the bodies of the storyteller and the listener. As we have seen, Carter's multifaceted explorations of the potential of each medium for telling the same story with different effects and implications attests the importance of continuing to adapt fairy tales across old and new media forms.

INTERGENERIC TRANSFORMATIONS

As the volumes in this cultural history of fairy tales dealing with the earlier periods indicate, the now commonly held view that associates the fairy tale with children's literature and pedagogical purposes began to be formed in the latter half of the eighteenth century and became consolidated after the Brothers Grimm's *Children's and Household Tales* (1812), in which the Grimms adapted oral fairy tales for the purpose of educating the children of the rising middle class in Germany, gained a wide readership in Germany as well as in many other parts of the world. In earlier times, oral folktales and fairy tales provided adults with imaginative entertainment as well as fictional spaces for exploring social, cultural, and gender norms. Early European literary fairy tales such as Italian poet and courtier Giambattista Basile's *Lo cunto de li cunti* (*Tale of Tales*) (1634–6), also known as *The Pentamerone*, and French author Marie-Catherine d'Aulnoy's *Contes de fées* (*Fairy Tales*) (1697) and *Les Contes nouveaux ou les fées à la mode* (New Tales, or Fairies in Fashion) (1698) were clearly targeted at adult audiences who would appreciate their sophisticated styles and understand their adult-oriented themes. D'Aulnoy's fairy tales, for example, can be read as critical comments on the various power relations in courtly lives in late seventeenth-century France.

The dominant association between fairy tales and pedagogy began to change in the early twentieth century when modernist and surrealist writers, such as Carrington and Djuna Barnes (1892–1982), began to turn to the fairy tale as a rich source of literary inspiration as Andrew Teverson discusses in the Introduction to this volume. It was in the 1970s, however, that the genre has regained its appeal and relevance for a much wider adult readership due, at least partly, to the development of feminist and psychoanalytic interpretations of fairy tales that invite adult readers to explore sociocultural and psychosexual subtexts for the tales with which they have been familiar since early childhood (I will come back to this point later).

Anne Sexton's (1928–74) *Transformations* ([1971] 2006) adapted traditional fairy tales into confessional poetry reflective of the inner lives of women in a modern society. Her poetic retellings of tales such as "Snow White" and "Little Red Riding Hood" focus on the various restrictions placed on women in a male-dominated society and use the familiar tales to transform the way we recognize our lives and desires. Olga Broumas (1949–), on the other hand, used well-known fairy-tale narratives such as "Cinderella" and "Sleeping Beauty" in her poetry collection *Beginning with O* (1977) to give voice to desires that are not bound by patriarchal and heteronormative values.

In *The Bloody Chamber*, Carter not only experimented with the intertextuality and the intermediality of fairy tales, as I have discussed above, but also incorporated different genres of fiction into her short-story adaptations of fairy tales. "The Bloody Chamber," an adaptation of Perrault's "Bluebeard," combines the literary conventions of gothic literature and pornography with the fairy-tale narrative, which makes the story suitable for adults rather than children in terms of both content and form. Gothicism also characterizes "The Company of Wolves," "The Tiger's Bride," "Wolf-Alice," and "The Lady of the House of Love," the last of which rewrites "Sleeping Beauty" in the mode of vampire literature. "The Erl-King," as the title indicates, references German Romantic literature while "Puss in Boots" is written in the style of the *commedia dell'arte* and is later adapted into a radio play by Carter. Carter's intergeneric writing explores new possibilities for the fairy-tale genre by creating hybrid spaces as well as interstices between different literary conventions.

Various other postmodern novelists have reworked traditional fairy tales in order to revise dominant cultural, social, and narrative conventions and expectations. Bacchilega's *Postmodern Fairy Tales: Gender and Narrative Strategies* (1997) analyzes the emerging canon of fairy-tale adaptations in postmodern and feminist fiction in English-speaking cultures, and explores works by Carter, Margaret Atwood (1983), Robert Coover (1969), Donald Barthelme (1967), and Tanith Lee (1983). These writers' self-reflexive and intertextual adaptations have played a major role in reestablishing the fairy tale as a genre for both adults and children, inspiring new approaches to the genre.

INTERDISCIPLINARY TRANSFORMATIONS

One of the most significant of the theoretical frameworks that have been used to transform approaches to fairy tales in the modern age is psychoanalytic theory. Along with myths, fairy tales play an important part in Sigmund Freud's work that sees fairy tales as symbolic expressions of the unconscious like dreams. For example, Freud's analysis of the Wolf Man, a patient who, according to Freud's analysis, suffered from castration anxiety caused by traumatic childhood experiences, is based on the comparison he makes between the patient's recurrent dream about wolves and the fairy-tale wolves in "The Wolf and the Seven Young Kids" and "Little Red Riding Hood" (Freud [1918] 2002), while his idea of the uncanny is developed through his close reading of German Romantic author E. T. A. Hoffmann's 1816 literary fairy tale "The Sandman" (Freud [1919] 2003). Freud's followers such as Otto Rank and Ernst Jones also used fairy tales to develop their ideas, while Carl Gustav Jung developed his own idea of the collective unconscious as a reservoir of universally shared images or "archetypes" that can be found in the symbolic narrative of myths, fairy tales, and dreams. Archetypal analyses of fairy tales have been developed worldwide; major works include Joseph Campbell's *The Hero with a Thousand Faces* (1949), Marie-Louise von Franz's *Shadow and Evil in Fairy Tales* (1974), Hayao Kawai's *The Japanese Psyche: Major Motifs in the Fairy Tales of Japan* (1982; English translation 1988), and Clarissa Pinkola Estés's *Women Who Run with the Wolves: Myths and Stories of the Wild Woman Archetype* (1992).

Among such psychoanalytic approaches to the fairy tale, Freudian psychoanalyst Bruno Bettelheim's *The Uses of Enchantment: The Meaning and Importance of Fairy Tales* (1976) can be said to have had the most significant impact on the reinterpretation of the fairy tale in both academic and general contexts. According to Bettelheim, the traditional fairy tale has a therapeutic effect on children by helping them resolve their unconscious fears and desires such as oedipal conflicts and sibling rivalry. Even though his heteronormative developmental model has been criticized especially by feminists, including Carter, who stated that her tales in *The Bloody Chamber* were "the result of quarrelling furiously with Bettelheim" (Haffenden 1985: 83), his psychoanalytic approach encouraged adult readers to revisit fairy tales from a different perspective and to explore their symbolism and underlying psychosexual meanings. Although he himself was strongly against the idea of making any kind of alterations or additions to the Grimms' tales in their 1857 edition, which for him represented the tales' original form, his work has provided a new framework for fairy-tale adaptations whose purposes go beyond children's education.

The development of feminist criticism since the late twentieth century has also made a significant impact on the modern reinterpretation and reevaluation of the fairy tale and has inspired fairy-tale adaptations from the perspectives of women, who have been historically marginalized within the twentieth-century fairy-tale canon, thanks largely to the impact Disney has had on our modern conception of the genre. Importantly, writers such as d'Aulnoy were viewed as canonical through the nineteenth century in England, France, and Germany, while German women informants, for instance, Dortchen and Marie Elisabeth Wild; Dorothea Viehmann; Marie, Amalie, and Jeannette Hassenpflug; and Ludowine von Haxthausen, among others, were indispensable to the Grimms' tale collection. However, by the mid-twentieth century, such voices were lost or edited out, giving way to the predominance of Perrault and select tales by the Grimms, as well as Disney.[4] Beginning with Simone de Beauvoir's *The Second Sex* (1949), feminist criticism has regarded twentieth-century canonical fairy tales such as "Cinderella" and "Sleeping Beauty" as examples of dominant narratives of patriarchy that inculcate the images of women as passive and powerless victims. Marcia Lieberman's "Some Day My Prince Will Come: Female Acculturation through the Fairy Tale" (1972), generally regarded as "a milestone in American feminist fairy-tale criticism" (Joosen 2011: 49), criticizes the way popular fairy tales of Andrew Lang and Walt Disney "serve to acculturate women to traditional social roles" (Lieberman 1972: 185). In *The Madwoman in the Attic: The Woman Writer and the Nineteenth-Century Literary Imagination* (1979), Sandra M. Gilbert and Susan Gubar interpret the Grimms' "Snow White" as reflective of the way in which patriarchal ideology, represented by the magic mirror, entraps women in twin images of the angel (Snow White) and the witch (the wicked queen). This kind of feminist reinterpretation of these modern classic fairy tales, especially concerning witch-like characters, has helped inspire more female-centered adaptations of fairy tales in diverse media, including *Maleficent* (2014), Disney's live-action film adaptation of "Sleeping Beauty" told from the viewpoint of the fairy who casts a curse on the princess in Perrault's tale.

Feminist fairy-tale scholarship has been flowering internationally and has continued to expand its scope until today. Early book-length studies on fairy tales from feminist perspectives include *Kiss Sleeping Beauty Goodbye: Breaking the Spell of Feminine Myths and Models* by Madonna Kolbenschlag (1979), *Grimm's Bad Girls and Bold Boys: The Moral and Social Vision of the Tales* by Ruth B. Bottigheimer (1987), *Don't Bet on the Prince: Contemporary Feminist Fairy Tales of North America* edited by Jack Zipes ([1987] 1989), *The Hard Facts of the Grimms' Fairy Tales* by Maria Tatar (1987), *From the Beast to the Blonde: On Fairy Tales and Their Tellers* by Marina Warner (1994a), and *Postmodern Fairy Tales: Gender and Narrative Strategies* by Cristina Bacchilega (1997). In addition, feminist scholarship that aims to revise our conception of fairy-tale history to recover lost female voices has appeared, including Lewis C. Seifert's *Fairy Tales, Sexuality, and Gender in France, 1690–1715: Nostalgic Utopias* (1996) and Jeannine Blackwell and Shawn C. Jarvis's *The Queen's Mirror: Fairy Tales by German Women, 1780–1900* (2001).[5] As Vanessa Joosen demonstrates in *Critical and Creative Perspectives on Fairy Tales: An Intertextual Dialogue between Fairy-Tale Scholarship and Postmodern Retellings* (2011), feminist fairy-tale criticism has developed in a close intertextual dialogue with feminist fairy-tale retellings. Fairy-tale adaptations by writers such as Carter, Atwood, and Emma Donoghue (*Kissing the Witch: Old Tales in New Skins* [(1993) 1997]) have both inspired and been inspired by feminist fairy-tale criticism that questions and subverts patriarchal and heteronormative ideology.

Such intertextual dialogues between newly emerging critical theories and fairy-tale adaptations can be also found in other areas. The development of postcolonial theory has informed, and has been informed by, various postcolonial, de-orientalizing, and anti-racist adaptations of fairy tales. For example, Patrick Chamoiseau's (1953–) short stories in *Strange Words* (1988; English translation 1994) adapt Martiniquan folktales to "provide a practical education, an apprenticeship in life—a life of survival in a colonized land" ([1988] 1994: xii). Helen Oyeyemi's (1984–) novel *Boy, Snow, Bird*

(2014), on the other hand, transposes "Snow White" to midcentury America and, as Weems's aforementioned photographic adaptation of the tale does, problematizes its color symbolism based on racist and Eurocentric ideology (see also Kimberly Lau's analysis in Chapter 8, this volume).

Postcolonial theory's emphasis on fairy-tale traditions from marginalized cultures has also led to inquiries into cross-cultural blending and fertilization—"creolization," to use Bacchilega's term—of fairy tales, a phenomenon that has become more widespread and more complex in the past century. As Bacchilega (2013) argues, *Dancehall Queen* (1997), a film adaptation of "Cinderella" set in contemporary Kingston, Jamaica, interweaves the classic European tale with contemporary Jamaican dancehall culture as well as traditional narratives of the West African trickster Anansi, remediating and creolizing the tale for antiracist and feminist purposes. As I discussed above, such cross- and transcultural fairy-tale adaptations can be found in various media such as Studio Ghibli's animation films, Yanagi's and Bae's photography, and Kōnoike's artwork, which have helped expand the scope of fairy-tale scholarship beyond the Euro-American-centric focus.

Finally, recent theoretical developments in the fields of ecocriticism and multispecies studies have inspired reinterpretations of fairy tales from a less anthropocentric perspective, as the chapter on human-animal relationship in this volume exemplifies (see Chapter 4, this volume). This new ecocritical framework has been intertextually engaged with modern fairy-tale adaptations that reflect current environmental concerns such as the climate crisis and mass extinctions of species caused by excessive human activities. The past few decades have seen a profusion of fairy-tale adaptations for both adults and children in various media that thematize human-animal relations and boundaries in a way that acknowledges more positive values in non-human animals than before. This emerging canon of animal-themed and more animal-oriented fairy-tale adaptations, based most frequently on "Little Red Riding Hood," "Beauty and the Beast," and "The Little Mermaid," seems to reflect our society's shift away from an anthropocentric perspective toward a more inclusive view that values interdependence and interconnectedness between human and non-human animals.

In the first sections of this chapter I have pointed out some of the major characteristics of fairy-tale adaptations in the modern age in terms of media, genre, and frame. I have argued that the technological development of the past century has expanded the possibilities of fairy-tale enchantment especially in its visual aspect while the change in the way fairy tales are framed theoretically has brought to light the genre's relevance and uses not only for pedagogic purposes but also for contemporary social, cultural, and political concerns. In what follows, I will conduct a case study of contemporary adaptations of "The Bremen Town Musicians" across diverse media and contexts, showing how these adaptations reflect current social, cultural, aesthetic, and ecological concerns.

CONTEMPORARY ADAPTATIONS OF "THE BREMEN TOWN MUSICIANS"

"The Bremen Town Musicians" is best known in the Grimms' version, which first appeared in the second edition of their collection in 1819 and remained almost in the same form throughout the later editions. The ATU system (for an explanation, see Chapter 8, this volume) classifies the story under "Animal Tales" as ATU 130 and calls this tale type "The Animals in Night Quarters" (Uther 2004: 99). The tale is described as follows:

> Donkey, dog, cat and rooster are ill-treated by their owners because they are too old to work. They run away [B296] and find a lonely house in the forest [N776]. Thieves come and begin to divide their money, the four animals climb on one another's backs and cry all at once [K335.1.4]. The thieves (robbers) are frightened and run away, leaving the money there. When the thieves try to come back the animals hide in various parts of the house and attack them with their characteristic powers [K116]. The four animals drive the thieves away and live happily ever after.
>
> (99)

In *The Oxford Companion to Fairy Tales*, Donald Haase attributes the tale's popularity in the twentieth century to its social theme:

> The story charts the triumph of the weak through resolve and cooperation. Facing death at the hands of their masters, who show no gratitude for the faithful service the worn-out animals provided, they each adopt the donkey's initial resolve to become a musician in Bremen. By developing a common plan of action and orchestrating their natural talents (braying, barking, meowing, and crowing), they empower themselves as a group, frighten the robbers who live off others, and reclaim a life for themselves.
>
> (2015: 72)

While the theme of "the triumph of the weak through resolve and cooperation" is clearly one of the main attractions of the tale as Haase points out, the tale's appeal can be also attributed to other elements that, as I argue below, are related to the particular mediality of the tale, which appeals to the visual and auditory senses, as well as to its potentially more animal-centered frame.

Visual images have played a particularly important role in the diffusion of "The Bremen Town Musicians." The most iconic image in the tale is arguably that of the four animals standing on each other's back in the order of their sizes, starting with the donkey at the bottom. The Grimms' telling describes this famous scene in a way that visually evokes the dynamic movements of each animal: "The donkey got up on his hind legs and put his legs down on the window ledge; the dog jumped up on the donkey's back; the cat climbed up on the dog; and finally the rooster flew up to the very top and perched on the cat's head" (Tatar 2014: 159). That the image of this acrobatic formation of the four animals has appealed to many readers is evident from the fact that it has almost always been included in the illustrations for this tale (Figure 2.1) and is often selected for the front cover of its picture-book adaptations. This tall creature with multiple heads suddenly emerging from the dark forest, combined with

FIGURE 2.1: Illustration by Leslie Brooke for *The House in the Wood and Other Fairy Stories* (1909). Source: https://static.torontopubliclibrary.ca/da/pdfs/37131032410516d.pdf.

the loud "music" that it produces (Tatar 2014: 159), scares away the robbers, who imagine this figure to be a monster with more-than-human power. It can be said that the fear that this visual image provokes in the robbers may reflect human beings' subconscious fear of those animals whose true otherness has been suppressed in their domesticated lives in the human sphere. In this tale, however, the reader clearly stands on the side of the non-human animals who have been used and abandoned, or even threatened to be killed, by their human masters.

Instantly recognizable in many parts of the world, the visual image of the animal tower from the Grimms' tale lends itself to commodification in various fields. For example, the German city of Bremen has adapted the tale into a tourist attraction for global fairy-tale tourism as pointed out by Haase: "While the social themes of just deserts and solidarity have made the story popular and motivated numerous twentieth-century adaptations, the story's identification with Bremen has made it a valuable commodity in that city's tourist industry" (2015: 72). Located in northwest Germany, Bremen is a Hanseatic harbor city historically characterized by its free and independent spirit, represented by the statue of the medieval military leader Roland, erected in 1404. Now the city is internationally much better known for the bronze statue of the Bremen Town Musicians (Figure 2.2), created by Gerhard Marcks in 1953, which has become one of the most popular photography spots for tourists in Bremen. The website

FIGURE 2.2: The statue of the Bremen Town Musicians by Gerhard Marcks (1953). Courtesy of BTZ Bremer Touristik Zentrale eine Marke der WFB Wirtschaftsförderung Bremen GmbH (https://www.bremen-tourism.de).

created by the official city directory of Bremen sums up the tale to emphasize the fact that Bremen figures as a utopian destination in the Grimms' tale: "The Bremen Town Musicians are without doubt the pride and joy of the Hanseatic city…. According to the story, a donkey, a dog, a cat and a rooster set off on a journey to Bremen in search of a better life" (Bremen 2020). Bremen also figures as the final destination of "The German Fairy Tale Route," a trail established in 1975 that starts in Hanau, the Grimm brothers' birthplace, and connects places related to their lives and their fairy tales leading all the way to Bremen.[6]

In addition, the fact that Bremen chose the image of the four animals standing on each other's back for their new official city logo shows the strong appeal of this image, which visually expresses solidarity among different beings, for those who actually live in Bremen. In their study of the place branding strategy of Bremen, Andreas Mueller and Michael Schade recount the municipal tourism office's adaptation of the tale as follows: "From the perspective of the place branding authorities in Bremen, who are challenged to unite a multitude of stakeholders behind a single branding concept, the symbol of four different animals (donkey, dog, cat, rooster) working together and reaching their common goal with combined strengths, was regarded as a perfect fit and as a symbol of authenticity for the city" (2012: 89). Furthermore, according to Mueller and Schade, when introduced to the new logo, "residents responded very positively and even started a discussion whether to build up additional statues of the Town Musicians at the city's entrances like the railway station and the local airport, in order to welcome visitors" (89). The image of the animal tower seems to function as a visual meme that carries the supposedly "authentic" identity of the city woven from the Grimms' tale, inviting people to "live" the tale as the motto on the official city logo states. That the four animals never actually reach Bremen in the Grimms' tale does not seem to hinder residents and tourists from identifying the city as a utopia where aging work animals dream of finding a new way of living free from abuse by humans.

Italian artist Maurizio Cattelan's two sculptures based on this tale, on the other hand, foreground the status of the four animals as animals rather than as metaphors for human characteristics and values. Cattelan's *Love Saves Life* (1995; see Figure 2.3), composed of four taxidermied animals stacked on top of each other, appropriates the aforementioned iconic bronze statue in Bremen with ironic humor. In this sculptural adaptation of the tale, the old, outcast work animals' desire to live is replaced by human beings' fascination with taxidermy, the art of preserving dead animals to simulate life, rendering visible human beings' ambivalent feelings toward both animality and death. Like Damian Hirst's series of works in which dead animals such as a shark, a sheep, and a cow are preserved in formaldehyde, postmodern art often uses animal remains to pose fundamental questions about the body as well as about art since the animal body used as an artistic medium lies midway between an actual animal and a representation of that animal.

FIGURE 2.3: Maurizio Cattelan, *Love Saves Life*, 1995. Taxidermied donkey, dog, cat, and rooster, 190 × 120 × 60 cm. Installation view: Una collezione trasversale. Da Duchamp a Nino Calos, da Cattelan a Entang Wiharso, ALT Arte contemporanea, Bergamo, Italy, June 29, 2009. Photogarph by Roberto Marossi. Courtesy of Maurizio Cattelan's Archive.

Two years after the creation of *Love Saves Life*, Cattelan created another sculpture, *Love Lasts Forever* (1997; see Figure 2.4), which mirrors the earlier work with a further ironic twist. Composed of the skeletons of the four animals stacked up, this sculpture transposes animal remains that have been processed to be used for the scientific study of the anatomy of the animal body into an artistic

FIGURE 2.4: Maurizio Cattelan, *Love Lasts Forever*, 1997. Donkey, dog, cat, and rooster skeletons, 186 × 120 × 60 cm. Installation view: Skulptur. Projekte in Münster 1997, Westfälisches Landesmuseum, Münster, Germany, June 22–September 28, 1997. Photograph by Roman Mensing. Courtesy of Maurizio Cattelan's Archive.

representation of fictional animals that are products of human imagination. Anatomy, a system of scientific classification founded upon the visual evidence of structural differences among species, has long functioned as one kind of truth that gives evidence of the supposedly intrinsic nature of each organism. If we follow Freud's dictum: "Anatomy is destiny," these animals' destinies are anatomically determined forever as objects to be classified and defined within a human-centered framework.

Cattelan's twin adaptations of "The Bremen Town Musicians" embody the fairy-tale animals in a way that foregrounds some of the ways in which human beings have used non-human animals as biological, socio-economic, and cultural resources. Cattelan's work also plays on the prioritizing of visual evidence—"seeing is believing"—not only in science but also in certain religious beliefs as exemplified by relics associated with saintly figures. As can be seen in his 1999 installation *La Nona Ora* (The Ninth Hour), a life-sized sculpture of Pope John Paul II struck down by a meteorite, Cattelan's work often takes a satirical look at systems of belief, including religion and politics. From this perspective, his sculptures made of real animal remains can be seen as a parody of a material evidence for the authenticity of the events recounted in the Grimms' tale, as if to claim: "These are the remains of the actual animals who appear in the tale." The four animals in Cattelan's sculptures do not allow human viewers any sentimental projection, forever frozen in the middle of making music as if in protest against human beings' belief in anthropocentrism.

The popularity of "The Bremen Town Musicians" can be attributed not only to its visual appeal but also to the idea of animals making music to survive. The extraordinary acrobatic formation of the four animals balanced on top of each other is accompanied by an equally extraordinary vocal orchestration: "When they were in formation, someone gave a signal, and they started making their music: the donkey brayed, the dog barked, the cat meowed, and the rooster crowed" (Tatar 2014: 159). In the Grimms' text, it is the donkey who first hits upon the idea of becoming a lute player in Bremen. The donkey then asks the dog to join the band as a drummer: "I'm on my way to Bremen to become a town musician. Why don't you join me and become a member of the band? I'll play the lute and you can play the drums" (157). They then recruit the cat and the rooster as singers: "Come with us to Bremen. As an expert in nighttime serenades, you'll make a good town minstrel"; "You have a fine voice! Why don't you come sing with us?" (158). Thus, music plays an essential narrative function in providing the story with a single aim, bonding the main characters, and leading the story to a happy conclusion.

It is no wonder, therefore, that the tale has been adapted into various types of musical works, including opera, musical theatre, choir, and popular music, as well as films incorporating musical elements such as Walt Disney's short animation film *The Four Musicians of Bremen* (1922), in which the four animals form a jazz band, and Jim Henson's Muppet television special *The Muppet Musicians of Bremen* (1972). It can be said that these musical adaptations take the word music in the literal sense and depict the four animals playing music just as human musicians do. In the Grimms' text, however, there are no descriptions of the animals actually making music, at least music as it is understood in the human sense.

The donkey's choice of his musical instrument seems to be related to the traditional motif of a donkey playing the lute found in the Greek saying, "Onos lyras," translated by Jan M. Ziolkowski as follows: "The donkey [hears] the lyre [but does not understand it]" (2009: 216). The donkey in this proverb represents the stupidity of nonhuman animals who would never appreciate music, an art form that is assumed here as one of the human prerogatives. In discussing the donkey in "The Bremen Town Musicians" and "The Donkey" (*Kinder- und Hausmärchen* [KHM] 144, ATU 430), an animal bridegroom tale in the Grimms' collection, Ann Schmiesing in *Disability, Deformity, and Disease in the Grimms' Fairy Tales* (2014) notes how the donkeys in these tales subvert the cultural stereotype imposed on them in different ways:

> It is telling that the first character introduced in the tale is the donkey, who informs the dog that he plans to become a lute player. If read in the context of the classical proverb that held that an ass could never learn to play music no matter how hard he studies, the donkey's plan seems implausible from the start. Whereas the protagonist in "The Donkey" defies this proverb and becomes a master lute player, the donkey and his companions in "The Bremen Town Musicians" never even reach their destination or embark on their intended livelihood. But they figuratively become musicians in the sense that the tale describes them scaring the robbers away with their "music" ("Musik") (KHM 7 1:163), and their plan to become town musicians points to their desire to have a voice where they have had none.
>
> (173)

It is important that, in "The Donkey" and other animal bridegroom tales containing the motif D721.3 "Disenchantment by destroying skin (covering)," such as "Hans My Hedgehog" (KHM 108), animal bridegrooms play the musical instrument—the bagpipes in "Hans My Hedgehog"—to the effect that their musical ability foreshadows their original human state underneath the animal skins. Both the donkey and the hedgehog turn out to be handsome human princes and, after their animal skins are burned to ashes, they do not revert to their animal forms. In this sense, it can be said that music in these tales also figures as the prerogative of human culture.

In contrast, the animals in "The Bremen Town Musicians" make music in order not to display their human abilities but to frighten off human beings and, more importantly, remain animals till the end of the tale. B. Grantham Aldred observes that, in folktales and fairy tales, music produced by animals tends to disadvantage the music makers as in "The Wolf Is Caught Because of His Singing" (ATU 100) and "Singing Donkey and Dancing Camel" (ATU 214A) (2016: 678). It can be said that, in these tales, animals who make music are considered to be transgressive of the human-beast boundary and, therefore, deserving of punishment. From this perspective, "The Bremen Town Musicians" is an exception in that the music made by the four animals obviously works to their advantage and does not cause them to be punished.

Nevertheless, the question remains as to what kind of music the animals make in "The Bremen Town Musicians." Even though it is referred to as "music" in the Grimms' tale, can the braying, barking, meowing, and crowing of the animals be regarded as music? If so, what kind of reconfiguration of music is needed for us to imagine these animal sounds as music, not simply in terms of human perception, that is, by anthropomorphizing the animals and their music, but also in terms of animal perception? In what follows, I discuss two different approaches to this question from a multispecies perspective.

The picture book *The Old Animals' Forest Band*, published in India in 2008, is based on an Indian oral retelling of Grimm's "The Bremen Town Musicians" and is illustrated by Durga Bai, an Indian artist who works within the Gond tradition of tribal art (Rao and Bai 2008).[7] Retold in English by contemporary Indian writer Sirish Rao, it was one of the tales that its publisher, Tara Books's editorial director V. Geetha, heard from her grandfather when she was a child, and she became aware of the tale's German origin much later.[8] Set in the Indian countryside, *The Old Animals' Forest Band* features a dog, a cow (who replaces the cat in the Grimms' tale), a donkey, and a rooster and follows the Grimms' tale except that the animals do not initially set out to become professional musicians in a town but end up becoming musicians in their own right. When the villagers, alarmed by the "terrible" singing, gather to the hut to investigate, they are glad to find their stolen gold and jewels that the thieves left behind. Their former masters now want to take these useful animals back home, but the animals refuse to leave the hut and decide to form the Old Animals' Forest Band instead. The four animals live happily ever after in the forest, singing and dancing to their hearts' content. The loud music that they make to scare a band of thieves away and continue to make for their own pleasure seems to stand for their freedom and independence from human society. In this picture-book adaptation, the role of music to give voice to the animals is given a stronger emphasis than in the Grimms' tale.

Moreover, the way the animals' music is represented visually in Durga Bai's illustrations presents a different approach to giving voice to animals without totally subjugating them to human-centered and language-centered frameworks. When the animals sing, their voices are made visible in a form resembling speech balloons that contain not words but irregularly painted small dots, a feature that is not simply attributable to Durga Bai's illiteracy—she was not given school education due to poverty (Gaur 2014)—but can be seen as a way of indicating that animals do speak but their language is not legible to us (Figure 2.5). Although the text uses standard English onomatopoeic animal sounds such as "cock-a-doodle-doo" for the rooster and "bow-wow, bow-wow" for the dog, the speech balloons are filled with dots rather than these onomatopoeic sounds.

FIGURE 2.5: Art by Durga Bai for *The Old Animals' Forest Band*, Original Edition © Tara Books Pvt. Ltd., Chennai, India (www.tarabooks.com).

You can tell to whom the balloons belong by their colors as they seem to match the color of each animal's body.[9] It is also important that these speech balloons are only used for animals; although human characters also speak in the text, none of them is given this visual form of speech in the illustrations. This is why the replacement of these dotted speech balloons with musical notes on the front cover seems to weaken, if not contradict, the more animal-oriented viewpoint

FIGURE 2.6: Art by Durga Bai for *The Old Animals' Forest Band*, Original Edition © Tara Books Pvt. Ltd., Chennai, India (www.tarabooks.com).

found in the other parts of this picture book's visual storytelling (Figure 2.6). Reorienting the concept of animal music through both text and image in this way invites the reader-viewer to reimagine "The Bremen Town Musicians" from a more multispecies perspective.

A more animal-centered adaptation of "The Bremen Town Musicians" that focuses on the musicality of animals may come from the field of interdisciplinary art installations and projects in the future. As Reinhard Gupfinger and Martin Kaltenbrunner observe in "Animals Make Music: A Look at Non-Human Musical Expression," animal music has largely been understood within a human-centered framework:

> The idea of animals becoming anthropomorphic musicians playing traditional acoustic instruments is much more common in ... literature [than in other fields such as music, art, and science]. Well-known fairy tales such as *The Town Musicians of Bremen* have popularized this concept. Since the middle of the twentieth century, this particular configuration has often been restaged in a circus environment, where, in general, various species including primates were capable of performing various musical tasks through conditioning.
>
> (2018: 3)

In addition, numerous videos have recently been circulating on the internet featuring dogs and cats playing the piano and other traditional musical instruments. In contrast to such "anthropomorphic musicians," Gupfinger and Kaltenbrunner argue, the African grey parrots in *metamusic*, an interdisciplinary art project by the artist group *alien productions* (Martin Breindl, Norbert Math, and Andrea Sodomka) in collaboration with zoologists, biologists, and zoo keepers that began in 2012, become authors or coauthors of music by using musical instruments designed to suit their specific capabilities, needs, and preferences. As Gupfinger and Kaltenbrunner point out, a number of biomusicological studies have found that "animals prefer sounds and musical arrangements that are biologically relevant for them" (2018: 8). Musical instruments created by *metamusic* include a digital DJ turntable for parrots that the parrots have been observed enjoying playing; by spinning its wheel with their beaks, the parrots can create different types of sounds and musical patterns, and the project is trying to find out what kinds of sounds and music are perceived as a positive experience by the parrots. Through these musical experiments in collaboration with the grey parrots, the project aims to enhance their well-being and create pleasure.

Such animal-centered music projects invite us to imagine what the musical aesthetics of animals may be like and to expand our understanding of music to include the sounds that non-human animals produce. The meaning of music to animals is yet to be explored from the perspectives of biomusicology and other interdisciplinary approaches. From such inquiries, a new interdisciplinary adaptation of "The Bremen Town Musicians" may emerge in which the four real animals play musical instruments biomusicologically developed to suit each animal's capabilities and aesthetics for their own happiness and pleasure.

This examination of fairy-tale adaptation, defined as dialogic relations among texts in an ever-changing media landscape, has sought to illustrate the crucial role that adaptation has played in the cultural history of fairy tales. In the modern era, as this chapter has argued, adaptation has expanded the intermedial possibilities of the genre of fairy tale and created new intertextual connections across generic and cultural boundaries. Adaptation of fairy tales, whatever form it may take in the future, will continue to evolve through repetition of the same stories with difference, combining old and new media forms, critical perspectives, and emerging creative and academic directions, as the history of its development in the modern age traced by this chapter indicates. The attraction of fairy-tale adaptation lies in its capacity to offer everyone—regardless of social, cultural, or any other status—the pleasures of experiencing a sense of wonder when encountering a new set of values in familiar stories that have been handed down from the past and have shaped the present.

CHAPTER THREE

Gender and Sexuality

JEANA JORGENSEN

Gender and sexuality have always loomed large in the fairy-tale tradition, through gendered tale structures, expectations of heteronormative happily ever afters, and patterns of sexual orientation and initiation that are baked into genre expectations as a whole, as well as in the contexts of the tales, with various cultures having their own gendered associations with the "appropriate" types of people to transmit and/or receive tales. In the modern era, however, the cultural history of the fairy tale has been significantly impacted by developments not just in world history but also in specific ways of thinking about gender and sexuality as distinct identities, as psychological traits, as pathologized behaviors, and more. Here, I argue that in tandem with technologies and progressive movements that have functionally and aspirationally liberated alternative genders and sexualities, the ways in which fairy tales depict and develop themes of gender and sexuality have also shifted. This is not to state that every producer, teller, or audience of fairy tales has uncritically embraced the same values around gender and sexuality, but rather to argue that there has been more explicit dialogue around gender and sexuality in fairy tales than in previous time periods, and with more nuance as well.

To make this argument, I first provide working definitions of gender and sexuality, and examples of how they operate in both fairy tales and their contexts. Next, I provide an overview of some notable events on the global/historical stage that have significantly impacted concepts of gender and/or sexuality. Finally, I provide three main areas of illustration for these claims: the Disney phenomenon in the West and in global contexts, the proliferation of folktale and fairy-tale collections from oral traditions published by folklorists and anthropologists in particular, and the popularity of revisions/retellings of fairy tales by contemporary authors, filmmakers, artists, and others who have deliberately sought to decenter conservative assumptions about gender and sexuality in their works (with varying degrees of success). Many of the texts under discussion here are written and filmed texts, though these should not be taken to represent the entirety of fairy-tale discourse in the modern era; fairy tales are also present in fashion, in games, in the digital realm, and so on.

In regard to that first claim, it is worth noting that I seek simultaneously to acknowledge the impact of significant Western formations of gender and sexuality, as expressed in Disney and promulgated globally through its form of cultural imperialism, and to decenter Eurocentric visions of gender and sexuality in the fairy tale. There is real danger in assuming that a Eurocentric view of the fairy tale (and the norms expressed therein) is universally valid or true (Bacchilega 2019; Haase 2019) but it is similarly facile to attempt to account for the contours of gender and sexuality in fairy tales of the modern age without discussing the role that Disney and its heirs have played on the global stage.

WORKING DEFINITIONS

Gender and sexuality are two traits that are often erroneously conflated; they may correlate or overlap in certain ways, but there are no guarantees. Certain complexities in how these traits are thought of are distinct to the modern era, with some scholars arguing that heterosexuality is in itself just over a century old (Blank 2012) and with much feminist thought on gender and sexuality emerging in the last century as well. Elsewhere I explain these terms as such:

> I define gender as the composite of culturally constructed characteristics of masculinity and femininity, best viewed on a spectrum rather than as a binary. Gender encompasses one's internal sense of identity, one's external expression, the roles one inhabits, and the norms and ideals one should—societally speaking—aspire to. Gender is distinct from one's anatomical, bodily, or genetic traits, often glossed as "sex," as well as distinct from one's sexuality, the constellation of desires and experiences that orient us relationally to others (and ourselves).
>
> (Jorgensen 2019: 260)

In many paradigms, gender is thought of as a social overlap atop the biological stratum of sex. As Hanne Blank writes:

> Gender refers to all the manifestations of masculinity or femininity that are not immediately, demonstrably biological. These include mannerisms,

conventions of dress and grooming, social roles, speech patterns, and more. A useful way to think about it is that we *have* biological sex—it is inherently present in our physical bodies—but we *do* gender.

(2012: xxi; emphases in the original)

This "doing" gender is a reference to the theory of gender performance that became popular in feminist theory from the 1990s onward, in which gender is seen less as an essential, internal, stable trait of identity and more as an iterative performance that has the potential to shift and change over time (see also Butler [1990] 1999). However, even the notion that gender is the social overlay of biological sex is fraught; scholars have also argued that sex itself is socially shaped in a number of ways (Dea 2016). Similarly, there remains extensive debate as to the degree to which sexuality is determined from birth, fluid over the course of one's life, or both.

None of these categories are as stable as they are thought to be, however many societies function as though they are, with gender markers required on legal documents and only certain sexual or romantic partnerships legally recognized, so it is important to begin any account of gender and sexuality in a cultural history with these caveats. Attempts to naturalize or essentialize gendered and sexual traits are stymied both by cross-cultural anthropological research demonstrating the constructedness of these categories as well as by biological research revealing that neither sex nor sexuality are stable categories in nature (see Roughgarden [2004] 2013). For example, by some estimates, the number of people who are intersex—their biological markers do not yield purely male or purely female characteristics, whether on a hormonal, genetic, genital, or other anatomical level—is between 0.2 and 1.7 percent of the general population (Dea 2016: 88). Further, while there is evidence that people whose gender identities and sexualities vary from the norm have always existed, suggesting that there is something innately human about sexuality and gender alternatives, it is only within the modern era that concerted human and civil rights movements have globally secured more rights for these populations than were previously available through institutional guarantees. The modern era has also yielded more precise language for some of these alternatives, such as not only naming people whose gender does not match up with that assigned at birth "transgender" but also labeling those whose gender *does* match up with that assigned at birth "cisgender," which is one way of no longer permitting the supposedly "normal" category to go unmarked.

Seeing gender and sexuality in fairy tales therefore depends on how these categories are perceived in the first place. As Kay Stone has shown, everyday consumers of fairy tales have sophisticated thoughts on gender norms and stereotypes in the tales (Stone 1985). In the context of contemporary fairy-tale studies, then, gender and sexuality inform our analyses in a number of ways.

The notion that certain tale plots (which professional folklorists codify as "tale types," e.g., using the Aarne-Thompson-Uther Tale Type Index to identify a tale plot's main features and locate other versions of the same tale) have a gender or are gendered emerged in the twentieth century and continues to be investigated and interrogated. A key feature of contemporary approaches to the tale type index includes an awareness that the very notion of tale type is often gendered, and sometimes in misleading or sexist ways (Lundell 1986). Danish folklorist Bengt Holbek famously proposed that there are "masculine" and "feminine" tales based on the gender of the cast-low protagonist at the tale's beginning (Holbek 1998). Likewise, Kathleen Ragan utilized analysis of a multitude of tale collections at the level of grammatical unit to make assertions about the gender of a tale and how it might relate to the gender of the storyteller, collector, and editor, thus demonstrating that "the predominant gender in a tale is related to the gender of the storyteller" (2009: 234). Moreover, Ragan's quantitative analysis allows her to claim: "If one studies tales, most of which have passed through a male editor, male collector, and male storyteller, one could not extend the conclusions from the study to the folktale as a genre, since there is a category of tales that is ignored—namely, female tales" (237). Thus, the myriad of ways in which gender impacts the performance and collection and structure of folk- and fairy-tale texts is still being investigated.

One further note about terminology: folklorists, narrative scholars, and fairy-tale specialists have devoted many works to distinguishing between folktale and fairy tale at the level of genre. Jack Zipes, for example, defines the folktale as "an oral narrative form cultivated by non-literate and literate people to express the manner in which they perceived and perceive nature and their social order and their wish to satisfy their needs and wants" (2002: 7) whereas the fairy tale is the "mass-mediated cultural form of the folk tale," which coincided with "the decline of feudalism and the formation of the bourgeois public sphere" (15). Somewhat differently, Cristina Bacchilega views the folk and fairy tale as coextensive genres, both serving as "ideologically variable desire machines" (1997: 7), a definitional hypothesis that hooks right back into the foundational importance of gender and sexuality to the genre (for we might ask: who is desiring whom, and how?). Here, the focus on fairy tale is maintained, with some reference to and inclusion of folktale materials for a few reasons: first, because these are etic or scholarly genres, which may not be as rigidly upheld in other cultures under discussion; second, because both genres share a focus on wonder and magic, which can, by outlining the limits of reality, reveal what is thought to be most real about gender and sexuality; and finally, because the intertextual web linking fairy tales from different authors and time periods (and indeed, linking these texts to critical scholarly impulses, as discussed in Joosen 2011) has always included less-canonical folktales as well as conventional tales of magic and quests. For these reasons, it is most useful to cast a wider net, to illuminate how fairy tale and folktale alike shape and are shaped by gender and sexual norms.

CULTURAL HISTORIES

For the purposes of this chapter, it is also useful to delineate some of the major movements for rights around gender and sexuality that occurred in the modern era, as well as their intersections with other identities. In some cases—as with second-wave feminism—these movements can be seen to have a direct impact on contemporary retellings of fairy tales (Joosen 2011). While the "wave" model of feminist movements has been criticized as Eurocentric and oversimplistic, it still provides some useful ways to correlate major historical events to cultural developments that, in turn, impact the formation of fairy tales and other expressive culture.

In a broad sense, the first wave of feminism started in the mid-1800s and lasted until the 1920s, when women in the United States and throughout much of Western Europe fought for the right to vote. In fact, nearly two dozen other countries granted women's suffrage before the United States permitted it in 1920 (Climent 2013). While much of the first wave's attention was bound up in issues of suffrage, these early feminists were also responsible for ensuring that

> a woman could hold property in her own name, even after marriage; she could keep the money she earned if she worked for pay; and she could enter into contracts as well as sue people. By 1920, a woman could go to college and earn higher degrees; she could enter the professions; and she could live on her own without the "protection" of a husband or male guardian.
>
> (Dicker 2008: 6)

Second-wave feminism was most active after the Second World War, blossoming in the 1960s and 1970s, and major concerns were the rights of (primarily white, heterosexual) women to work outside the home for equal pay; addressing systemic issues of sexual harassment and violence, and access to contraception and abortion (Dicker 2008: 57–101). Notably, second-wavers were largely dismissive of lesbian feminists as a "lavender menace" (93), revealing that a progressive attitude toward gender roles did not automatically include a similar deconstruction of attitudes toward sexuality. The third wave of feminism is thought to have started in the early 1990s, with more emphasis on including those whose voices had previously been marginalized (women of color; women who are not heterosexual), with an increased focus on issues of sexual violence and intersectionality (109, 119).

Each wave of feminism conceived of gender and sexuality in different ways, tending to move from more essentializing to more culturally constructed and inclusive views over time. The concept of intersectionality is crucial to understanding these nuances, even though the term itself is fairly recent. Introduced by black legal scholar Kimberlé Williams Crenshaw in 1989 (though with a longer conceptual history as detailed by Anna Carastathis [2016]), intersectionality refers to the ways in which those with multiple marginalized identities (such as women of color, who suffer under both patriarchy and white supremacy) experience unique forms of oppression and erasure. Intersectional approaches, as Carastathis points out, "insist that multiple, co-constituting analytic categories are operative and equally salient in constructing institutionalized practices and lived experiences" (2016: 54). Relevant to the cultural history of fairy tales is the fact that gender- and sexuality-based modes of oppression have both continued and been contested in the modern era and, moreover, that these modes of oppression overlap with others. The many writers who interrogate the sexism of fairy tales do so in a context where sexism impacts white women and nonwhite women differently, for example, which is why bringing an intersectional lens to this discussion is important.

Further, there are a number of major world events that left indelible marks on the cultures of the modern age, such that attempting a cultural history without mentioning them would be unwise. There may not, for example, be many fairy tales that explicitly describe vaccinations or the birth control pill, but it is crucial to take these developments into account when setting the stage for how fairy tales depict, for instance, the dissolution and formation of families (which can be described as structures that use gender roles to regulate sexuality). The sociocultural movements of the post–Second World War era, ranging from student activism and the counterculture movements to second-wave feminism and the civil rights and anti/de-colonial and anti-racist movements, set the stage for large-scale cultural discourse on normative identities and regimes that derive much of their power from being hegemonic or naturalized to the point of fading into the background.

Specific to the topics of gender and sexuality, the modern era saw a boom in governmental policies regulating sexuality, a flourishing of research on sex, and an uptick in technologies that impacted daily and lifelong gender roles. Multiple nations implemented some form of sex education in the early to mid-twentieth century, while many of those same nations also had laws making it permissible to indefinitely detain women suspected of being prostitutes or having venereal diseases (Stern 2018). As of the 1940s, many of these long-feared diseases such as syphilis, chlamydia, and gonorrhea could be cured with penicillin, and yet a few decades later the HIV epidemic would create a new atmosphere of fear around sexual activities, one with homophobic implications. The new field of sexological research, pioneered by scholars such as Alfred Kinsey and William Masters and Virginia Johnson, also meant that scientific insights around human sexual behavior became more a part of common knowledge than ever before. Finally, the invention of household technologies such as the washing machine and dishwasher freed up many women from domestic activities that would have continued to consume their time, even as marriage became less of a defining factor in women's access to legal and economic freedoms (Traister 2016). These factors all meant more open—if not necessarily more progressive—dialogue around gender and sexuality than in previous time periods, alongside increased attention to the role of medical, scientific, and educational institutions in governing public versus private ways of viewing gender and sexuality.

DISNEY, GENDER, AND SEXUALITY

Without a doubt, one of the major forces in the cultural history of fairy tales in the modern era, and the shaping of gender and sexuality in these fairy tales, has been Disney. The successes of Disney in the modern age, and the types of stories it has sold to audiences worldwide, are in turn predicated upon significant historical events. As Tracey Mollet details, Disney and the American Dream worked in tandem to reinforce the "rags to riches" storyline as a major part of the American worldview, a storyline that in turn has gendered ramifications: "While many characteristics of Disney princesses have changed over time, however, their nature and temperament has not changed. Disney princesses are all as universally kind and good as Snow White, while Disney villains always embody the jealousy and superficiality of the Wicked Queen" (2019: 223). The specifics of the plot may change but, as Zipes points out, all the major animated Disney films "follow conventional principles of technical and aesthetic organization to celebrate stereotypical gender and power relations and to foster a world view of harmony" (2011: 23). Thus, the structures and the functions of Disney fairy-tale films are inextricable from their messages about gender.

During the Great Depression that persisted throughout the 1930s in the United States, which destabilized the American Dream as well as the economy and the major foundations of social life, the animated shorts of Disney were wildly popular (Mollet 2019: 222). Further, Disney's first full-length animated film, *Snow White and the Seven Dwarfs*, was released in 1937. Dubbed "Disney's folly" (Bodden 2009: 10) the film was an immense success. As the Depression era transformed into the Second World War, which meant a revitalized economy for the United States and the upending of gender roles as increasing numbers of women entered the workforce, Disney adapted to the changing cultural context.

The postwar years, furthermore, meant a reevaluation of gender roles, which were also reflected in Disney films: "Domesticity was celebrated in the postwar years as it had been in the Victorian era. Even if they had enjoyed their wartime labor, women were asked to make their families and homes the center of their lives" (Dicker 2008: 65). The emphasis on domesticity appears in postwar films such as *Cinderella* ([1950] 1997) and *Sleeping Beauty* (1959), which feature heroines confined to the private sphere. Further, an increased emphasis on commodification within the domestic sphere began to characterize the Disney franchise. As Rebecca Traister observes of gender roles after the Second World War:

> Advertisers sold women and men on an old, cult-of-domesticity-era ideal: that the highest female calling was the maintenance of a domestic sanctuary for men on whom they would depend economically. In order to care for the home, these women would rely on new products, like vacuum cleaners and washing machines, sales of which would in turn line the pockets of the husbands who ran the companies and worked in the factories that produced these goods.
>
> (2016: 64)

Cleverly adapting to changing values in North American contexts, while also beginning to expand its global reach, Disney continued to maintain an emphasis on stereotypical gender roles and simultaneously commodified its popular films into an endless array of products: dolls, toys, clothing, theme park experiences, and more (Zipes 2011: 25–6). These items solidified the links between femininity and the domestic sphere (dolls can be played with anywhere, but have a complement of outfits and accessories that must be meticulously sorted and cleaned), and between womanhood/girlhood and consumer/beauty culture. The global marketing of Disney films and products has led to a form of cultural imperialism, which includes the gender roles being tacitly endorsed by the films and attendant products.

Of course, as cultural changes have occurred (such as the third wave of feminism with its broader reach and appeal, as described above), Disney has kept pace. Heroines of their films no longer need marry to have a happy ending; as Mollet observes: "In the case of *Frozen*, *Brave*, *Tangled*, and the latest Disney princess release, *Moana* (2016), the princess' 'happily ever after' doesn't contain a prince at all" (2019: 227). These are notable changes, but the overwhelming assumption is still that these heroines are most likely heterosexual, and moreover that they are cisgender and not intersex.

Regarding sexuality in Disney, heterosexual and monogamous relationships are the norm. Most princesses end up paired off with a different-gender long-term lover (or spouse) at the end of the film, and many of the villains are unmarried and queer-coded (e.g., displaying traits of a different gender, or appearing to have a transgressive sexuality). Examples include Ursula from *The Little Mermaid*, who was modeled off drag queen Divine (Sells 1995), and the femininized and racialized features of Jafar from *Aladdin* and Scar from *The Lion King* (thereby also invoking Orientalism). Notably, in the live-action remake of *Beauty and the Beast*, the villain Gaston's sidekick Lefou was depicted as openly gay, which did not automatically make him a villain nor disqualify him from receiving a tentative happy ending of his own, as he is depicted in the film's end dancing with another man (discussed in Mollet 2019: 228).

There have always been dissonant voices alongside Disney in the realm of fairy-tale films; the racy takes on "Little Red Riding Hood" by Tex Avery in the 1930s and the "Fractured Fairy Tales" produced for the *Rocky and Bullwinkle* cartoon show in the 1950s and 1960s have offered carnivalesque spins on the happily ever after, with few of their stories ending in heterosexual marriage (Zipes 2011: 67). However, as Zipes notes, by 1959 with Disney's production of *Sleeping Beauty*, "the artistic and ideological recipe and approach to making animated fairy-tale films in the Disney studio became cemented" (89), leaving a legacy that future fairy-tale films would have to work within or knowingly subvert, especially when it comes to depictions of gender and sexuality.

Other filmic traditions have relied less on Disney for providing molds; these include films that retell tales such as "Little Red Riding Hood" and "Bluebeard," of which Disney did not provide early iconic images (Disney in fact created a short animated "Little Red Riding Hood" in 1922 but it is not well known; discussed by Zipes [2011: 137–8]). These tales are particularly relevant to the discussion of gender and sexuality because their plots revolve directly around sexual violence. As Zipes summarizes the films adapting "Little Red Riding Hood," there were two distinct phases: the first one, in the silent film period and up through the 1940s and 1950s, "focuses on the gullibility of Little Red or the rapacity of a stupid wolf, both who need governing and policing by an armed huntsman," while in the second phase, primarily after 1979, "the films are more concerned with depicting a more forceful young woman intent on following her desires and breaking with the male gaze of domination" (2011: 135). Contemporary films that disrupt or depart from the Disney mold include queered retellings of "Little Red Riding Hood" such as that created by David Kaplan (discussed in Orme [2015]), French director Catherine Breillat's 2009 *Bluebeard*, which decouples curiosity from sexual infidelity (see Bacchilega 2013: 90–2), and Mexican director Guillermo de Toro's *Pan's Labyrinth* (2006) and *The Shape of Water* (2017) with their ambiguously (un)happy endings, their depiction of corrupted masculine power and deviant femininity, and in the latter case, their representation of love and desire across species boundaries (see Jorgensen 2020).

GLOBAL FOLKTALE AND FAIRY-TALE COLLECTIONS

While many of the "classic" fairy-tale collections that are regarded as canonical today originated in the nineteenth century, such as those of Jacob and Wilhelm Grimm and Hans Christian Andersen, the twentieth century saw the publication of many other collections of folk and fairy tales that have been influential and important both to the expansion of the field of folk narrative and to the consideration of gender and sexuality therein. Bacchilega refers to the "canonized Perrault-Grimms-Disney triad" (2013: 27) as a major authority, but one that is "no longer *the* central pretext for their adaptations in literature, film, or other media" (27; emphasis in the original). In the next section, the deliberate feminist adaptations of fairy tales will be addressed; here, the focus will be on folk- and fairy-tale texts that come more directly from various oral traditions, which in both their content and their framing encourage readers to think of gender and sexuality in new ways.

As Karen Rowe (1989) among others has argued, fairy tales have long been associated with women: women as traditional taletellers, women as skilled weavers of story, women as mistresses of maintaining and transmitting oral tradition. What is new in the modern era is a sustained focus on not just a few star tellers—such as the female informants of the Grimms or the salon writers of seventeenth-century France—but on robust, female-dominated oral taletelling traditions that continue on into the twentieth century. The centrality of gender to these tale collections is noteworthy, and has implications for sexuality as well, and further, the global reach of these collections provides a useful basis for comparing and contrasting cultural attitudes about gender and sexuality worldwide.

Folklorist Richard Dorson's *Folktales of the World* series provided a number of texts that directly present gender roles in their cultural contexts. With books documenting the tales from Norway, Egypt, France, Germany, Chile, and England, among other countries, Dorson's series marks an important contribution to global understandings of gender roles. At the same time, other collections represent the opportunity to dive in deeper to local understandings of gender and sexuality. In their collection of Palestinian-Arab folktales *Speak, Bird, Speak Again*, Ibrahim Muhawi and Sharif Kanaana write "that society considers the telling of these tales to be a woman's art form" (1989: 2). As such, the tales provide an artistic portrait of society, with a mix of direct representations of gender norms (such as the emphasis on chastity and modesty for women) and fantastic wish fulfillment outside those norms. In terms of sexuality, the authors

> find women's sexuality and their emotional needs largely affirmed. Indeed, women play a much more active role with regard to their sexuality in the tales than in real life. For example, they actively choose their mates at least as frequently as the men do, whereas in the society they play a passive role, being chosen by the family of their potential mates and then having merely to accept the decision their guardians make on the subject.
>
> (Muhawi and Kanaana 1989: 34)

And indeed, the tales reflect this interplay between norm and fantasy, with adventurous heroines and bashful heroes starring in the stories.

The notion of gendered tales mentioned above bears out in the work of James Taggart, whose ethnographic collection of Spanish tales in the 1980s follows gendered lines. Taggart's main premise is that "Spaniards tell many folktales that describe in metaphorical language how a maiden and a young man emerge from their parental families and bond with each other in heterosexual love" (1990: 3). And yet, these tales do not always uphold heteronormative patterns; as Pauline Greenhill and Emilie Anderson-Grégoire document in their survey of tale-type 514 or ATU 514 (for an explanation, see Chapter 8, this volume), "The Shift of Sex," there are numerous twentieth-century versions of this tale, featuring "cross-dressing, genderfucking, and possible lesbianism/bisexuality of the protagonists" (2014: 70), which do not seem to attract negative commentary from narrators.

As described above, the patterns in global folk- and fairy-tale collections tend toward an already multifaceted understanding of local gender and sexual norms. Rather than uncritically assuming that traditional tales even in the modern era are simplistic in their depiction of gender and sexuality, scholars should bear in mind that encounters between local and global forces yield the active reshaping of identities within the tales.

REVISITING/REVISING GENDER AND SEXUALITY: FEMINISM AND THE CARTER GENERATION

A notable feature of fairy-tale texts in the modern era is their explicit engagement with themes of gender and sexuality. Occasionally, these texts are explicit in the most literal sense, with erotic and pornographic retellings of tales produced for mass-market audiences (see Jorgensen [2008] for an overview of fairy tales eroticized in popular fiction). However, this is not to imply that the fairy tales of previous time periods did not address issues of gender and sexuality—one has but to learn about *The Arabian Nights* or the French *conteuses* to disprove this assertion—but rather to point out that increasing attention to gender and sexuality in tales, as well as increasing attention to gender and sexuality in larger cultural contexts, combined to make this a powerful focus for many taletellers, writers, artists, producers, consumers, and more.

As Sarah Bonner says specifically of European female visual artists, "particularly since the 1960s and 1970s ... the female voice in fairy tale has been further strengthened by the emergence of female fine artists who have taken on the mantle of soothsayer and through their work explored the possibilities of gender representation in the visual fairy tale" (2019: 439). Bonner continues: "These female artists are radical in their retellings; sisters of their literary forebears, their protagonists speak of independence, action, courage, dissent, rebellion and darker motivations that do not align easily with the conventional female characters that have dominated the popular fairy tale" (439). What

Bonner writes of the fine arts is true of other media as well: the ways in which many contemporary retellers of tales engage with gender (and sexuality) is often more transgressive than it is complacent, though as we will see, there are a few notable exceptions to this general statement.

Much scholarship has already focused on Western authors and artists who have reworked gender and sexuality in fairy tales in contemporary times; here, I will summarize some of those findings before moving on to more global examples as well as a few specific case studies that illustrate this general focus on interrogating gender and sexuality. As Vanessa Joosen points out, "a remarkable increase in the production of fairy-tale criticism and retellings" occurred in English- and German-speaking contexts in the 1970s, with especial links to "the 1968 movement and the second wave of feminism" (2011: 4). Ideas from second-wave feminism permeated fairy-tale retellings, such that Joosen observes: "One of the earliest, simplest, and most popular strategies to correct the patriarchal model of representation in traditional fairy tales was the reversal of gender roles" (86). Tales that invert the gendered active/passive dichotomy often observed in both canonical fairy tales and their Disneyfied counterparts exemplify this trend, though as noted above, even Disney has started to deliver more active heroines as well as heroines who do not simply succumb to heterosexual marriage at the film's end.

As examples of fairy-tale retellings that address gendered stereotypes by reversing them, one can look to children's literature, young adult fiction, and adult literary fiction. The children's picture book *Princess Smartypants* (1987) features a princess who does not wish to marry, and thus sets impossible tasks for her princely suitors to preserve her independence, including transforming the one successful prince into a frog (Cole 1987). In the young adult genre, Francesca Lia Block's book *The Rose and the Beast* (2000), a collection of dreamy, urban-set short stories retelling individual fairy tales, also presents a series of feminist-influenced inversions: the Snow White character chooses a life with the dwarfs over reentering the human world and Thumbelina's ambient magic transforms a human boy into a person her size so they can be together.

In terms of adult literary fiction, an important and influential cluster of writers emerged in the 1960s, 1970s, and 1980s, dubbed the "Carter generation," including the eponymous Angela Carter, A. S. Byatt, Salman Rushdie, and Robert Coover, among others. Often characterized as postmodern retellings, the works of these authors are notable for their use of hybrid literary strategies to interrogate the ideologies of canonical folktales. As Stephen Benson observes of these writers: "The revision and retelling of the canonical fairy tales in new fictions ... becomes one aspect of the deconstruction of narratives of patriarchy, allowing for a critique of the way such narratives function and including illustrations of the effects of, and alternatives to, such historically dominant codes of behavior" (2003: 168).

Perhaps one of the most notable approaches to gender and sexuality in these authors involves interrogation of the linking of women's worth with sexual behavior. To take one example from Carter, her story "The Company of Wolves," a "Little Red Riding Hood" (ATU 333) retelling, features a heroine who joins the wolf (in this case, a werewolf in the shape of a man) in bed. Recognizing that he has killed her grandmother, but also recognizing that fear does not serve her, she undresses and joins him in bed, where the two have sex, which saves her life: "See! sweet and sound she sleeps in granny's bed, between the paws of the tender wolf" (Carter 1979 [2006]: 118). As Kimberly Lau observes, Carter's revision embraces "Little Red Riding Hood's sexual agency in the tale's seduction, overturning the bourgeois morality of [Perrault's] coda in verse" (2015: 124). In contrast to earlier versions of the tale type, in which joining the wolf in bed means death in his jaws, or death followed by miraculous rescue by a woodcutter, Carter's version offers another view of sex as not determining a heroine's worth (e.g., equating loss of virginity with death or dishonor). Instead, as Lau proposes: "through this other erotic, this animal intimacy, Carter unveils the hegemonic order of heterosexual relations ... a sexual moment no longer chained to a dominant erotic that limits the sexual possibilities of men and women but one that emerges from our deepest drives" (137).

Another noteworthy pattern is that femininity and women's gender roles have been interrogated more thoroughly and widely than masculinity and men's gender roles, at least until fairly recently (in North American fairy-tale literature specifically, this trend is discussed in Jorgensen [2019]). This tendency can be linked to how femininity has been more thoroughly theorized than masculinity, with the academic fields of women's studies and feminist theory predating the field of men and masculinity studies by a few decades at least, depending on how one measures the start of a discipline. Just as Carter and her colleagues started many of these trends, other authors, auteurs, and artists have stepped forward to expand these ideas.

REVISITING/REVISING GENDER AND SEXUALITY: THE CONTEMPORARIES

After the Carter generation's revisions, as well as later retellings that carried forward much of the same second-wave feminist momentum in questioning gender roles, a series of global retellings has continued this creative practice whilst simultaneously exploring other directions in gender and sexuality. Retellings that question the primacy of heterosexuality have noticeably been slower to appear, perhaps in conjunction with the slow rate at which social movements accept nonheterosexual identities as valid and worth defending. Recall, as noted above, that second-wave feminism tended to exclude lesbians, to say nothing of the erasure of bisexual people, and this continues in many cultural contexts today (Germon 2008). As Joosen notes: "From the feminist fairy-tale criticism of the 1970s and 1980s, the issue of homosexuality seems virtually absent" (2011: 111). Queer fairy-tale scholarship has begun to fill this gap in the last decade (see Turner and Greenhill 2012), but in another instance of the retellings and the scholarship mirroring one another, fairy-tale revisions that are explicitly queer or nonheterosexual have been slower to appear than those that simply question heteronormative gender roles. Further, it is important to avoid conflating texts with explicitly queer content (some of which will be discussed below) with those texts that lend themselves to queer readings; Pauline Greenhill works with a number of contemporary films that retell "Cinderella" that conform more to the latter than the former. Greenhill writes: "Two single mothers, two illegal immigrants, and a lesbian opera singer queer the conventional idea of Cinderella as an innocent ingenue" (2019: 257). While it is certainly important to use queer theory to examine how many fairy-tale retellings "queer" or call into question hegemonically linked gender and sexual identities, it is also key not to lose sight of how many texts contain explicit nonheterosexual and/or non-cisgender identities and behaviors.

One of the most famous examples of a queer fairy-tale collection is *Kissing the Witch: Old Tales in New Skins* by Emma Donoghue ([1993] 1997). Published in 1997, the thirteen stories are linked structurally: the protagonist of each story asks another character how they came to be who or where they are today, and that character then tells their story next. Donoghue revises a number of canonical tales, positing for instance that Thumbelina felt small and insignificant rather than being tiny in reality, and thus she fled her controlling husband. While characters like this one are heterosexual, many of Donoghue's heroines find love with other women, whether in romantic and/or sexual relationships (as in her revisions of "Cinderella" and "Beauty and the Beast") or whether focusing on the power of platonic or familial love (as when the "Snow White" character eschews marriage with the prince to return to her stepmother and stay by her side).

However, as Joosen notes, even these sexually liberated tales fall back on older gender stereotypes at times:

> The binary opposition of males and females is largely retained in *Kissing the Witch*, and the rise of women in Donoghue's tales more often than not happens at the expense of men. Their roles are limited and reside mostly in the negative: some have incestuous feelings for their daughters ("The Tale of the Apple" and "The Tale of the Skin") or abuse their wives and children ("The Tale of the Cottage").
>
> (2011: 90)

The question of whether same-sex desire mandates strict gender roles is one that receives ongoing attention, both in cultural outlets and in the fairy-tale retellings. A handful of "Cinderella" retellings illustrate the imbrication of gender and sexuality. As Mark Macleod discusses, gay male Cinderella characters in young adult fiction get to experience a "fabulous Cinderella moment" such as "acceptance by members of the Gay-Straight Alliance, or attending prom night with a same-sex partner" (2016: 203). Even the "triumphant gay fairy tale" (2016: 211), however, risks reifying gender roles, with various hypermasculine and feminizing stereotypes being expressed in the gay male characters of which Macleod writes. In the novel *Geekerella* by Ashley Poston (2017) the Cinderella character, Elle, is heterosexual, but one of her stepsisters ends up falling for the donor figure Sage (a green-haired, heavily pierced fellow teenager who makes Elle's dream of cosplaying as a favorite sci-fi character come true). While this Cinderella character is straight, one of her stepsisters cruelly teases her by insinuating that she's a lesbian, apparently not knowing that she is insulting her own sister. Finally, in the novel *Ash* by Malinda Lo (2009), the Cinderella character has a dalliance with the fairy man Sidhean, but ultimately falls in love with the king's huntress Kaisa. In all of these "Cinderella" retellings, characters who are not heterosexual receive some pushback from straight characters, but ultimately they are able to craft happy endings for themselves.

A major thread that continues from the Carter generation, and indeed pushes gender and sexual norms further, is the unlinking of fairy-tale happy endings from women's sexual purity. This will be seen in the *Lost Girl* TV example discussed below, and is also seen in the fantasy series *A Court of Thorns and Roses* by Sarah J. Maas (2015), wherein the first novel of the series of the same title sets up a "Beauty and the Beast" plot. In it, the female human protagonist Feyre is paired with a male faerie protagonist, whom she must help disenchant through what ends up being a fairly traumatic sequence of torture and trauma, given that the power-hungry faerie queen who had cursed him tries to destroy the human lover as well. In the second novel, *A Court of Mist and Fury* (2016), Feyre suffers from severe trauma, what might be diagnosed as post-traumatic stress disorder (PTSD) in another context. Forced by a magical bargain to spend time at another faerie court, she eventually falls in love with its leader instead of the Beast from the first novel in the series. In stark contrast to the fairy tales from previous time periods, Feyre falls in love with and has passionate sex with more than one man (sequentially, not simultaneously). Similarly, in one of the novels discussed above, *Ash*, the protagonist chooses to give herself to the fairy man Sidhean for one night to fulfill the bargain that has had him acting as a donor figure in her life, and after, she is free to pursue her love for Kaisa; and this sexual encounter does not leave her marked as damaged goods.

Indeed, a focus on sexual violence and trauma have been major themes from the 1970s (such as in Anne Sexton's poetry) to the present. As Laura D'Amore demonstrates using recent American retellings such as the films *Snow White and the Huntsman* (2012) and *Hansel and Gretel: Witch Hunters* (2013) as well as the novel *Sisters Red* (2010), contemporary fairy-tale revisions that explicitly depict women combating sexual violence with violence of their own involves a "powerful feminist fantasy in which girls and women can be hardened into weapons that destroy those who seek to harm them" (D'Amore 2017: 402). D'Amore identifies this phenomenon as vigilante feminism, and it is also evident in stories from Block's and Donoghue's collections, where certain heroines fight back violently against their oppressors.

These themes and adaptation strategies appear at different rates and with differing emphases all over the world. Mayako Murai summarizes the "Grimm boom" in the 1990s in Japanese art and literature, noting that although "the Grimm boom lasted for only about two years, this vogue radically changed the public perception of the Grimms' tales in Japan, where the tales had previously been circulating widely but mostly in heavily sanitized versions intended for a young audience" (2015: 31). Books such as Matsumoto Yūko's *Tsumibukai hime no otogibanashi* (Fairy Tales of Sinful Princesses) (1996) and Kiryū Misao's *Hontō wa osoroshii Gurimu dōwa* (Grimms' Tales Really Are Horrific) (1998) displayed an "obsession ... with violence and sexual transgression" (2015: 32) that paved the way for a number of literary and artistic fairy-tale retellings that Murai discusses in *From Dog Bridegroom to Wolf Girl*, many of which both "resist and subvert the eroticization of girls" and challenge essentializing approaches to gender, thereby offering "more complex views of women and their relationship with the Other" (2015: 142). In a later work, Murai further notes the publication of the innovative anthology *Ankoku Gurimu Dōwashu* (Dark Grimm's Tales) in 2017, wherein all of the tales "either question or subvert gender stereotypes and hierarchy, and none of them has a conventional happy ending with a royal marriage, reflecting the changing values of contemporary Japan" (2019a: 348). The tales summarized by Murai include a retelling of "Bluebeard" wherein the Bluebeard figure's latest wife, who is a cyborg, mutilates and kills him in a move that makes her even more humanlike and desirable to him; and a retelling of "Hansel and Gretel" where the witch is a maligned figure: "the talented and independent woman is cast in the role of the witch by various members of society who distort reality so that it matches their perceptions of the truth" (349). Murai argues that these tales reject heteronormative gender roles, or alternately critique those who would seek to uphold them as misguided. In particular, Japanese adaptations of Andersen's "The Little Mermaid" have also challenged gender roles that mark women as passive, and have often yielded pessimistic endings fraught with cannibalism and sexual violence (Fraser 2017). For example, prior to the "Grimm boom" Kurahashi Yumiko published the notable collection *Cruel Fairy Tales for Adults* (1984), and in her revision of "The Little Mermaid" (titled "A Mermaid's Tears"), the mermaid has sex with the prince while he is unconscious after she rescued him from the storm. This sex act is not framed or (apparently) experienced as rape, since when the mermaid is transformed into a human, the prince happily resumes a carnal relationship with her. The tale ends with a disaster, causing the mermaid and prince to become halfway fused, with the mermaid's legs and lower half paired with the prince's upper body, leading to neither one being quite complete or happy. Kurahashi concludes with the moral, "The nether parts are not for loving" (2008: 177). This perplexing phrase encourages readers to consider whether the nether parts—often thought of as the locus of sexual feeling and desire—are in fact a necessary part of the fairy tale's happily ever after.

Similarly, in Korean fairy-tale films, gender roles are heightened especially in connection with sexual violence, trauma, and memory. As Sung-Ae Lee demonstrates, multiple Korean films utilize local traditional tales—such as those featuring female ghosts or fox women—to tell stories rooted in local ideas about gender and sexuality. For instance, ghost women characters reveal important contextual information about identity: "Since in Korea a woman's social value is still determined by biological reproduction, childcare and home management, the most feared ghost is the virgin ghost, a young woman who has died without fulfilling the conventional female roles of sexual partner, wife and mother, and therefore, in this patriarchal gendered culture, may bitterly resent the living" (2019: 358). The unremarked-upon murder of women as background for these stories, and the working-out of trauma through telling them, demonstrates how "South Korean film and television drama uses adaptation of well-known traditional folktales and a small number of Western fairy tales as a significant domain in which to comment on Korean social, political, and economic life" (366), including facets of gender and sexuality.

However, simply paying more explicit attention to gender and/or sexuality does not guarantee doing so affirmatively, or being progressive in regard to other identities. The novel *Boy, Snow, Bird* by Helen Oyeyemi exemplifies this. A "Snow White" retelling set in mid-twentieth-century North America, the novel adheres to Joosen's observations about recent "Snow White" retellings, wherein "the disappearance of magic helps to increase the contact with contemporary reality" (2007: 237). The main character, a woman named Boy, escapes an abusive parent she nicknames the Ratcatcher, marries a widower, and sends away the prior child (Snow) when Boy gives birth to a child they name Bird, whose dark skin reveals that the husband's family has been passing for white. With finicky mirrors and uncanny doublings, the novel, as Kimberly Lau observes, "suggests alternatives to the feminine modes of sociality locking Snow White and the Evil Queen in an eternal battle predicated on female jealousy" (2016: 388). The doubled emphasis on gender roles as well as on racial identity also demonstrates intersectionality at work in the text; the non-passing female members of the widower's family, for instance, face special hardships in the beauty standards to which they as African American women are held. However, this innovative approach to gender roles that ends with "female allegiance and play" (2016: 388), and with Boy no longer playing the role of wicked stepmother but rather uniting all the women in her family to go on a quest, works only because it fundamentally misunderstands another phenomenon: the relationships between gender identity and sexual trauma.

One of the novel's main plot twists is that the abusive father, Frank (whom Boy has nicknamed the Ratcatcher), is actually Boy's mother, Frances. Boy's longtime friend Mia digs up this fact and talks to Frank to get his life story, learning in the process that Frances had been a stellar student, someone who had been studying homosexuality and society until she was raped. After giving birth to Boy, she looked in a mirror, saw a man instead, and became Frank. The novel ends with this revelation, with Boy interpreting Frank's transgender identity as a spell to be broken. Lau, whose focus is more on racial identity than gender identity in the novel, remarks in a footnote that while this ending

> might make sense in a novel about mothers and daughters, it nonetheless discounts the Ratcatcher's chosen identity as a man by assuming the possibility of a suppressed interior female identity. It seems worth noting that the novel's final turn to female solidarity and collaboration depends on a dismissal of the Ratcatcher's male identity as an authentic and self-determined one.
>
> (Lau 2016: 391)

This mild criticism misses the mark on two main fronts. First, Oyeyemi's suggestion that transgender identities emerge as a response to trauma and are not valid on their own is mistaken. Second, trauma (especially sexual trauma) does not cause people to then become abusive. Texts such as the Oyeyemi novel contribute to misunderstandings of transgender experiences and traumatic experiences alike.

As Neal A. Lester observes of erotic fairy tales retold for adults:

> These authors and these stories … do not address race and culture, and when they do, even they maintain and sustain the patriarchal ideal of heteronormativity and of binary gender roles in same-sex unions. Rarely do single adaptations—revisions, reimaging, and reimaginings take into account intersectional perspectives that involve age, gender, sexuality, race, class, ability, religion, body type, and the like at once.
>
> (2019: 233–4)

Or, in the case of Oyeyemi's novel, when race comes to the forefront, complexities of gender and sexuality are left behind. This is unfortunate, as identities such as gender and sexuality are co-constituted with other identities like race, class, nationality, (dis)ability, and so on.

Films and TV shows that retell fairy tales also do intriguing work with gender and sexuality, and in some cases fall short in similar ways as Oyeyemi's novel. For example, the Canadian TV show *Lost Girl* (2010–16) combines elements from multiple genres of global folk narrative (with a monster-of-the-week plot that incorporated creatures from myth, legend, and folktale/fairy tale alike) but ultimately borrows heavily from fairy-tale structures. The protagonist, Bo, begins as a "lost girl" in a nameless North American city, where she learns that she is actually of fae descent, specifically a succubus, meaning that she draws sustenance from sexual encounters. As the series progresses over its five seasons, Bo learns that she is both hero and princess, and must make alliances among fae nobility and royalty to save the world, as well as grapple with her own nature, suspended between the human and fae worlds. The show's obsession with the main character's mysterious yet royal lineage, with prophecy, and with quests make it as much a fairy-tale retelling as any other genre. Notably for the purposes of this chapter, Bo is bisexual, taking lovers that are men and women alike, and she demonstrates many nonmonogamous behaviors without reproach or slut-shaming, because her magical nature requires her to engage in sexual activity to thrive.

However, it is impossible to label *Lost Girl* as unilaterally sex-positive or progressive. In season three, episode one, "Caged Fae," Bo rampages through the city until she is arrested and sent to a Fae prison for women. This is a ruse to allow her to investigate suspected unethical practices inside the prison: the Amazons who staff the prison are forcing rare female fae to give birth so that their offspring can be sold at high prices. While this is an intriguing comment on issues of women's reproductive coercion and oppression, the plot is resolved when the lead Amazon is revealed to be a male impostor, either a type of cross-dresser or failed trans woman, leading the remaining guards to depose her and let the prisoners go free. Dragged off by angry Amazons, the impostor shouts, "My mother was an Amazon! I'm one of you!" The episode ends with Bo and a human doctor, Lauren, deciding to finally give their romance a shot and begin dating. Thus, while the show demonstrates a progressive attitude toward sexual orientation, with a same-gender partnership being affirmed, it simultaneously relies on transphobic plot devices that essentialize gender identities to one's genitals and one's assigned-at-birth gender.

The Oyeyemi and *Lost Girl* case studies help demonstrate the point that many of the most marginalized identities around gender and sexuality—people who are transgender, asexual, aromantic, and so on—continue to remain marginalized in fairy tales. Exploring and exploding gender roles within an assumption of a cisgender identity has been quite popular; writing characters who are agender or transgender or non-binary, less so.

In certain cases, the most marginalized voices are finding representation on the margins; specifically, on the internet rather than through mainstream channels that go through levels of committees and production. A post on Tumblr (a social media website and mobile application) offers a revision of Cinderella with the following text:

> Yo ok what if there was a Cinderella story where Cinderella is a trans woman and that's really why her stepmom treats her like shit and won't let her go to the ball and when the prince and his men come looking to try the slipper on every woman in the land her stepmom tells the prince there aren't any women left in the house because she insists that Cinderella is a man, but Cinderella comes out and the prince recognizes her and says something along the lines of "well I'd say that's a woman if I ever saw one."
> (Bells Does Tumblr n.d.)

A follow-up comment to the Tumblr post reads: "That would explain the shoe size not being common among women as well." Indeed, this is a significant revision of the classic fairy tale that decenters the assumption that the protagonist would be cisgender. In contrast to some of the global tales mentioned above that are fruitfully interpreted through a transgender studies lens, this snippet of a revision foregrounds the nonnormative status of a classical heroine, which is a notable phenomenon of the modern era's fairy tales.

CONCLUSION

Despite the many innovative approaches to gender and sexuality in fairy tales in the modern era, the legacy of earlier gender/sexuality systems and earlier texts remains strong. As noted above, the Grimms were active in the nineteenth century, but the influence they continued to exert globally, specifically in regard to gender roles, is noteworthy. To mention a few examples from Spain and India, respectively, "Francoist ideology clearly affects Spanish variants of the Grimms to reaffirm conservative notions of gender" (Hernández and Martín-Rogero 2014: 68) while in contrast, Indian author Harikrishna Devsare's twentieth-century Hindi translation of the Grimms' tales for child audiences weaves in a "progressive" attitude toward gender roles in a "largely patriarchal society in which female feticide remains a rampant and horrifying reality" (Roy 2014: 44). The authors and translators of contemporary fairy tales clearly respond to notions of gender and sexuality in their cultural contexts, whether driven by the desire to uphold current normative regimes or to restructure them.

Major developments in cultural arenas surrounding gender and sexuality have also impacted the structures, textures, and audiences of fairy tales in the modern era, with changes in the legal freedoms granted to women and lesbian, gay, bisexual, transgender, queer/questioning, and other (LGBTQ+)

people impacting the roles available to such people in fairy tales. More "accepted" acts and identities still get more screen time than those that remain marginalized, as examples above like the ones from *Lost Girl* and feminist-inspired retellings, which sometimes valorize gay and lesbian identities over bisexual or transgender ones, reveal. Folk and fairy tales have always dealt with themes of gender and sexuality, both shaping and responding to social developments in these arenas; as the modern era continues, with a spate of both progressive policies as well as backlash, global consumers and creators of fairy tales alike will continue to explore these ideologically variable desire machines in new media and in new ways.

CHAPTER FOUR

Humans and Non-Humans

Nature, Anima, Matter

AMY GREENHOUGH

INTRODUCTION

The prowling, six-legged wolf sculptures of Japanese artist Tomoko Kōnoike are made from shards of mirrored glass. When inside, they reflect the artificial lights of exhibition rooms, seeming to laugh as they walk away from their discarded pelts into the kaleidoscopic patterns created by their mirrored embodiment, as in the installation *The Planet is Covered by Silvery Sleep* (2006; Figure 4.1). When outside in the forest, however, as in *Donning Animal Skins and Braided Grass* (2013; Figure 4.2), the wolves reflect and inevitably refract the ecosphere of the woodland. Surrounded by the closed landscape of the forest, in the mirrored skin of Kōnoike's wolves, we might feasibly see both ourselves and the non-human world contorted and fractured. By disturbing the lines of sight, the artwork suggests a distortion, not only of the non-human animal itself (or herself, in the case of the wolves) but also of what we see in her reflective skin: *everything else*.

The wolves of these pieces allude to the wolves of folk and fairy tale from across the globe; yet another reflection of humanity. Such is the reach of those narratives and, to use A. S. Byatt's (2004) phrase, the "narrative grammar" of their imagery, that to create sculptures of fantastical wolves adorned with mirrors is to invite comparisons with stories of wolfish metamorphoses, magic mirrors, and even little girls alone in the forest. In her analysis of Kōnoike's wolves, Mayako Murai suggests that "in myths and fairy tales, mirrors do not

FIGURE 4.1: Tomoko Kōnoike, mixed media sculpture, *The Planet is Covered by Silvery Sleep*, 2006.

FIGURE 4.2: Tomoko Kōnoike, mixed media sculpture, *Donning Animal Skins and Braided Grass*, 2013.

simply reflect appearances but refract the surfaces of reality to reveal another level of meaning hidden beneath them" (2015: 136). In Kōnoike's mirrors, this refraction of the "surfaces of reality" reveals—and metaphorically represents—the suggestion that storytelling, and particularly storytelling about the non-human world, is a distortion, and that in our stories of non-humanity we have only ever been able to tell stories of humanity itself.

The evolution of folk and fairy tale has consistently reflected the changing narratives of human existence. Not least in the twentieth and twenty-first centuries, when the literary fairy tales of Europe evolved dramatically in contemporary poetry, fiction, film, and mixed-media art forms (including advertising) to embrace psychoanalytic, anthropological, feminist, postcolonial, Marxist, queer, and ecocritical modes of retelling, to name but a few. These changes are not, however, limited to the European tradition. As Murai suggests of contemporary Japanese fairy tale: "especially notable has been the change in the role of women as (re-)creators of stories as well as the difference in the way they are represented in the genre, as women have increasingly recuperated their own voices and autonomy both in and outside stories" (2015: 9). As the popularity of fairy- and folktale revisions rose, the breadth of stories they told of humanity widened, with contemporary fairy-tale "(re-)creators" able to "recuperate" the voices of those previously silenced by traditional models and dominant narrative and ideological structures, and therefore attempt to alter the representations of their stories in the genre.

Though this form of revisioning has been hugely successful, particularly for female writers/creators, for the wolves of those fairy-tale narratives—as well as for the tables and chairs, the trees and flowers, the metals, minerals, bears, and tigers—such recuperations are more complex. Non-human subjects are unable to become the creators of stories and therefore remain written *about*. Their voices can only be recuperated from a human viewpoint, thus affecting a one-sided dialogue in which the creators of contemporary fairy tales must imagine the voice of the non-human through their own (limited) perceptive lens. Timothy Clark suggests that the non-human world is largely "unseen" in canonical literature, despite appearing in various forms, because "any study of a text on the non-human always becomes a study of the human in some sense" (2011: 187). Though contemporary fairy tale has responded to the political, social, and critical debates that surround the non-human world and its discursive depictions, such depictions remain limited and partial, and the recuperations merely an imagined and, therefore, fantastical vision of non-humanity.

Of course, fairy-tale depictions of non-humanity have traditionally always been aligned with fantasy and imagination, consciously avoiding any attempt at realism and opting instead for the wonder of possibility. Famed for their anthropomorphic portrayals of speaking animals, singing objects, and elaborate metamorphoses, fairy- and folktale representations of non-humanity have been deliberately distorted through the medium of magic. If, as Jane Bennett suggests, for many "the world appears as if it consists only of active human subjects who confront passive objects and their law-governed mechanisms" (2010: xiv), in fairy tales, perceptions of subjectivity are often subverted, with objects, animals, and even landscapes playing active roles in the narratives and avoiding any such reliance on "law-governed mechanism." "All the natural laws of the world [are] held in suspension here" ([1979] 2006: 50), Angela Carter's Beauty observes; anything is possible in these stories, and so while the non-human world in fairy tale is alive in the most anthropomorphic sense of the word, it is also alive with the potential to think beyond the anthropocentric.

Since the late 1970s, scholars have identified the ways in which the fairy tale communicates contemporary preoccupations and ideologies concerning class, gender, race, and sexuality. But in our current cultural climate, the depictions of animals, materials, objects, and technologies in twentieth- and twenty-first-century fairy-tale creations can also reveal—as well as highlight and inform—contemporary discursive engagements with non-humanity. Catherine Parry observes that "human relationships with animals are inflected through political, economic, gendered, legal, social and cultural discourse, and fictional animal representations, because they are conditioned by these multiple concerns, constitute a discursive nexus" (2017: 5), an assessment that can be applied to non-humanity more broadly. Though often perceived to be inane or childish, fictional representations of animals—as well as materials, objects, and environment—are crucial to our conception of them and to the discursive narratives we form about both ourselves and what we consider to be everything else.

From the curious and attentive woodland creatures of Walt Disney's *Snow White and the Seven Dwarfs* (1937) to the numinous forests of Angela Carter's *Bloody Chamber* ([1979] 2006), the objects of Nalo Hopkinson's *Skin Folk* (2001), and the mirrored wolves of Kōnoike, changes to the contemporary fairy tale and its depiction of human/non-human relations reflect changing cultural and theoretical approaches to anthropocentrism. The animism and suspension of disbelief in fairy tales has long been a vehicle through which human-animal-object engagement could be interrogated, and even earlier traditional fairy tales highlight the fairy tale as a genre in which species and materials are fluid and in flux. In recent years, as the ecocritical, object-oriented, new material, and posthuman theoretical movements have gained pace in the latter part of the twenty-first century, fairy-tale revisionists have responded. Spanning the course of contemporary fairy- and folktale reworkings and their radical revisions of human/non-human binaries from the 1920s to the present day in Europe and worldwide, this chapter will focus on some of the dominant trends in the representation of non-humanity in contemporary folk and fairy tale. It will look first at the use of anthropomorphism and its relationship to anthropocentrism in early fairy-tale film and psychoanalytic theory, before considering Carter's engagement with human/non-human relations, the deconstructive emphasis of the postmodern fairy-tale movement and the implications of poststructuralism for non-humanity. Finally, this chapter will examine the move into more materially engaged, posthuman revisions that disrupt, in various ways, the anthropocentricism embedded in the earlier models.

For Cristina Bacchilega, "the tale of magic's controlling metaphor is the *magic mirror*, because it conflates mimesis (reflection), refraction (varying desires), and framing (artifice)" (1997: 10). Fairy- and folktale reworkings offer a mirror into our evolving attitudes to non-humanity, but like the magic mirror of "Snow White" and the fractured mirrors of Kōnoike's wolves, they are not only reflective but also refractive and, ultimately, artificially constructed. However, as our theories and attitudes toward the non-human world change, such changes are reflected in our stories. This chapter will interrogate where the human and non-human begin and end in contemporary fairy tale, asking what tensions are revealed at the borders between them and what role anthropomorphism plays in our depictions of non-humanity. By broadly mapping out the changing representations of non-humanity in contemporary folk and fairy tale, I will demonstrate how these reworkings grapple with the complexities of the human/non-human debates, and suggest that in our current age these new texts may use the traditional stories to enable as well as reflect contemporary challenges to anthropocentric thought.

A HUMAN IN WOLF'S CLOTHING: ANTHROPOMORPHISM AND THE FASCINATION WITH THE HUMAN MIND

The long-standing relationship between anthropocentrism and anthropomorphism finds a comfortable home in the fairy-tale tradition, where animals, objects, and the environment are often given human abilities and personalities. According to Parry, "the story of the human in the West tells us that we are not like other animals, that there are humans and there are animals, and that animals are part of a world ready and waiting for us to use" (2017: 1). This model of thinking was solidified by René Descartes in the 1700s, when his separation of thought from matter served to initiate a legacy of human/non-human duality, which continues today in the stories we tell about non-humanity. To think of the non-human world in fairy tale is to think, I would argue, primarily of animals, and fairy-tale tellers and writers have used animals in their narratives repeatedly as a reflection and representation of humanity, giving them human abilities and characteristics that often (intentionally or not) further a human-centric worldview. Marina Warner observes that a tradition of articulate, anthropomorphized creatures of every kind is as old as literature itself: animal fables and beast fairy tales are found in ancient Egypt and Greece and India, and the legendary Aesop of the classics has his storytelling counterparts all over the world, who moralize crows and ants, lions and monkeys ... to mock the follies and vices of human beings.

(2014: 27–8)

The most prominent fairy-tale retellings of the earlier part of the twentieth century not only reflect this anthropomorphic tradition but also simultaneously affirm the characterization of animals as "part of a world ready and waiting for us to use." While Disney's fairy-tale remakes capitalized on the anthropomorphism of the fairy-tale tradition to create an all-but-inescapable legacy of animals as friendly helpers of humans, iconic films such as Jean Cocteau's *La Belle et la Bête* (*Beauty and the Beast*) (1946) used animality as a costume through which to discuss human relationships and, in the background, psychoanalytic trends presented animals as reflections of unconscious human desires. Still regarded by most as innocent and benign stories for children, the fairy tales of the mid-twentieth century highlight the continued centrality of the human and demonstrate the tendency toward humanizing the animal as a way to confront and/or engage with its supposed Otherness.

The impact and reach of Disney Studios' animated fairy-tale films cannot be underplayed, and perhaps more than any other creator of fairy-tale reworkings, these films solidified, at least in the Western cultural consciousness, a specific and pervasive image of anthropomorphic non-humanity that still echoes through our fiction, film, and cultural engagements with fairy tale today. As David Whitley suggests: "Disney's animated features make a play for our feelings; inventing animals with exaggerated features that enhance their cuteness; creating characters out of stereotypes that are finessed by charm and humor" ([2008] 2016: 2). Since the first of Disney's feature-length fairy tale films, *Snow White and the Seven Dwarfs*, was released in 1937, the role of the non-human animal in animated fairy tales has been characterized by wide-eyed innocence. In a development from Jacob and Wilhelm Grimms' "Schneewittchen" ("Little Snow White," *Kinder- und Hausmärchen* [KHM] 53), in which wild animals leap out at Snow but do not harm her, Disney's Snow White finds that the animals she had so feared in the darkness of the forest are in fact curious and friendly: rabbits, deer, turtles, chipmunks, racoons, and birds who comfort her with their huge eyes, soft features, and perfect pitch. Such tropes reverberate through Disney Studios' fairy-tale films, from *Cinderella* ([1950] 1997) to *Tangled* (2010). Though the Disney humanization of animals may endear us toward them, the portrayal of animals as comedic props, side-kicks, or helpers with little-to-no narrative experience of their own outside that of the human protagonist sets a dangerous precedent. In some cases, such as *Cinderella*, the helpful animals are a direct link to the earlier literary fairy tale, but Disney's wildly successful formula relies on this human/non-human model, and so it is repeated in almost all of Disney's fairy-tale films, irrespective of its appearance in the stories from which they draw. As Henry Giroux notes, "pleasure is one of the defining principles of what Disney produces ... [but] [a]t the same time, these films are often filled with contradictory messages" (1999: 91). As sweet, sometimes sassy sidekicks, the animals of Disney films are held in the tension created by this kind of comfortable anthropomorphism: while they behave and sometimes even speak like humans they remain the Other, contained by their stereotypical and saccharine depictions, and appearing in forests as if their existence relies entirely on their discovery by a human protagonist.

Another aspect of the relationship between humans and non-humans in fairy tale that has been drawn upon frequently in contemporary reworkings is that of humans transforming into animals (and back again). Although in later twentieth- and twenty-first-century incarnations of the fairy tale, metamorphoses across species/material lines have enabled radical subversions of human/non-human boundaries, in the earlier texts of the modern age, such transformations can affirm rather than disturb the trope of non-human-as-other. In Cocteau's *La Belle et la Bête*, the magic centers (as it does in the literary narratives) on the curse of a prince who has been transformed into a beast, and alongside this central metamorphosis, Cocteau enchants his film with "*trompe l'oeil*: dematerialization, animation of inanimate objects, and transformation, as, for example, a magic necklace which turns into burned rope in the hands of the wrong person" (Galef 1984: 97). The film has been lauded for its surrealist visual imagery as well as its apparent psychoanalytic subtext, but its depiction of the beast as monstrous but loveable has limited potential for non-humanity if he retains the sensibilities of a human.

Unidentifiable as any specific animal, Cocteau's Beast wears the otherness of non-humanity as a costume, while retaining a sense of his own humanness. As Cynthia Erb suggests, Cocteau "envisioned the Beast as a deeply romantic, introspective hero whose self-doubts and inner torment attain virtually Byronic proportions" (1995: 54). His transformation back into a charming and physically untainted human prince in the closing moments of the film might also suggest that his residence in the non-human world was a temporary glitch of little consequence when he so easily regains his former splendor as human man. However, the response to the transformation was one of "terrible disappointment" for viewers, who, like the filmmaker Noël Simsolo, perhaps lamented the loss of his beastly appearance: "isn't the Beast more beautiful than Beauty?" (quoted in Popkin 1982: 101). That Beauty comes to love the Beast in his monstrous form and that audiences mourn the transformation back to mere man hint at a desire from creators and consumers to see boundaries blurred between the human and non-human. Yet, the Beast's performance of non-humanity as courteous and tormented instead upholds anthropocentric models of animality, and in returning to human form, the potential for any cross-species relationship is refuted just at the moment it might occur, leaving the human/non-human boundary intact.

According to Bryan L. Moore: "since Plato at least, anthropomorphism and anthropocentrism have long worked in tandem, the former representing the world in human terms and the latter in proclaiming the whole world for human ends" (2008: 12). Though fictional fairy-tale texts themselves are crucial to any study of human/non-human relationships, the landscape of twentieth-century fairy tale has also felt the effects of psychoanalytic approaches to the narratives that furthered both anthropomorphic and anthropocentric thought. One major (and much critiqued) psychoanalytic study of fairy tale comes in Bruno Bettelheim's *The Uses of Enchantment* (1976). In his analysis of some of the key European literary fairy tales, Bettelheim upholds an anthropocentric viewpoint through his presentation of animals as archetypal representations of the "violent, potentially destructive tendencies of the id" (1976: 172) and his acceptance of human dominance over and ownership of the rest of the world: "The fairy tale offers the child hope that someday the kingdom will be his. Since the child cannot settle for less, but does not believe that he can achieve this kingdom on his own, the fairy tale tells him that magic forces will come to his aid" (133). The "magic forces" that come to his aid may, of course, take non-human form, and so the cyclical system of "representing the world in human terms" and "proclaiming the whole world for human ends" is complete. As Rosi Braidotti argues: "for the narcissistic human subject, as psychoanalysis teaches us, it is unthinkable that Life should go on without my being there" (2007: 6). Bettelheim's readings of fairy tales were ruthlessly challenged in both fiction and scholarship in the years that followed (see Dundes 1991; Haase 1993; Teverson 2013: 117–23; Zipes [1979] 2002), but his views serve as a reminder that contemporary engagement with the literary fairy tale has been embedded with and upheld by anthropocentric thought.

CARTER, POSTMODERNISM, AND THE CULTURE OF NATURE

The burst of fairy-tale inspired writing that occurred in the second half of the twentieth century and began with a collection of writers famously coined "the fairy-tale generation" (Benson 2008: 2) coincides with the move toward a postmodern, poststructural literary theory that began in the late 1960s and saw a focus on language, text, ideology, and representation over material realities (Heise 2006: 505). Through the lens of postmodernism, the literary fairy tale was critiqued and reevaluated, rewritten, and reimagined by writers such as Salman Rushdie, Carter, Robert Coover, Byatt, and Margaret Atwood who wished to break away from the stereotypical representations of gender, race, class, and sexuality embedded in the classical fairy tales such as those commercialized by Disney, and often upheld by psychoanalytic theory as well as literature and film. By highlighting the construction involved in any kind of storytelling, undermining grand narratives masquerading as truths, and denying the assumptions of naturalness in those narratives, the fairy-tale authors of this generation reshaped the genre to reflect current ideological concerns regarding social inequality. The result of these radical reworkings was twofold in the context of the non-human/human divide. By approaching nature "as a sociocultural construct that had historically often served to legitimize the ideological claims of specific social groups" (Heise 2006: 506), postmodern fairy-tale writing often (and perhaps inadvertently) served to ostracize the non-human world from the perceived agency, fluidity, and creativity of the human mind through its emphasis on the constructive capabilities of language. And yet, through this focus on language and attempts to deconstruct the concepts of animal, nature, object, and human, these reworkings enabled a critical and contemporary approach to the depiction of the non-human world in the fictions and criticism that followed.

The complexities of the postmodern approach to the non-human world (that it is a fiction created by language, but that this fiction can be altered to give rise to newer, less anthropocentric depictions) are reflected in Carter's collection *The Bloody Chamber and Other Stories* ([1979] 2006). Carter's "tales in which nothing is … natural" (Day 1998: 2) came in many ways to define the contemporary fairy tale and were seen to have borrowed the "overarching project of denaturalization" (Heise 2006: 505) from poststructural literary theory. Because of this, Carter's position is often viewed solely through a poststructural lens, making hers a potentially uncomfortable bedfellow for a reimagined non-humanity. How could a vision of life and nature as constructed by and through language disrupt anthropocentrism? Yet, the tales of Carter's much-discussed collection embrace the complexities of human/animal relations in a way that can be seen to play out alternative and subversive realities for human and non-human characters, as well as highlight the inadequacies of fixed notions of existence. Depending on which side of the debate one falls, Carter's phantasmagorical depictions of the sometimes-intangible lines between the human and non-human have either the potential for a radical destabilization of the conception of what it is to be human and the primacy of that role, or they serve only to affirm the capacity of language to shape and reshape both human and non-human realities—thus furthering the Otherness of the non-human, non-linguistic world.

According to Brian McHale, postmodern fictions are often "fictions *about* the order of things, discourses which reflect upon the worlds of discourse" ([1987] 2001: 164; emphasis in the original). Carter's work can certainly be seen to reflect upon those worlds and their ideologically bound order.

However, unlike postmodern fictions that, as McHale continues, "participate in that very general tendency in the intellectual life of our time toward viewing reality as *constructed* in and through our languages, discourse, and semiotic systems" (164; emphasis in the original), *The Bloody Chamber* demonstrates a focus on materiality and non-humanity that suggests a refusal to accept the postmodern implication that language is the sole constructor of reality. As Anja Müller-Wood has observed, from inside the postmodern, linguistic turn of deconstruction, Carter "reveals that the shaping influences of individual identity are not exclusively cultural, and the deconstruction of social codes is up against powerful material realities" (Müller-Wood 2012: 105). Although Carter's stories are in many ways "*about* the order of things," they can also be seen to align with the voices of postmodernism—such as Gilles Deleuze, Félix Guattari, and Donna Haraway—whose work encouraged a deconstruction of language without a denial of material experience and embraced a more vitalist engagement with non-humanity. The material realities of her collection are animal, mineral, flora, and fauna; the non-human world in all its forms, and her linguistic deconstruction of the "natural" does not undermine the non-human, but merely attempts to liberate it from the trappings of fixity and inertia.

Carter's skepticism toward the accepted stereotypes of human and non-human engagement combined with her focus on materiality enable a portrayal of non-humanity that disrupts human centrality. In *The Bloody Chamber*, environments, bodies (human and non-human), and materialities are charged, visceral, and sensory. The earth is "moist, heavy"; milky moonlight falls and glistens on "frost-crisped grass" (Carter [1979] 2006: 142); and the "brown light of the end of the day" drains into the earth (101). From the mist rolling over the woodland, to the wolves and their metamorphic pelts, the non-human world is depicted as an active rather than a passive participant in these stories. In "The Tiger's Bride" the narrator declares: "He and I and the wind were the only things stirring" (Carter [1979] 2006: 63), aligning subjectivity with human, animal, and weather and defining them all as the collective "things." Carter's conscious enlivening of those varied manifestations of nature calls forth that fairy-tale tradition in which the birds, the flowers, and the climate take on their own characterization irrespective of their non-human manifestation; a tradition in which: "even when a tree has been cut down and turned into a table or a spindle, its wood is still alive with the currents of power that charge the forest where it came from" (Warner 2014: 21).

Although Carter does not shy away from anthropomorphic techniques, the anthropomorphism has potentially radical potential for reconceptualizing the non-human. In "The Erl-King," the wood feels alive with, in Warner's words, "currents of power" (2014: 21) despite the encroaching death of winter, due to its many eyes. The animals, alert and curious, watch the protagonist as she enters the forest, which itself watches with its own "intimate perspectives" (Carter [1979] 2006: 97). Carter's descriptions of the plants and fungi growing slowly, imperceptibly, though at times pointedly eerie, encourage an engagement with non-human existence as alive with animism. While the forest and the creatures watching the protagonist may be anthropocentric in their focus, the many eyes of the forest also suggest a subjectivity for beings that are so often relegated to object status. In a Deleuzean sense, "any eye that sees is already a flow of life, anticipating a future and propelling from a past" (Colebrook 2002: 51). Carter's watchful woodland thus enables this flow and offers possibilities for non-human, material agencies. When the narrator describes ferns that "one by one ... have curled up their hundred eyes and curled back into the earth" (Carter [1979] 2006: 97) the woods are made multiple, possessing myriad eyes with which to observe. The many tiny eyes of the ferns and their sensuous curling motion evoke the desires of the wood and its inhabitants; desire in the Deleuzean sense of a creative, productive force that is not limited to human beings. Mark Halsey notes that Deleuze's theory of "'immanent deterritorialization' means that every*body*—whether it be a flower, bird, forest, regulatory institution, or whatever—continually faces, intermingles with, draws energy from, or opens onto other bodies *which are themselves multiplicities*" (2006: 79; emphases in the original). Carter's denial of a singular natural element through a detailed depiction of the multiplicities of wildlife as well as the differing behaviors of varying species of flora and fauna encourages multiple flows between human and non-human gazes and desires, and Carter's anthropomorphic depictions of the woodland open up possibilities for new understandings of non-human experience.

However, it is Carter's engagement with non-human *animals* that has most often captured imaginations. Carter's wolf tales, "The Werewolf," "The Company of Wolves," and "Wolf-Alice," have long been subject to critical discussion, and it is in these tales that we see the metamorphic transitions between the human and non-human world come most obviously into being. For many, the wolf stories highlight Carter's personal brand of feminism through which women might be associated with an animalistic nature buried by patriarchal constraints. As Zipes suggests in *Don't Bet on the Prince* "writers such as Carter ... insist that women seek contact with the 'wolfish' side of femininity, that is, their sensuality, to be proud of their animalistic ties to nature" ([1987] 1989: 25). Yet, such an assessment continues that long-standing tradition of viewing the non-human animal as merely a vessel through which the human can be better understood, and perhaps neglects another revolutionary aspect of her narratives as they grapple with the complex entanglements of human and non-human animality and identity.

Carter's deconstructive efforts may have been a denial of any sense of the "natural," but they do not immediately deny the non-human world itself, and nor do they serve only as reflections of the human—despite the use of anthropomorphism. As Lucile Desblache observes:

> Carter uses animals as agents for the deconstruction of traditional archetypes, not as natural creatures …. Animals in her work do not represent the other as such or function as reflections of the self but rather reveal the other as a figure of transgression or alienation. They are meant to be subversive tropes of myths, archetypes and beliefs to be deconstructed or challenged.
>
> (2005: 385)

As figures of "transgression or alienation" who combine with the human in various and complex ways, Carter's non-human animals deny the fixity of the human subject and undermine its dominance. When Carter's narrator describes how coupling with the Tiger Man (his very name a confusion of boundaries) leads to him licking away her skin—"each stroke of his tongue ripped off skin after successive skin, all the skins of a life in the world, and left behind a nascent patina of shining hairs" (Carter [1979] 2006: 75)—she entirely reimagines human/non-human relations, bringing us closer to David Abram's conception of "becoming animal":

> Tuning our animal senses to the sensible terrain: blending our skin with the rain-rippled surface of rivers, mingling our ears with the thunder and the thrumming of frogs, and our eyes with the molten gray sky. Feeling the polyrhythmic pulse of this place—this huge windswept body of water and stone. This vexed being in whose flesh we're entangled.
>
> (2010: 3)

Carter's fairy tales are not asomatous fictions, but viscerally corporeal and material, brimming with life—paving the way for the continued reworking of human/non-human relations in fairy-tale literatures to come.

ANIMALS, OBJECTS, AND ENVIRONMENTS: NON-HUMANITY POST-CARTER

As Bacchilega observes, "whether they have read Carter or not, writers (re)-turning to the fairy tale in the 1990s and into the twenty-first century have her fairy-tale phantasmagoria as one of their potential pre-texts" (2008: 181). Though Carter's material emphasis was not always at the forefront, in the decades that followed the appearance of *The Bloody Chamber*, her focus on the deconstruction of what is natural enabled in new fictions both a critique of previously accepted narratives around animals, landscapes, and materials, on the one hand; and a vehicle through which the non-human world could be used metaphorically to unpick the assumptions around fixity of meaning and representation, on the other. Heise suggests too that "by the early 1990s

... the theoretical panorama in literary studies had changed considerably ... Ecocriticism found its place among this expanding matrix of coexisting projects" (2006: 505). The growing environmental concerns of the era certainly impacted the approach to non-humanity in the contemporary fairy tale. Through the continuation of deconstructive techniques alongside emerging ecocritical perspectives, many fairy-tale revisionists of the 1990s emphasized the role of non-humanity in their narratives, creating alternate perspectives and opening up further discussion about anthropocentricism.

In Agha Shahid Ali's poem of 1987, "The Wolf's Postscript to 'Little Red Riding Hood,'" the wolf reflects on his role in the narrative with incredulity while simultaneously revealing the limited anthropocentric (and Eurocentric) perspective of the traditional tale. "Couldn't I have gobbled her up / right there in the jungle?" he asks wryly. "Why did I ask her where her grandma lived? / As if I, a forest-dweller, / didn't know ... As if I couldn't have swallowed her years before?" (Ali 1987). Ali's critique ridicules the anthropomorphism of the earlier narratives that denies the wolf's skill as a hunter and knowledge of the forest (or jungle), highlighting the inadequacies of the construct; "as IF" that could be true, his wolf laughs. Through his own anthropomorphic characterization, Ali encourages an alternate view of the wolf as a creature of vast knowledge outside of human realms of perception. Ali's approach is deconstructive and pointedly postmodern, and none the less so in its alternate viewpoint—offering a depiction of the wolf that ties in with the growing ecological and ecocritical discourse of the time.

Environmental concerns about treatment of the non-human world are reflected too in Salman Rushdie's fairy-tale inspired children's book *Haroun and the Sea of Stories* (1990). In the novel, water represents the fluidity of stories and language, the ability for narrative to run freely and coalesce with other narratives:

> He looked into the water and saw that it was made up of a thousand and one different currents, each one a different colour, weaving in and out of one another like a liquid tapestry of breathtaking complexity ... those were the Streams of Story ... and because the stories were held here in fluid form, they retained the ability to change, to become new versions of themselves, to join up with other stories and to become yet other stories.
>
> (Rushdie 1990: 71–2)

But the Ocean of Stories is under threat; the stories and the water are draining away and the protagonist, a young Haroun, "must save the world by saving its stories" (Harris 2017: 179). As Rosalía Baena suggests, the "the moral values transmitted in *Haroun* [are] freedom of speech and human ecological guardianship of earth and sea" (2001: 72). Yet, Rushdie's emphasis on the centrality of narrative and language also have potentially difficult implications for the human/non-human boundary. For Jean Hillier, the flow of words in the text are emancipatory in a Deleuzean sense for both the human and the non-human, and to save words is to save the stories of all experience, not only that of humans: "in the Ocean of Stories ... we see human and non-human stories, flowing, interconnecting, congealing and transforming as molecular and molar lines" ([2007] 2017: 225). However, in Rushdie's attempts to highlight the power of narrative to alter reality, his portrayal of stories as solely linguistic can also be seen to deny the experience of other beings. Although the novel warns against the dangers of misuse of the non-human environment, as metaphor, does the environment merely become, like Kōnoike's shards of mirrored glass, a distorted reflection of the human power over the world around us? If the quest of a protagonist is to save the world from ecological collapse (even metaphorically) how do we avoid the trap of some forms of environmentalism, which posit that because man is the "dominator and exploiter" of a previously harmonious nature, he must too be the "steward" and savior of Nature as passive victim (Herzogenrath 2008: 2–3)? As Heise suggests, if poststructural texts present nature as "purely a discursive construction," this has the potential to play "into the enemy's hands by obfuscating the material reality of environmental degradation" (2006: 512).

The prevalence of non-humanity in fairy-tale fiction continued throughout the 1990s and into the new millennium, as fairy-tale writers grappled with the growth of technology, the changing theoretical perspectives on the body, and the developing scientific and theoretical perspectives on ecology and the environment. When Donna Haraway issued her "Cyborg Manifesto" in 1984 and made an "argument for *pleasure* in the confusion of boundaries and for *responsibility* in their construction" ([1984] 2016: 7), she may not have predicted how this call to action would manifest in the fairy-tale fictions that followed. From Philip Pullman's *His Dark Materials* ([1995–2000] 2011) trilogy and its object-centered narratives in which the divisions between thought and matter are undermined, to Byatt's collections *The Djinn in the Nightingale's Eye* (1995), *Elementals* ([1998] 1999), and *The Little Black Book of Stories* ([2003] 2004), many writers of this period saw the folk and fairy tale's animist engagement with objects, nature, and transformation as an instrument through which to engage with contemporary discourse on what it means to be human.

Byatt's collections, for example, frequently challenge the inertia of matter, animality, and environment. In "The Glass Coffin," the tailor must allow himself to be carried by the wind without resistance; in "The Stone Woman," a woman watches as her body turns slowly and beautifully into stone; and in "Cold," a princess grapples with the oppositional forces of Ice and Fire and their power over her identity. Far from focusing on non-human animals, these fictions invariably turn to the more supposedly inert aspects of non-humanity—flora, minerals, weather, objects—to reevaluate the experience of existence through an engagement with external materialities.

In Nalo Hopkinson's *Skin Folk* (2001), inspired by African American, Caribbean, and European folklore and fairy tale, the non-human appears in various guises, from supernatural beings to objects, to non-human animals. In her tale "Precious," based on ATU 480 (on the Aarne-Thompson-Uther Tale Type Index, see Chapter 8, this volume, for more information) "The Kind and the Unkind Girls," she imagines the reality of being the recipient of the supposed reward given to the kind girl in the earlier narrative, of having a flower, a precious metal, or a jewel fall from her mouth whenever she spoke. As in *Haroun and the Sea of Stories*, Hopkinson's use of these non-human objects is metaphorical, as the protagonist must learn to speak up for herself and use the power of words (and the jewels, flowers, and currency that come with them) to free herself from the spell. The preciousness of language is mirrored by the precious stones that fall from her mouth; she must take her banker "another shoebox crammed with jewelled phrases, silver sentences, and the rare pearl of laughter" (Hopkinson 2001: 249). Diana Coole suggests that "the predominant sense of matter in modern Western culture has been that it is essentially passive stuff, set in motion by human agents who use it as a means of survival, modify it as a vehicle of aesthetic expression, and impose subjective meanings upon it" (2010: 92). In an echo of Coole's analysis, Hopkinson's jewels, flowers, and stones are shaped and formed by the thoughts of the protagonist—"emeralds green with jealousy; seething red garnets, cold blue chunks of lapis" (Hopkinson 2001: 254)—the passive creations of human agents.

However, the coalescing and transfiguring bodies of Hopkinson's wider collection—a collection that "as the 'skin folk' metaphor suggests, *hinges* on transformation" (Bacchilega 2008: 183; emphasis in the original)—in many ways reflects the theoretical conceptions of the body (particularly, but not exclusively, the female body) of the 1990s, over the later theories of objects that emerged into the 2000s. According to Braidotti, "the body emerges at the center of the theoretical and political debate at exactly the time in history when there is no more unitary certainty or uncontested consensus about what the body actually is …. The body has turned into many, multiple bodies" (1994: 19). In *Skin Folk* bodies are certainly multiple, fluidly becoming other bodies, with their "transformations externalized." After all, "for feminist and sociohistorical critics, transformation is a process that can enact a range of possibilities, an enabling move that is subject to multiple permutations" (Bacchilega 2008: 183). The transformation of flesh and skin in the stories evidences these conceptions of bodies as active and unfixed as a challenge to the passivity of Cartesian extended matter. For Hopkinson, the liberation is of the body, specifically the female body, and as her characters interact with and become embedded in the human and non-human worlds, we might recognize that a challenge to the fixity of human flesh has potentially positive political implications for non-human materiality, even as her metaphor in "Precious" reveals the continued impact of postmodern deconstruction over non-human existence. Interestingly, the publication of *Skin Folk* coincides with the publication of Bill Brown's essay "Thing Theory" in 2001. Brown argues that "as they circulate through our lives, we look *through* objects (to see what they disclose about history, society, nature, or culture—above all, what they disclose about us), but we only catch a glimpse of things" (2001: 4; emphasis in the original). If Hopkinson is guilty of looking *through* the jewels, flowers, and precious metals that drop from the mouth of her protagonist, she does so as part of a genre which frequently—and perhaps unavoidably—uses non-humanity to shed new light on the complexities of the human.

CONTEMPORARY TRANSFORMATIONS BEYOND ANTHROPOCENTRISM?

Byatt has observed that "myths, like organic life, are shape-shifters, metamorphic, endlessly reconstituted and reformed" ([2000] 2001: 125). Folk and fairy tale have long been acknowledged as a "metamorphic genre"; from form to plot, fairy tales enable the shapeshifting they so often gloriously depict, and as Teverson acknowledges when he argues that the genre has been "shaped and reshaped by shifting attitudes to the concept of 'folk,'" these tales have always shapeshifted according to external influence and cultural attitudes (Teverson 2013: 8). If the theories of postmodernity had the tendency to favor the language of humanity over the materialities of the non-human, how has the contemporary fairy tale adjusted to this growing understanding? How can stories written by humans for humans about invented worlds ever avoid or even positively disrupt anthropocentrism? The fairy tales of the present day have transformed (of course) to reflect the enormous changes to cultural worldviews. In the latter part of the twentieth century they tended to be used to emphasize specific social justice issues (gender, race, class, sexuality), while the fairy-tale creators of the new millennium have been faced with the enormity of globalized perspectives, intersectional thinking, and the recognition of inevitable environmental catastrophe caused by humanity. Alongside the new and ever-expanding theories of the twenty-first century—of posthumanism, new materialism, and ecocriticism, as well as further leaps in scientific knowledge and the conception of the term the Anthropocene—the fairy-tale genre has seen the beginnings of a more contemporary model of writing about non-humanity in which humanity is not the center or the leader but simply one part of an interconnecting web of experience.

The move in cultural theory toward a more material engagement with existence has been growing steadily over the past three or four decades.

Postmodern thinkers such as Deleuze, Guattari, and Haraway laid the groundwork for the shift away from an emphasis solely on the discursive models of existence and into the so-called "Material Turn" and the corporeal feminism of Elizabeth Grosz and Braidotti, emerging as what has come to be known as new materialism and posthumanism. Drawing from Haraway's "Cyborg Manifesto" and Deleuze and Guattari's rhizomatic theories of existence, posthuman and new materialist discourses align materialities with language, offering a radical reconceptualization of human/no-human divides. The centers of theoretical concern have shifted to reflect, then, the scientific developments regarding non-human experience—the complex networks in the activity of a tree's roots, for example—as well as the growing dissatisfaction with the earlier linguistic models of female lived experience as purely culturally constructed. As Diana Coole and Samantha Frost suggest, "the more textual approaches associated with the so-called cultural turn are increasingly being deemed inadequate for understanding contemporary society, particularly in light of some of its most urgent challenges regarding environment, demographic, geopolitical, and economic change" (2010: 2–3). These theoretical developments run parallel with a growing understanding about the human impact on the planet and a recognition of the global impact of personal lifestyle. And our emerging fictions reflect the understanding that to ask "what does it mean to be human" is inadequate in its focus on the human as singular subject. When the world is so clearly and unavoidably interconnected, the question to ask now might instead be: "what does it mean to exist?"

In American writer Karen Russell's short-story oeuvre, fairy-tale tropes run freely alongside myth, fantasy, and a growing sense that the non-human world (natural and supernatural) may not be as separate from humanity as it once seemed. In "Reeling for the Empire" from her collection *Vampires in the Lemon Grove* (2013), Russell's protagonist is an unmarried Japanese woman (Kitsune) with an ailing father and her family's catastrophic debt. In a twist on stories about women whose lives are signed away by careless fathers, Kitsune signs a contract to work in a new generation of silk production factories, only to find that the initiation tea she forced herself to drink was actually a drug that would transfigure her body into that of a silkworm. At first, the transformation seems to homogenize the women (she is not the only one) whose "bodies begin to resemble one another" when "the polar fur … covers our faces, blanking us all into sisters" (Russell 2013: 23), blanking them all too, perhaps, into the non-human Other. They become "reelers"—"some kind of hybrid creature, part *kaiko*, silkworm caterpillar, and part human female" (24)—and their bodies begin to produce the silk they are contractually obliged to provide: "You will manufacture silk in your gut with the same helpless skill that you digest food, exhale" (29). The skill is deemed to be passive, physical, and therefore inert, instinctual, and lacking in intelligence. Yet, as the story progresses, the relationship between Kitsune's body and mind begins to shift, and so too does the depiction of non-humanity. When Kitsune realizes that she can alter the color of her thread through her thoughts, she reconnects her physicality with her thought processes, creating what Braidotti might consider an "embodied and embedded" (2002: 13) vision of existence in which the two seemingly polarized aspects of life are interwoven. She realizes that she can both "channel these dyes from [her] mind into the tough new fiber" and "change the thread's denier" (Russell 2013: 46), as well as recognizing the potential of her body to carry out the tasks she knows she must undertake: "Without my giving a thought to what step comes next, my hands begin to fly" (47). Russell's protagonist does not surrender to the non-human/material element of herself, nor does she rebel against it; instead, she finds a path through which she can be and serve these seemingly separate but ultimately inseparable aspects of her existence.

Aligned with much of the new materialist and posthuman discourse of the current era, Russell's narrative destabilizes anthropocentrism through her challenge both to language and the centrality of the human mind, and in so doing, suggests alternate visions that reflect the interconnectivity of experience. When Kitsune recognizes the power she has as hybrid creature, turning her silk black and spinning her own cocoon, she learns too that communication can also alter through this state of in-betweenness. "Words seem to be unnecessary now between me and Tsuki," she notes, "we beam thoughts soundlessly across the room. Perhaps speech will be the next superfluity in Nowhere Mill. Another step we *kaiko*-girls can skip" (Russell 2013: 47). The magic of the transformation invites suggestions of language's inadequacy at expressing all of the world's experiences, and also evokes images of collective consciousness between creatures—a more fluid and collective vision of existence that feels radical and exciting against the backdrop of an atomized, autonomous Cartesian human subject. In an echo of new materialist discourse, rather than surrendering the mind in full pursuit of the body, the story's metamorphic nexus forms around Kitsune's transformation into yet another creature, as her internal and external experience are fully intertwined. In a vision of Cyborgian hybridity, we come to see Kitsune as moth woman, transformed once more and now surrounded by other moth women, all unable to distinguish the parts of themselves that are human and non-human; which material and which thought. Like Karen Barad's conclusions on matter and meaning, the human and non-human in Russell's moths are "inextricably fused together, and no event, no matter how energetic, can tear them asunder" (2002: 3). From the ashes of Kitsune's catastrophic choice comes a posthuman insect in whom the human and non-human are interwoven, with the capacity (at the very least) to fly.

Russell's reflections on human/non-human relationships invite questions about capitalism and production, the manufacture of goods, and the creation of supposedly sustainable alternatives that maintain the lifestyles of humans, reflecting and refracting the anthropocentrism of not only our stories but also our modes of living. Such questions are unavoidable in contemporary Western discourse. As Bennett observes:

> The quarantines of matter and life [affirmed by the dominant trends in Western philosophy] encourage us to ignore the vitality of matter and the lively powers of material formations, such as the way omega3 fatty acids can alter human moods or the way our trash is not "away" in landfills but generating lively streams of chemicals and volatile winds of methane as we speak.
>
> (2010: vii)

Yet, contemporary discussions of the Anthropocene make us potently aware of our impact not only on the planet and the human slave laborers making our clothes but also on the non-human creatures of all kinds subjected to the distortions of capitalist labor to serve a species who subjugates and abuses them. Russell's story of fairy-tale metamorphosis recognizes both the mistreatment of women and non-Western workers (so often tied to the non-human Other), and that of non-humans, who, in Braidotti's words, "are manipulated, mistreated, tortured and genetically recombined in ways that are productive for our bio-technological agriculture, the cosmetics industry, drugs and pharmaceutical industries and other sectors of the economy" (2013: 7). Only in refusing the delineations of human/non-human and rejecting the confines of capitalist oppression does the protagonist—as hybrid creature of fiction—flourish: "the last thing I see before shutting his eyes is the reflection of my shining new face" (Russell 2013: 52).

In the Netflix film *Okja* (2017) a young Korean girl forms a bond with a genetically engineered super-pig, bred as a "sustainable" alternative to pig farming. Though perhaps more of sci-fi setting, the magical realist elements of this narrative recall fairy-tale non-human/human relations, and the girl's quest to save Okja from the capitalist system uses the anthropomorphic tendencies of fairy tale and children's literature (Okja is as loving and intelligent as any human) to challenge assumptions about the consumption of animals. For Michelle Gunawan, Okja's "very existence confuses the legal categorization of non-human animals and highlights the law's arbitrary double standards when regulating the treatment of animals" (2018: 264). As Braidotti notes, "advanced capitalism and its bio-genetic technologies engender a perverse form of the posthuman. At its core there is a radical disruption of the human-animal interaction, but all living species are caught in the spinning machine of the global economy" (2013: 8). Like the women in "Reeling for the Empire," spinning yarn for capitalist torturers, the super-pig Okja, as a mixture of science and nature, embodies the posthuman subject as the tool of capitalism trapped in the machine of global economy. Okja and Kitsune in different ways both disrupt the concept of the human, asking, as Haraway did, "which identities are available to ground such a potent political myth called 'us,' and what could motivate enlistment in this collectivity?" ([1984] 2016: 16–17). When Mija sleeps between the paws of the tender super-pig, the anthropomorphic tropes of traditional fairy tale that ran through Carter's fairy tales as well as so many others are used to disrupt, rather than perpetuate, anthropocentricism. Perhaps, as Bennett suggests, "we need to cultivate a bit of anthropomorphism—the idea that human agency has some echoes in nonhuman nature—to counter the narcissism of humans in charge of the world"? (2010: xvi).

The fairy-tale inspired creations of the twenty-first century often use tropes of hybridity or metamorphosis or focus on human/non-human embodiments to engage with contemporary concerns about the human relationship with the world around us. In an age where our relationship to the non-human world is being more and more widely recognized as embedded in our political, social, ecological and economic structures—stories that engage with such concerns highlight our continued attempts to write new ways of seeing the world. In many ways it is the magic of these narratives that enables a challenge to the fixity of our previous dichotomous structures, as the characters are free to shapeshift or love other creatures in ways that disrupt anthropocentric norms. Recent contemporary fairy tale has given us the turn-of-the-century sculptures of Kiki Smith, in which women are birthed from deer (*Born*, 2002) or step out from the abdomen of wolves (*Rapture*, 2001); and the films of Studio Ghilbli, such as *The Tale of Princess Kaguya* (2013), in which the landscape feels alive and as much a part of the narrative as the princess born of a bamboo shoot. It offers Sarah Hall's award-winning short story "Mrs. Fox" ([2013] 2017), depicting a husband's attempts to cope with his wife's transformation into a fox, and Marlon James's recent fantasy and folklore-inspired *Black Leopard, Red Wolf* (2019), in which the human and non-human are perpetually drawn together in a physicality-centered epic. The fascination with human/non-human boundaries in fairy-tale texts is far from abating, and such interest enables, in the current critical climate, critique of the anthropocentric systems that have long infiltrated (and continue to infiltrate) the telling of stories. When the protagonist of "Mrs. Fox" sits "for hours, thinking, silent—every time he speaks he feels the stupidity of words" (Hall [2013] 2017), he recognizes the inadequacies of the human mind and acknowledges that there are some things language cannot control. When his wife, as fox, "produces a low sound, like a chirp, a strangled bark," he admits, quietly countering centuries of human "knowledge" of animals, that "he does not know what it means" (Hall [2013] 2017), and does not try to guess.

CONCLUSION

In *An [Un]likely Alliance*, Michael Mikulak cites Neil Evernden: "we are not *in* an environmental crisis, but *are* the environmental crisis," because it is "our way of knowing and being in the world [that] is the problem" (2008: 67; emphases in the original). The human preoccupation with our own knowledge and existence has perpetuated dualistic and hierarchical engagements with non-humanity in all its shades, with human superiority as the model through which our lifestyles, our policies, and our stories have been shaped, and folk and fairy tales are no exception. But if our sense of being and knowing in the world is to change, it will do so through the stories we tell. As a site of magic and transformation, the contemporary fairy tale can be the vehicle through which we explore the possibilities of material fluidity, inter-species relations, and metamorphosis in ways that do not further anthropocentric assumptions but create new, disruptive visions of interconnectivity and experience outside the confines of the human and non-human dichotomy. Braidotti suggests that a "range of new, alternative subjectivities ... emerged in the shifting landscapes of postmodernity. They are contested, multi-layered and internally contradictory subject-positions. They are hybrid and in-between social categories" that offer an "embedded and embodied form of enfleshed materialism" (2002: 13). When the fairy-tale creators of the last century combine fur with flesh, objects with thought, matter with language, blurring the boundaries and creating hybrid forms from the seemingly oppositional, they do so with the magical traditions of folk and fairy tale behind them. Our representations of the non-human world (and of ourselves) will always be representations, but envisioning materiality as "changing and changeable, as *transformable*" (Birke 1999: 45; emphasis in the original), just like the fairy-tale storytelling tradition itself, might—if we pay enough attention—enable us to reimagine our ways of knowing and being in the world. Our mirrors may be distorted, but perhaps it is only by distorting accepted notions of existence and experience that we can envisage new, inclusive ones.

CHAPTER FIVE

Monsters and the Monstrous

CHRISTA JONES AND CLAUDIA SCHWABE

Twentieth- and twenty-first-century tales recycle a myriad of universally popular monster figures, including devils, dragons, dwarves, ghosts, ghouls, giants, beasts, ogres, sorcerers and sorceresses, trolls, werewolves, vampires, witches, and other mythological and fantastic figures. Etymologically, the word "monster" is derived from the classical Latin *mōnstrum*, referring to either a monstrous creature, a wicked person, a monstrous act, an atrocity, or a portent. The root of *mōnstrum* is *monēre*, which means to warn, the verb *monstrāre* signifies to show. According to the *Oxford English Dictionary* (OED), there are multiple significations of the term "monster," including mythical creatures that are "part animal and part human," combining several animal forms, and "frequently of great size and ferocious appearance" (OED n.d.-b). Later on, the term referred to any big, ugly, and scary fantastic creature. Further meanings of the term include "something extraordinary or unnatural; an amazing event or occurrence; a prodigy, a marvel," and "a person of repulsively unnatural character, or exhibiting such extreme cruelty or wickedness as to appear inhuman; a monstrous example of evil, a vice, etc." (OED n.d.-b). Another denotation of "monster" is a person, animal, or thing considered ugly or deformed. Monsters—whether animal or human—are bothersome, attractive and repulsive, because they are outside the norm of what constitutes, in generally accepted biological terms, a human being or an animal, and thus defy any efforts of traditional scientific categorization.

Monster figures traditionally epitomize human fears that are exteriorized, namely, projected outside of the self, so they can be safely contemplated from a distance. These fears can be linked to future events or developments, to dangerous or antisocial behaviors, physical disabilities or suffering, morally reprehensible urges, and ultimately, the inevitable spectre of human mortality. The beast in Jeanne-Marie Leprince de Beaumont's "Beauty and the Beast" ("La Belle et la Bête")—adapted to the screen by Jean Cocteau (1946), Christophe Gans (2014), and the Disney corporation (1991, 2017)—was supposedly inspired by the "monster man" Pedro González (1537–1618), a Spaniard who suffered from hypertrichosis, a congenital condition that causes uncontrollable hair growth (Stockinger 2004). Likewise, David Lynch's *The Elephant Man* (1980) was also inspired by a real-life story, that of Englishman Joseph Merrick (1862–90), who was put on display at fairs. In some cases, such as in the subversive tales of Frenchman Pierre Gripari (1925–90), traditionally evil or wicked monster figures such as witches or devils are portrayed as heroes. Indeed, there appears to be an ambiguity linked to monstrosity today. Monsters are no longer predominantly malicious and frightening but their physical or moral flaws elicit human compassion, their features are appealing and attractive, their deeds are heroic or therapeutic, and their characters are sometimes reimagined to be comedic and hilarious. After all, as consumers of fairy-tale films or texts, it is perhaps more pleasant, more commercially palatable to laugh than to scream in horror.

The psychological depth of contemporary monster figures leaves readers and viewers wondering whether they should laugh, condone, or condemn their "monstrous" characteristics and their ambivalent actions. Nonetheless, traditional monsters such as evil ogre characters or serial killers remain popular in contemporary fairy tales, both in text and on screen. In twentieth-century North African folktales, for instance, ogre and ogresses (in Arabic called *teryel*), characters that feast on human flesh and particularly enjoy devouring small children, abound. Bloodthirsty anthropomorphic ogre figures generally represent powerful father figures whose main function it is to reinforce and preserve the patriarchal order, which calls for a gendered division of space: men are allowed in the public sphere, while women are relegated to the domestic sphere (cooking, household chores, and childrearing). In that role, the ogre figures admonish girls to obey and preserve their virginity, a very important aspect in the Maghreb tale "Une histoire d'ogre" ("An Ogre Story"). Traditional North African ogre tales continue to be told as primarily cautionary tales today, though female storytellers such as Nora Aceval and Salima Aït Mohamed have published women-centered tales. A modern, Canadian rendition of the ogre figure sheds a much more modern and positive light on him. *L'Ogrelet* (The Ogreling, 1997) by French Canadian playwright Suzanne Lebeau, discusses an identity crisis suffered by a child ogre figure who rejects his origins and resists his cannibalistic penchants. Ogrelet—meaning little ogre—is the nickname of a six-year-old boy called Simon who lives in the woods with his mother. His father—an ogre—has left in search of a cure for his murderous needs. Ogrelet gradually realizes that he is radically different from the other boys in the village. Not only is he as tall as an adult but he is deeply attracted and repulsed by the sight of blood. When he learns that he had six younger sisters all of whom were devoured by his father, he refuses to be called Ogrelet any longer, sets out to become human, and succeeds. Likewise, in Tomi Ungerer's *Zeralda's Ogre* (1967), an ogre changes his human diet for love. The ogre terrorizes the inhabitants of a city by eating all the children until he meets a country girl called Zeralda, who cooks a feast for him. She moves in with him in his castle and spends the days cooking signature dishes for him. The ogre ends up marrying Zeralda, and he and his fellow ogre friends renounce cannibalism thanks to her excellent cooking skills.

Thus, in contemporary literary and cinematic adaptations, fairy-tale monster figures are not simply Manichean forces of evil. Rather, they take on different personas, from therapeutic agents, helper figures, sexually attractive creatures, and cute or funny beasts to human monsters or serial killers such as Bluebeard. Physically impressive yet emotionally unstable and therefore vulnerable ogre figures abound in contemporary retellings by authors and filmmakers such as Olivier Dahan (*Le Petit Poucet*, 2001), Patrick Chamoiseau ("Une affaire de mariage," 1988), Margaret Atwood (*Bluebeard's Egg and Other Stories*, 1983), Angela Carter (*The Bloody Chamber and Other Stories*, [1979] 2006), and others. Catherine Breillat's made-for-television remake of Charles Perrault's Bluebeard tale (*Barbe bleue* 2009) features an ugly, middle-aged, complex, paternal ogre-husband figure. In her filmic Bluebeard remake, the "monstrous serial killer is ironically depicted as an intellectual loner" (Zipes 2012b: 51), overweight yet somehow sensitive and weirdly likeable (Figure 5.1). Bluebeard (Dominique Thomas) openly discusses his vulnerability and his cannibalistic tendencies with his teenage wife Marie-Catherine (Lola Créton). He blames society for making him a monster:

> BLUEBEARD   I am a monster.
> MARIE-CATHERINE   Certainly not.
> BLUEBEARD   Everybody looks at me like a monster. I am very aware of this and end up becoming a monster, sort of an ogre, do you understand?
> MARIE-CATHERINE   Yes.
> BLUEBEARD   And I don't scare you?
> MARIE-CATHERINE   No, I am much more afraid of wickedness that cannot be seen.

Thus, humans are partially responsible for creating monsters by labeling individuals as such and marginalizing them on account of their physical, sexual, or other character traits that are widely considered to deviate from the norm.

Belgian writer Amélie Nothomb's palimpsestic retelling of Perrault's tale *Barbe bleue* (2013) also takes a few liberties with Perrault's tale, depicting Bluebeard

FIGURE 5.1: Film still from Catherine Breillat's *Barbe bleue* (2009).

as a somewhat eccentric but not altogether despicable individual. The tale is no longer cautionary (it does not contain any explicit morals), and the emancipated young Parisian heroine named Saturnine Puissant (Powerful) ends up becoming a monster herself by killing the Bluebeard character called Elemirio. Like Breillat's monster, Elemirio is also an intellectual loner, who shuns the company of others. As Nothomb points out, "Elemirio is a contemporary ogre figure. He's a dandy ogre, very refined, mythical and esthetical. He has nothing of a Don Juan. His attitude is closer to [that of] the Faustian wager" (2015: 149). Interestingly, Nothomb put much of herself in her heroine. Saturnine Puissance is Belgian and she is a champagne connoisseur (like Nothomb, who owns a fridge filled exclusively with bottles of champagne). Her luxurious appetite shines through in her very name, Saturnine, derived from the Greek *Cronos*, which unmasks her as an ogress and hence the equivalent of the male monster figure. If the classic Bluebeard tale is "about power among other things; and who is in control of power, and why power should always be in the hands of men" (Zipes 2012b: 53–4), Nothomb's feminist retelling clearly gives this power to the shrewd and active heroine. Saturnine adamantly refuses to give up her independence by marrying the forty-year-old Elemirio. By the same token, it is Saturnine Puissance who ultimately becomes a monster since she shuts Elemirio into his darkroom where he joins the eight female corpses already there. As her name underlines, Saturnine does not need to be told what to do or to watch out for: rather, it is Bluebeard who should watch out for himself. Like Breillat's human Bluebeard monster, Elemirio is a fine example of "moral monstrosity," a constellation that links monstrosity to both the ethical and the esthetical and manifests itself in indifference, cupidity, ambition, authority, vengeance, and pleasure (Pharo 2009: 157). Indifference and arrogance are character traits that define Nothomb's couple that indulges in intellectual exchanges—the French art of conversation—sarcasm, and culinary pleasures.

Alex Garland's science-fiction thriller *Ex Machina* (2014) features a Bluebeard story with a feminist edge. In this film, Caleb Smith (Domhnall Gleeson), a programmer working for the internet company Blue Book, wins a contest that allows him to spend a week at the isolated but luxurious estate of the company's mysterious CEO, Nathan Bateman (Oscar Isaac). Nathan, the egotistical, muscular, head-shaven Bluebeard character sporting a bushy hipster beard, is intellectually brilliant but morally ambiguous. He has created Ava (Alicia Vikander), a beautiful android or fembot with artificial intelligence, and asks Caleb to determine her capabilities and consciousness. Although Nathan pretends to be a casual, laid-back, beer-sharing buddy, his domineering, omnipresent surveillance style and his prison-like home with its auto-locking doors appear threatening to Caleb. Reminiscent of Perrault's Bluebeard tale, Nathan gives Caleb a key card that enables him to enter certain rooms while other doors remain locked. This makes Caleb the "bride" of the Perrault tale who is permitted to explore Bluebeard's entire castle except for the forbidden room. After Ava tells Caleb that Nathan is a liar and cannot be trusted, Caleb takes advantage of Nathan's drunkenness, steals his security card and enters Nathan's private chambers. In Nathan's bedroom, Caleb finds four closets, each containing a "dead wife," the lifeless bodies of Nathan's previous AI attempts. Nearly all of the female robots are naked and dismembered, missing several limbs and parts of their skin. Caleb also discovers that Nathan's mute servant, Kyoko (Sonoya Mizuno), is a robot and effectively his sex slave.

Ex Machina presents Nathan as a monstrous Bluebeard figure who wields his hegemonic and violent masculinity against oppressed females, here the imprisoned androids who are far more self-aware than either Caleb or Nathan imagined. However, similar to Saturnine in Nothomb's retelling, Ava is also portrayed with monstrous features. She is deceptive and manipulates Caleb's emotions successfully by making him believe that she has romantic feelings for him so that he may aid her escape. Ava now takes over the role of Bluebeard's "bride" and relies on a male figure for help, paralleling the fairy tale where the brothers of Bluebeard's victim must come to save the day. In a feminist twist of the story though, Ava collaborates with Kyoko in murdering Nathan and flees the compound. She leaves a screaming Caleb behind who is trapped in one of the locked rooms without hope of rescue, thus dooming him to a slow death. No matter that she was created by a more forbidding monster, the narcissistic, arrogant, brute Bluebeard figure in the form of Nathan, Ava merely clothes herself in humanity. After getting damaged during the struggle with Nathan, she strips the female androids who came before her of their body parts to fully appear human. Ava refuses to be objectified but her desire for freedom and agency come at any price. To some extent, the film's narrative evokes that of Mary Shelley's *Frankenstein; or, The Modern Prometheus* (1818), one key difference being that Victor Frankenstein creates a male monster whereas Nathan creates a female monster that he can exploit sexually.

MONSTROUS IMAGINATIONS IN CONTEMPORARY FAIRY-TALE FILMS AND MEDIA

Monsters in various shapes, such as wicked witches, nasty ogres, cannibalistic giants, furious dragons, evil fairies, terrible trolls, crafty wolves, and other savage beasts, are a staple of the fairy tale. They slither, crawl, swim, fly, trot, and stamp through fairy-tale landscapes in the stories we tell, the books we read, and the films we watch. Ever since the latter third of the twentieth century, however, imaginations of the monstrous in cinematic and televisual fairy-tale adaptations have begun to deviate from the villainous, horrific creatures that are traditionally associated with the term "monster." Instead, a new trend is noticeable on the small and silver screen that portrays monstrous beings in a positive light and desirable fashion. The following section illuminates how twentieth- and twenty-first-century media celebrates the beauty of Otherness and promotes alterity in fairy-tale films. Some of the films examined are perhaps not, strictly speaking, fairy-tale films but the motifs, characters, and plots have been borrowed from fairy tales. The figure of the serpent-like, ferocious dragon is just one example of a popular fairy-tale monster that has recently received a "makeover" in contemporary cinema: in Disney's live-action films *Pete's Dragon* (1977) and its 2016 remake the dragon Elliot is a child-protective and funny creature; the West German fantasy film *Die unendliche Geschichte* (*The NeverEnding Story*, 1984), based on Michael Ende's novel, features the fluffy, white, benevolent Luckdragon Falkor; in the British-American film *DragonHeart* (1996) the dragon Draco saves the life of a human by sharing his heart; the ruby-colored she-dragon Fergie in the *Shrek* films (2001, 2004, 2007, 2010) produces adorable hybrid children with Shrek's hilarious sidekick

Donkey; in *Eragon* (2006), based on Christopher Paolini's novel, the blue she-dragon Saphira is the wise, fearless protector of the Dragon Rider Eragon; and in *How to Train Your Dragon* (2010) the cute dragon Night Fury befriends the Viking teenager hero Hiccup.

The 2017 fairy-tale film, *The Shape of Water* by Guillermo del Toro, is an erotic monster tale that addresses Otherness favorably by introducing audiences to a sexualized, heroic amphibian man-beast (Doug Jones) as an embodiment of the noble savage. Set in 1960s Baltimore, Maryland, the story revolves around a vocally impaired woman, Elisa (Sally Hawkins), who works as a cleaning lady at a high-security government laboratory and falls in love with a creature captured from the Amazon river. The mute woman bravely manages to rescue the fish man, who is viewed as a God by his people, from imprisonment. At the end of the diegesis, the amphibian man's healing touch allows Elisa to grow gills and breathe under water so that both can live happily ever after together. The film is a fairy tale about interspecies love that crosses all barriers, the ugliness of discrimination, overcoming disability, and the transcendent beauty of differentness (Figure 5.2).

Del Toro's work foregrounds the fact that the "monster" and the "freak," the merman and the mute heroine, are in effect more humane than the common people surrounding them. Viewers are invited to identify not only with the Other but also to relate to the protagonists' unique love relationship and to commiserate with their struggles. The film suggests that the true monsters in our society are those people who discriminate against and are abusive of individuals who are different. At the forefront is the sadistic government agent Strickland (Michael Shannon) who uses torture and intimidation to wield power over everyone in his path. Strickland is a layered monster made of fleshy white privilege and entitlement who resorts to a high-voltage electric shock cattle prod to torture the amphibian man and sexually harasses Elisa in his office. In the year of the #MeToo movement, it seems especially fitting that Strickland with his toxic masculinity is found out to be the real monster and villain of the film. As the narrative goes on, Strickland's character grows more despicable, metaphorically reflected in his increasingly "monstrous" physicality. After having two fingers slashed off by the merman creature, Strickland has them reattached in a desperate attempt to be "normal," a "whole," "complete" man, again. His disfigurement makes him "abnormal" in his eyes, and he cannot stand it. However, over the course of the film, the reattached fingers turn gangrenous and drip with pus. The rotting flesh on his hand renders him physically hideous, further emphasizing the monstrosity of his malign nature.

The film also implies that "monsters" are still considered threats in North American society, and that there is no place for them just as there is very little space for immigrants from "undesirable" countries. Whereas *The Shape of Water* is set during the height of the Cold War era, del Toro's dark tale *Pan's*

FIGURE 5.2: Film still from Guillermo del Toro's *The Shape of Water* (2017).

Labyrinth (*El laberinto del fauno*, 2006) unfolds against the backdrop of fascist Spain in 1944, five years into Franco's regime. The film follows Ofelia (Ivana Baquero) who is sent along with her mother (Adriadna Gil) to live with her new stepfather Captain Vidal (Sergi López), an officer in the Spanish Army. Similar to the childlike, voiceless heroine Elisa, the child protagonist Ofelia is overlooked by those around her and builds a relationship with a monster underground. The monster, which is only visible to the girl, is a faun (Doug

Jones), a towering figure with a goat-like face and horned head, but made of dirt, leaves, trees and rocks. Intricate, decorative, circulate patterns adorn his flesh as if carved into tree bark. The faun tells Ofelia that she is a princess but must prove her royalty and immortality by surviving three gruesome tasks. If she succeeds she will return to the underworld and be reunited with her true father, the king.

As the messenger of the king of the underworld, the faun appears to be a fairy-tale helper sent to aid Ofelia. However, as Jack Zipes has aptly noted, "the trustworthiness of the faun, who is immense and weird-looking, ancient and sphinxlike, is clearly meant to be ambiguous; he appears to be kind and gentle sometimes and mean and menacing at other times" (2008: 238) (Figure 5.3). The faun is essentially a trickster figure, neither good nor bad. Like the forces of nature, he is a creature of destruction, on the one hand, and a creature

FIGURE 5.3: Film still from Guillermo del Toro's *Pan's Labyrinth* (2006).

of nurturing and life, on the other. Whereas the figure of the faun remains ambiguous, oscillating between parental concern and a questionable desire for Ofelia, the film presents fascism, personified by Captain Vidal, as the true horror in the girl's life. The supernatural toad and the Pale Man, a child-eating monster, can be read as expressions of Vidal's monstrosity viewed through the lens of Faerie. Vidal is del Toro's gender reversal of the wicked stepmother, the "monster" that supplants the good but dead parent at the beginning of the story. Reminiscent of Strickland, Vidal's body becomes increasingly disfigured as the narrative progresses so that his physicality mirrors his internal monstrosity. It is up to the audience to decide whether the mystical beings and monsters that Ofelia encounters are "therapeutic" fictions of her imagination created to help her cope with the harsh realities of a fascist Spain, or whether they are real.

A monster as therapeutic agent who helps a child cope with trauma and grief is also the theme of J. A. Bayona's *A Monster Calls* (2016) based on Patrick Ness's eponymous novel. The film tells the tragic tale of a young boy named Conor O'Malley (Lewis MacDougall) and his journey to overcome the passing away of his mother (Felicity Jones) through the power of imagination and creativity. Conor's biggest comfort during this dark time is his mother's sketchbook full of watercolors and a monster in tree form conjured up by his imagination, that helps him to overcome his angst, fury, and anguish. Voiced by Liam Neeson, the monster is a giant humanoid yew tree that tells Conor three "true" stories, after which the monster expects the boy to tell his own story, the truth of his recurring nightmare. Although Conor is afraid of the gigantic tree monster at first, it turns out that the creature is a therapist in disguise, dispensing psychological truths along with each empowering tale it tells. Just like Pan who is only visible to Ofelia and seems menacing at times, the tree monster is a frightful creature that can only be seen by Conor, the boy who summoned him. The humanoid yew tree is taller than a house with burning hot insides, glowing red eyes, and spiked branches for a spine.

The therapeutic approaches of the gruff tree monster are unconventional but effective. When Conor is scared, the yew tree does not tell him to stop being afraid but forces the boy to lean into the fright. Instead of calming Conor's anger, the tree monster encourages the boy to wreak havoc on a parson's house in his imaginary realm that, in reality, turns out to be his grandmother's living room. At school, the monster tells Conor the story of an invisible man and spurs him on to beat up the school bully. During these emotional outbursts of rage, Conor draws on the monster's strength and both appear to become one entity. Although Conor thinks the anthropomorphic yew tree came to heal his mother from her terminal cancer, he ultimately learns that the tree only came for his sake (Figure 5.4). The monster becomes Conor's guide and enables him to accept the truth at the heart of his recurring

FIGURE 5.4: Film still from *A Monster Calls* (2016), directed by J. A. Bayona.

nightmare, and that he must not feel guilty for wanting his mother's disease to be over so that he does not have to feel pain anymore. Bayona's film highlights the monster not so much as the horrible Other within us that needs to be feared, tamed, and overcome but, rather, as a metaphor for our own intrinsic truth, courage, strength, and faith.

Whereas del Toro's and Bayona's fantastic creatures still display beastly and intimidating features, other monstrous visualizations in fairy-tale adaptations have been stripped of their monstrous looks and demeanor entirely. Popular examples include the reimagination of trolls and ogres for purposes of comic relief as seen in the *Shrek* films, in *Harry Potter and the Philosopher's Stone* (2001), in *The Hobbit* film series (2012–14), and more recently in Disney's *Frozen* (2013) and in the computer-animated musical film *Trolls* (2016). The animated Shrek character (voiced by Mike Myers), a large green ogre with a Scottish accent, is a grumpy, misanthropic, cranky creature who is generally peaceful and does not want to hurt anyone. Traditionally, ogres are associated in fairy tales, such as "Puss in Boots" and "Little Thumbling," with monstrous traits, especially cannibalism and a taste for infants. However, the *Shrek* films promote the notion of a friendly, funny, and heroic ogre and draw viewers' attention to the tropes of outsiderness, alterity, and marginalization. Shrek prefers to live secluded in his swamp because people have either teased him, screamed at him in fear, or tried to kill him for being an ogre. During a conversation with his sidekick Donkey (voiced by Eddie Murphy), Shrek explains that he became a recluse after trying and failing to find acceptance by the outside world. He laments that he is always judged by others simply for being different: "Look, I'm not the one with the problem, okay? It's the world that seems to have a problem with me. People take one look at me and go 'Aah! Help! Run! A big stupid ugly ogre!' They judge me before they even know me. That's why I'm better off alone" (Shrek 2001). Indeed, the *Shrek* films are based on the 1990 fairy-tale picture book *Shrek!* by William Steig, an award-winning cartoonist known for writing on themes of marginalization, isolation, and transformation. The animated adaptation emphasizes the beauty of the marginalized Other when Princess Fiona (voiced by Cameron Diaz) transforms permanently into an ogress after kissing her true love Shrek who makes her realize that she is indeed beautiful.

Closely related to the ogre as a fairy-tale monster is the troll, a creature mostly found in Norse mythology and Scandinavian folklore and generally described as extremely old, very strong, dim-witted, slow, and a man-eater. Cinematic fairy-tale adaptations today draw on the figure of the troll for comic relief, similar to the ogre character Shrek, or infantilize the troll to appeal to child audiences. In *Harry Potter and the Philosopher's Stone*, a gigantic mountain troll threatens Hermione (Emma Watson) in the girls' bathroom at Hogwarts before Harry (Daniel Radcliffe) manages to successfully distract the troll by jumping on its back and shoving his wand up the troll's nose. Ron (Rupert Grint) knocks out the troll by using the previously mastered Levitation Charm to hit it in the head with its own club. After the troll falls onto the floor, Harry extracts his wand, which is covered in goo, with the words "Ew. Troll bogies." The scene trivializes the troll by turning the creature into a comical character. Troll snot jokes are also used in a scene from *The Hobbit: An Unexpected Journey* (2012) when several stone trolls gather around the fire to cook their supper. After one troll sneezes, sending snot into their cooking pot, another troll remarks that this might improve the flavor. The sneezing troll reaches behind him to grab his handkerchief but instead grabs the hobbit Bilbo (Martin Freeman) and blows his nose all over him. The troll looks down, sees Bilbo in his hand, and shouts, "Aah! Blimey! Bert! Bert, look what's come out of me hooter! It's got arms and legs and everything!" Similar to the humorous portrayal of the troll in *Harry Potter*, these trolls are less monstrous and more hilarious.

Other examples of film trolls that have been "cutified," exploited for comic effect, utilized for musical entertainment, and stripped completely of their monstrous attributes can be found in the fairy-tale adaptations *Frozen* and *Trolls*. In Disney's *Frozen*, which is a very loose adaptation of Hans Christian Andersen's fairy tale "The Snow Queen," a community of small, magical trolls tries to convince the protagonists Anna (voiced by Kristen Bell) and Kristoff (voiced by Jonathan Groff) to get married in a troll ceremony. The trolls, which have the ability to transform at will into rock balls for purposes of fast transportation, are portrayed as overbearing, loud, and meddlesome but well-meaning "love experts." The film foregrounds the trolls as loving and family-oriented beings whose song "Fixer Upper" highlights love's ability to triumph over imperfection. Because they appear to be in a perpetual state of happiness, singing, dancing, and hugging all day, they evoke their candy-colored, hairy "cousins" in DreamWorks Animation's *Trolls*. The animated musical follows two trolls, Princess Poppy (voiced by Anna Kendrick) and Branch (voiced by Justin Timberlake), who embark on a journey to save their village from destruction by the Bergens, creatures who feed on trolls to be happy. Based on the 1960s marketed "Good Luck Troll" dolls created by Danish woodcutter Thomas Dam, the film presents the wild-haired trolls as hyper-cute, glittery characters on a musical adventure to spread the moral message that "Happiness comes from within."

The trend of endowing monstrous characters with cutesiness, humor, and appeal has increased tremendously since the twenty-first century. Pixar's computer animated comedy film *Monsters, Inc.* (2001) comes to mind with its two friendly monsters James P. "Sulley" Sullivan (voiced by John Goodman), a huge, furry, blue monster with horns and large purple spots, and his buddy Michael "Mike" Wazowski (voiced by Billy Crystal), a round, green, opinionated, feisty, short, one-eyed monster with skinny limbs. The loveable monsters are the top scare team at Monsters, Inc., the scream-processing factory in Monstropolis. However, when a little human girl enters their world by accident, it is the monsters that are scared silly, and it is up to Sulley and Mike to get her back home. The film promotes the idea that monsters can be cute, funny, and endearing, and features the twist that monsters are more scared of children than vice versa, because monsters consider human children to be toxic. *Monsters, Inc.* was a box office hit and marked the beginning of the Monsters, Inc. franchise, which includes several films, video games, theme park attractions, toys, apparel, costumes, accessories, stuffed animals, and so forth.

The multinational toy manufacturing company Mattel has capitalized on the idea of the "attractive" monster by launching the American franchise Monster High in 2010. The franchise, which includes different consumer products and media productions, promotes monstrous fashion dolls for girls. These ghoulish dolls, which are propagandized to be cool and desirable, are bone-thin "goth barbies" equipped with monstrous attributes, such as fangs, stitches, wolf ears, fins, bandages, and snakes. The idea behind the brand is that all people are somehow "monstrous," because of their idiosyncrasies, perhaps quirky characteristics, and individual flaws. The logo of the franchise, a skull with eyelashes and a pink bow tie, feminizes death, on the one hand, and beautifies the monstrous, on the other. The logo, together with the slogans of the franchise, "(Where) Freaky Just Got Fabulous!" (2010–11) and "Be Yourself, Be Unique, Be a Monster!" (2011–16), suggests that monstrosity represents a marketable concept in North American society today. Whereas the Monster High app is targeting teenage girls as primary consumers, other apps promoting trivialized monsters in fantastic worlds and augmented realities have young and adult followers all over the world. Two popular examples of such digital entertainment are My Singing Monsters, launched in 2012, and Pokémon Go, launched in 2016. Numerous media outlets, such as *The New York Times*, have referred to the surge in popularity of chasing after the cute pocket monsters as "Pokémania" (Isaac 2016).

Consumerism and the pursuit of a cute monster are also amongst the central tropes of the eco fairy-tale film *Okja* (2017), a South Korean production directed by Bong Joon-ho. *Okja* tells the fantastical story of a girl named Mija (Ahn Seo-hyun) who travels to Manhattan from Korea to prevent Lucy Mirando (Tilda Swinton), the CEO of the eponymous, sinister multinational meat company looking for a revolutionary product, from kidnapping her best friend Okja, a massive, genetically modified "super-pig." With some help from the Animal Liberation Front (ALF), a group of animal activists, Mija rescues Okja from a slaughterhouse along with a little piglet and returns to her life in the countryside with her grandfather. Not unlike a giant Pokémon in design, the computer-generated imagery (CGI) created monster in this live-action film is an adorable, pig-like creature resembling a cross between a huge hippopotamus and a hairless dog. *Okja* invites viewers to connect personally with its characters and their relationships, especially the close bond between Mija and her beloved pet pig (Figure 5.5). The lumbering pig hybrid is portrayed as almost as intelligent and emotionally developed as a human being with the mannerisms of a friendly pet.

By drawing on the notion of the lovable monster, the film is a morality tale that tackles themes of corporate greed, the ethics of meat consumption, animal cruelty, muddled intentions of activists, and the loss of innocence. Although Okja's genetically modified origin might label her a monster, there is nothing monstrous about her. Instead, Bong Joon-ho presents the viewers with the true unnatural horrors: the South Korean factory-farming system that evokes images of concentration camps when Okja is being forced up a ramp leading

FIGURE 5.5: Film still from Bong Joon-ho's *Okja* (2017).

into a slaughterhouse and greedy, capitalistic corporations, like Mirando, that hide their cruel and unethical practices from the general public. These horrors become personal because the issue of animal cruelty is not a distant reality or fantasy far from those consumers who enjoy the consumption of meat all over the world.

HUMAN/MONSTER/ANIMAL AFFINITIES IN TALES FROM FRANCE AND ARGENTINA

Another notable pig-monster tale is the female protagonist and narrator of Marie Darrieussecq's *Truismes* (1996, translated as *Pig Tales*, 1997), a fantastic, dystopian tale of animal transformations (reminiscent of Franz Kafka's *Metamorphosis*) set in Paris at the turn of the third millennium. The major preoccupation of the characters in the tale concerns sanitary conditions (related to mind, body, and infrastructure) in a very dystopian urban setting. The first-person narrator, a young woman, is kicked out by her mean, unloving mother once she finds a job selling luxury perfumes and administering (sexual) massages in a perfume shop. She recounts her gradual transformation into a sow. Her sexual appetite grows at the same rate as her bulging monstrous body. The narrator builds self-esteem, successfully fights victimization, and validates her sense of selfhood by using her appealing sexuality. Efforts to control her gradual and unstoppable metamorphosis (frequent lap swimming, makeup to cover up her pink skin, etc.) prove unsuccessful but land her a boyfriend, Honoré, an employee at the Aquatic Center. At first, monstrosity is positive and desirable. She wins sexual appeal but her voluptuousness becomes increasingly repulsive as animal characteristics clearly take the upper hand and make her day-to-day life difficult.

The French title, *Truismes* (Self-evident Truths), hints that women's sexuality generally speaking is overabundant, overflowing, and hence perceived as grotesque and monstrous. The female protagonist is increasingly dehumanized, as she starts bursting out of her clothing, walks on four legs, grunts, and wallows in the mud. Darrieussecq explores a female body that is coerced by society—both men and women—into monstrosity, "because there is this aspect, which perhaps is not accepted by some women, that the female body is like a monster, contrary to the better known male body, which is leaner and more muscular" (Leprince 2016). At first, the only apparent monster in the text is the female narrator, who recounts her slow descent into monstrosity. Female animal-like monstrosity mirrors alienation and revolt against daily humiliation in the workplace, where she is used by men as an object of desire: she willingly puts up with sexual advances and sodomy, because, she thinks, this is what attractive women are supposed to do. The pig lady suffers from an intense female rivalry, as her coworkers envy her voluptuous curves and then despise her once she becomes more pig-like. In the age of plastic surgery, breast augmentation, #MeToo, and an overall obsession with weight control, exercise, and diet, the text suggests that female curves are needed and attractive but only up to a certain point at which they become repulsive. Thus, Honoré, her boyfriend, is disgusted by her impressive physical transformation and kicks her out of his apartment. Thinking that she is pregnant, she has several "abortions" in a futile attempt to tame her bulging belly. Is she a woman, a monster, or an animal? Her fluid identity appears to be all-encompassing.

The narrator recounts the gestation of her own monstrosity. As she grows heavier and her body takes on a pinkish glow, bestiality takes over. She starts growing an additional nipple on her chest (and, eventually six udders), her hair falls out in bushels, hair starts growing all over her body, her nose starts looking like a pig's snout, and she grows a small tail. In the text, which presents itself as a witness account of subsequent monstrous transformations into animal shape and back into human shape, monstrosity reflects a psychological instability, estrangement, fear, immoderation, and an ever-growing, unwholesome consumer appetite for unbridled sex. In the end, monstrosity wins as she fails to reverse her bodily changes (with creams, lotions, hair removal, waxing, etc.).

The female monster inevitably becomes a social outcast in an increasingly misogynous society: the pig lady quits her job and ends up on the street, where people stare at her with fear in their eyes, and justifiably so, since she is developing strong cannibalistic urges that are difficult to contain. Once, she even tries to eat a baby:

> I opened my mouth but managed to produce only a sort of grunt. The baby gave me a quizzical look and sobbed all the harder. The sight of me seemed to frighten the woman ... I nudged the baby with my nose, the woman began to yell, and as for the baby, I don't know whether it was laughing or crying. I think—how should I put this—that I could easily have eaten the baby, sunk my teeth into that really rosy flesh, or that I could have carried it off, if the woman had given it to me.
>
> (Darrieussecq 1997: 79–80)

Eventually, other secondary characters also take on animal shape, mirroring the downward spiral of a corrupt and brutal society into sheer chaos. A politician called Edgar who uses the pig woman on electoral posters to advance his political campaign turns into a horse and starts neighing. A businessman called Yvan with whom she falls in love, periodically turns into a werewolf at full moon and eats humans. When the authorities grow suspicious after discovering numerous corpses on the river Seine embankment, Yvan and the pig lady hide inside his luxury apartment. To avoid being devoured by Yvan at full moon, she orders pizza for delivery. While she eats the pizza, Yvan the werewolf devours the delivery person. The human/animal couple move apartments and order from a different pizza delivery service every month so that Yvan may satisfy his monstrous appetite. One day, they are found out. Yvan the werewolf is shot dead after decapitating three policemen and his pig lady lover is taken to a pound from which she escapes in human shape, first to kill a TV presenter, then to pay her mother a lethal visit.

The overall structure of *Truismes* is characterized by four functions: transformation (from human to animal and vice versa), random human/animal encounters (individual and collective), overflowing sexuality, and random wanderings in the city of Paris (see Willocq 2008), essentially to hide from the authorities and from animal control trucks. Paris has become a surreal, threatening, extremely hostile urban environment, even the sewers are populated by crocodiles and piranhas. Many major tourist sites and landmarks such as the Arc de Triomphe and Mirabeau bridge have been destroyed after a war, the borders are hermetically closed. After Yvan's death, the narrator pays a final visit to her mother, who is now dating her former boss. She has moved to the countryside, where she raises her own cows and pigs and sells meat on the black market. After a catastrophic final mother/daughter standoff, her mother reluctantly offers her temporary refuge in the stable, only to attempt to butcher her with a knife. In the end, her daughter shoots her and seeks refuge in the woods: "Afterward I went off into the forest. Some of the pigs followed me, while the others, too attached to the comforts of their modern pigsty, were probably taken away by the SPCA or by another farmer, but in any case, I wouldn't want to be in their place today" (Darrieussecq 1997: 150). The pig lady roams freely and happily in the countryside where, once a month—during full moon—she fondly thinks of Yvan, takes on human shape, and writes down her experience in a world that has gone topsy turvy and has lost its human characteristics.

Pierre Gripari (1925–90), a French writer of Greek-French descent is known for his tales, including: *Diable, Dieu et autres contes de menterie* (*The Devil, God, and Other Tales of Untruth*, 1965), *Le gentil petit diable et autres contes de la rue Broca* ([1967] 1988, translated as *The Good Little Devil and Other Tales*, 2013), *Contes de la rue Broca* (*Tales of Broca Street*, 1967), *Histoires du Prince Pipo de Pipo le cheval et de la princesse Popi* (*Stories of the Prince Pipo, Pipo the Horse, and Princess Popi*, 1976), *La Sorcière de la rue Mouffetard* (*The Witch of the Rue Mouffetard and Other Tales*, 1980), *Patrouille du conte* (*Tale Patrol*, 1983), *Contes de la folie Méricourt* (*Tales of Folie-Méricourt*, 1983), *Jean-Yves à qui rien n'arrive* (*Jean-Yves to Whom Nothing Happens*, 1985), and *Contes d'ailleurs et d'autre part* (*Tales of Elsewhere and Otherwise*, 1990). Having penned numerous novels for adults, Gripari is remembered for his modern tales, which he considers also suitable for adults (Paucard 1985: 21). Though Gripari takes his inspiration from Charles Perrault, the Grimm brothers, Alexander Pushkin, and Alexander Afanasyev, the majority of his humorous tales feature friendly witches, fairies, dragons, ogres, and devils, which he finds "amusing" (89). Gripari's tales are anchored in realistic settings where the fantastic is accepted as constituting part of reality: he was convinced that reality and dreams are intertwined (Peyroutet and Gripari 1964: 77).

Gripari's fantastically realistic tales are colorful, funny, entertaining, and beautifully illustrated. They use a simple language that speaks to children and, thirty years after his death, have become modern classics of French literature. "Le gentil petit diable" ("The Good Little Devil") for instance, recounts the story of a social misfit who yearns for a radically different life: "There was once a charming little devil who was red all over, with two little black horns and two bat-wings. His daddy was a big green devil and his mother a black she-devil. All three of them lived together in a place called Hell, which can be found right in the centre of Planet Earth" (Gripari 2013: 137). The little devil stubbornly disobeys his parents: he wants to come into his own and refuses to be evil. At school, he earns good grades instead of bad grades and when his father orders him to help cook the sinners in a large cooking pot, he refuses to fan the fire that boils the sinners and instead helps them to think of God so they can redeem themselves and are instantly sent to heaven. One day, as he is punished to work in a coal mine, the little devil pierces a thick wall with his pickaxe and miraculously ends up in the Parisian Métro system. In the city, he tries to befriend all the humans he meets but they all run away terrorized because of his devilish appearance. He finally talks to a priest who sends him to the pope in Rome who in turn sends him to heaven where he passes tests administered by baby Jesus, God, and Mary. Having passed all the tests (reading, writing, and calculus), he is admitted to Heaven and becomes an angel himself: "Now the little devil lives in heaven. And if Paradise were not Paradise, the other angels would be envious of his fine red skin and his black horns" (Gripari 2013: 160–1).

Although the tale contains no morals, its underlying message to children is that monstrosity—the radical difference of the little devil in hell and then in heaven—is acceptable. Gripari's little devil rejects his biological identity as well as his upbringing and opts for a radical change. The tale suggests that it requires courage to embrace radical change to find happiness and fulfillment in life. The struggle to achieve individuality and to face one's own monstrosity is better than giving in to pressure from relatives and trying to adapt to conditions that are not conducive to happiness: we are responsible for creating our own heaven, even at the risk of being perceived as monsters by others. Gripari's tales mock normative thinking, as he explains:

> Obviously, it's an initiatory tale. What I liked about it, is to retell the story of the perverted [individual] that makes his parents despair: here, he is a nice little devil that makes his parents feel ashamed; and everything turns out very well for him. The moral would be the following: be a good little boy, not for your parents, but for yourself!
>
> (Peyroutet and Gripari 1964: 43; my translation)

A well-known French author, Marcel Aymé (1902–62), dedicated his anthropomorphic animal tales cycle *Les contes du chat perché* (1939, translated as *The Wonderful Farm*), to "children between the ages of four to seventy-five" (Paes-Kada 2014: 143). In 1956, Aymé wrote in a letter that he did not intend to write these tales solely for children:

> I did not write for children. I wrote the first *Conte du chat perché* tale ["Le loup" or "The Wolf"] that was published, because I wanted to, without asking myself whether or not it would or would not be read by under twelve-year-olds. As for the subsequent tales, I knew that the publisher [Gallimard] intended them for children, but the framework and the characters were already established. So, I just had fun without worrying just about the first target group.
>
> (Paes-Kada 2014: 138–9; my translation)

The tales that "oscillate between the marvellous and realism" (Paes-Kada 2014: 136) tell the daily life of Delphine and her younger sister Marinette, who live with their parents on a farm in early twentieth-century rural France. Much of their days are taken up shepherding and tending to various anthropomorphic farm animals, who for the most part have a friendly disposition toward the sisters, while the parents are ogre figures, always criticizing, admonishing, or shouting orders at the girls. The opening tale, titled "Le loup" ("The Wolf") revisits Perrault's "Petit Chaperon rouge" ("Little Red Riding Hood"), the Grimm brothers' "Der Wolf und die sieben jungen Geißlein" ("The Wolf and the Seven Young Goats"), and references Jean de La Fontaine's fable "Le loup et l'agneau" ("The Wolf and the Lamb"). In Aymé's cautionary tale, which reads like a twentieth-century sequel to Perrault's tale, Delphine and Marinette are warned by their parents not to let in anyone during their absence. As expected, the wolf knocks at the door but the girls do not let him in right away, because they have internalized Perrault's moral, never to trust strangers. When he encounters the girls, the wolf is convinced that he has finally become good, though secretly suspects he has not. The girls are no fools, recognize the wolf for what he is, and do not open the door. Disappointed, the wolf says: "You know, people tell many stories about wolves, you mustn't believe everything people say. The truth is that I am not bad at all" (Aymé 1939: 11). After much deliberation, the girls finally let the wolf in and they have a jolly good time playing all sorts of games until Delphine, the older sister who is more skeptical than Marinette, asks the wolf about Little Red Riding Hood: "It's true, I did eat little Red Riding Hood. But I can assure you that I have had a lot of regrets. If I had to do it again … Take my word for it, if I had to do it again, I'd rather starve to death" (13). The wolf's sincere apologies are accepted. He asserts that he never ate the grandma and downplays his murder of the girl as a mere youthful indiscretion.

Delphine reproaches him for having eaten (La Fontaine's) lamb, to which he counters that he is a carnivore—as they are, as well—and that he simply will not, as Delphine suggests, become vegetarian. She ends up accepting his sincere apologies. The wolf and the girls make up and they become the best of friends. The girls take delight in the wolf's excellent storytelling skills, while he becomes more human: he learns how to play and have fun. Yet, the wolf remains a predator and Aymé masterfully uses digression, a key ingredient of folktales at the end of which death awaits, as Italo Calvino reminds us: "The digression is a strategy for putting off the ending ... Flight from what? From death of course" (1988: 46). In the end, the wolf remains a wolf and Perrault was right when he cautioned not to socialize with him. A week later, the wolf calls again to play with the girls. Overexcited by a wolf game ("loup y es-tu?") in which the girls run away from the wolf, the animal gets carried away. The wolf wants to do a good job impersonating himself and this implies that he must eat the girls, so he does. When the parents return, they cut open its belly and free the girls. The repenting wolf promises never to be a glutton again and to run away when he sees children. He does not promise never to eat any children ever again, though. And though the ending asserts that "people *believe*" he kept his promise, readers are led to conclude that the wolf's sudden metamorphosis into a model of virtue is wishful thinking and that the cycle is about to start all over again if not in the twentieth century, then certainly in the twenty-first, for a monster cannot escape from its intrinsic monstrosity, even if it has the best of intentions.

Jorge Luis Borges's tale "The House of Asterion" ("La Casa de Asterión"), written first for a magazine edited by the Argentinean writer in May 1947, then republished in various anthologies, revisits the ancient Cretan myth of the Minotaur (a beast with a human body and the head and tail of a bull) caught inside a labyrinth. Borges wrote the a short palimpsestic tale in a single day:

> And I thought that the whole point lay in the fact of the story being told by, in a sense, the same scheme as "The Form of the Sword," but instead of a man *you had a monster telling the story*. And also I felt there might be *something true in the idea of a monster wanting to be killed, needing to be killed*, no? Knowing itself masterless. I mean, he knew all the time there was something awful about him, so he must have felt thankful to the hero who killed him.
>
> (Burgin and Borges 1969: 41; emphasis added)

Classic monster tales are one-dimensional, archetypal, lack psychological depth, and primarily focus on the hero's obstacle course, his quest and accomplishments. They take any potential monsters and their monstrous qualities more or less for granted without dwelling too much on them other than to point out their dangerousness or cruelty. In Borges's tale about the Minotaur, a hybrid figure oscillating between a wise, superhuman beast and an incarnation of the regression of the human to bestiality, readers gain access to the monster's psyche, inner thoughts, and worldview. The suffering solitary monster yearns for death: a long-awaited delivery from solitude. The one time he tries to socialize, people run away frantically due to his horrid physical appearance, half monster, half human:

> One afternoon I did go out into the streets; if I returned before nightfall, I did so because of the terrible dread inspired in me by the faces of the people—colorless faces, as flat as the palm of one's hand ... The people prayed, fled, fell prostrate before me ... I cannot mix with commoners even if my modesty should wish it.
>
> (Borges 1998: 221)

Caught inside the labyrinth constructed by Daedalus and Icarus, the Minotaur patiently awaits to be killed by the hero, Theseus, who, at the end of the tale quips: "Can you believe it, Ariadne? ... The Minotaur scarcely defended itself" (Borges 1998: 222). This is because the man/monster wanted to be killed, and thus be delivered from his inherent torturous duality, the impossibility of accepting his half-human, half-monster nature. The non-human animallike quality of the Minotaur is reflected by his obstinate refusal of intellectual activity. The beast spends his time playing inside the labyrinth or sleeping: "I have never grasped for long the difference between one letter and another. A certain generous impatience has prevented me from learning to read. Sometimes I regret that, because the nights are long" (220–1). Yet the human side tells a different story: the Minotaur is an introvert that yearns to conquer the world. The beast yearns for unity and redemption, it is caught in an internal quandary from which it cannot escape. He/it yearns for a Doppelgänger/soul mate to communicate with, and like Marie Darrieussecq's pig lady, he clearly also has some intellectual faculties, since he/it is able to tell his own story, express his anguish, hopes, and desires:

> But of all the games, the one I like best is pretending that there is another Asterion. I pretend that he has come to visit me, and I show him around the house. Bowing majestically, I say to him: *Now let us go this way, now, out into another courtyard* or *I knew that you would like this rain gutter* or *Now you will see a cistern that has filled with sand* or *Now you will see how the cellar forks.* Sometimes I make a mistake and the two of us have a good laugh over it.
>
> (Borges 1998: 221; emphasis in the original)

The Minotaur reflects on his labyrinthine open-ended house—the world—and the creator, perhaps himself? He also wonders about the form and shape of his redeemer: "Will he be bull or man? Could he possibly be a bull with the face of a man? Or will he be like me?" (Borges 1998: 222). In all of the above monster tales, the "monstrous condition" is ultimately perceived by the monsters themselves (pig lady/devil/wolf/Minotaur) as conflict-ridden, burdensome and unwanted in societies that struggle to accept radical differentness.

To conclude, postmodern fairy-tale monsters—on screen and in literature—tend to be portrayed as less frightening, less threatening, and less beastly than traditionally seen in fairy tales. Instead, fantastic creatures, such as the ogre, the troll, the witch, the dragon, or the fairy-tale wolf, have undergone significant character changes that recast these creatures in a favorable light. Equipped with positive attributes, for example, a sense of humor, heroic ambitions, therapeutic or helpful properties, feelings of remorse or a guilty conscience, cute features, or an attractive physique, formerly villainous creatures appear awe-inspiring, appealing, and redeemed. In some cases, they arouse sympathy in viewers and readers, especially when accompanied by a traumatic backstory that explains why such creatures may have committed evil deeds in the first place. By humanizing fairy-tale monsters and by endowing them with positive traits, such creatures invite identification and allow audiences and readerships to relate to them on a personal level. We see contemporary fairy-tale monsters reimagined as admirable beings or marvels (one of the meanings of the term monsters), which complicates our notion of what makes a fairy-tale monster truly "monstrous."

Today's fairy-tale adaptations oftentimes unsettle the simplistic dichotomy of good versus evil and present us with complex characters that destabilize our traditional understanding of monstrosity. What if the fairy-tale wolf no longer chases after Little Red Riding Hood and her grandmother but instead prefers to be vegan? This is the case in the American television series *Grimm* (2011–17), where Monroe (Silas Weir Mitchell) is a reformed "Blutbad" (bloodbath), or rather "Wi(e)der-Blutbad" (again/against blood-bath). The character, who can transform into a wolf-like creature or human-lupine *Wesen* (being), explains to Nick Burkhardt (David Giuntoli) that he is not the Big Bad Wolf found in fairy tales. Instead, Monroe tells Nick that stories about the Wesen-hunting Grimms, Nick's ancestors, "scared the hell" out of him when he was a child. This particular scene enlightens viewers, on the one hand, about stereotypical perceptions of the monstrous Other and stresses, on the other hand, that monstrosity is a subjective concept and matter of perspective, as for Blutbaden the Grimms are the true monsters.

> MONROE   You people started profiling us over 200 years ago. But as you can see I am not that big, and I am done with the bad thing.
> NICK   Well, how do you … ?
> MONROE   How do I stay good? Through a strict regimen of diet, drugs and Pilates. I'm a reformed Blutbad. A Wieder Blutbad. It's a different church altogether.
> NICK   Wait, you guys go to church?
> MONROE   Sure. Don't you?

Given the less clear-cut, no longer intrinsically obvious and undisputable evil nature of postmodern hybrid monsters—they often resemble humans given their imperfections and sometimes psychologically tormented nature, which makes them appear less threatening, but rather weak and human—the term "human beast" might more aptly describe them. The term beast, derived from the Latin word *bestia*, according to the *Oxford English Dictionary* refers to animals as well as to an "inhumanly cruel, violent, or depraved person," "sex beasts," "a person's brutish or untamed characteristics," or an "objectionable or unpleasant person or thing" (OED n.d.-a). Hence, monsters defy any efforts of simple categorization. They come in many different packages and our definition of what constitutes a monster appears to be based upon personal or societal interpretations of what is deemed monstrous.

CHAPTER SIX

Space

The Magically Real Spaces of Twentieth- and Twenty-First-Century Fairy Tale

SARA UPSTONE

In the unfortunate absence of an explicit opening phrase "Once upon a place," it is therefore apparently necessary for the student of folktales to invent it in order to draw attention to the spatial facets of story, on the one hand, and to the perhaps surprising but undeniable realisation, on the other, that the past is as much located in space, whether as namable place or not, as in time; in other words the past is a place as well as a time.
—W. F. H. Nicolaisen (1991: 4)

In the summer of 2019 the UK television viewing public were gripped by the third season of the reality dating show *Love Island* (2015–). Screening six nights a week for more than two months, the show achieved live and catch-up streaming figures of over thirteen million. While the sun blazed with record temperatures, the bars emptied at 9:00 p.m. as people rushed to follow the lives of a group of twentysomethings looking for love.

Love Island is nothing more (or less) than a fairy tale, if by this we take the meaning of that term to be—as I do in this chapter—works that adopt the influence of traditional folk- and fairy-tale narratives, whether as an explicit intertextuality or an unconscious resonance resulting from widespread cultural incorporation. *Love Island*, which falls under the definition of the latter, seems impossible without tales such as "Cinderella" and "Sleeping Beauty," relying on the premise of love at first sight—that two strangers meet and find an instant connection transcending the temptations of everyday life. As each couple forms, new contestants serve the role as ugly sisters (or brothers), threatening to disrupt the outcome. Resolutely heteronormative, the final satisfaction is a metaphorical crowning of the prince and princess who receive a shared £50,000, the golden ticket to a future in which audiences are promised they will live "happily ever after."

The reality TV fairy tale is thus the most striking example of the contemporary desire for the fairy tale made "real." At the center of this "reality," however, is a spatiality that is anything but real. The show is filmed in Mallorca, but contestants are never to refer to it as anything other than "the Island." On that island the show contains contestants in a villa set apart from the outside world, only permitted to leave for fixed excursions, created to drive forward particular relationships. Within the villa, a private swimming pool, outside kitchen and high-end furniture creates an ambience of luxury. Yet dormitory beds, designed to drive the show's romantic plot, and fake grass—intended to look ceaselessly immaculate over the show's long run—remind viewers constantly of the artificiality of arrangements.

While short contemporary fairy tales do exist that continue the spatial abstractions of traditional tales—see, for example, the late twentieth-century inclusions in Angela Carter's *Virago Book of Fairy Tales* ([1990, 1992] 2005), Sara Maitland's *Gossip from the Forest* (2012), or Emma Donoghue's *Kissing the Witch* ([1993] 1997)—*Love Island* marks the limit point of a trajectory in twentieth- and twenty-first-century fairy tale toward an engagement with real-world spatialities, drawn out via short story cycles, the novel, television, cinema, art, and opera. These spatialities are nevertheless predicated on elision and imaginative reconstruction of the real to maintain a continued sense of fantastic unreality and magical possibility. Recognizing such spatializations is not only about understanding the evolution of fairy tale within the modern and contemporary cultural imaginary, but also about identifying its contribution both to the contemporary spatial imaginary and a globalized cultural politics that rests upon a conterminous investment in the ethico-political specificity of location and the utopian abstraction of magical space.

IN PORTLAND, EVERYTHING LOOKS LIKE A FAIRY TALE

As Marnie Campagnaro notes, there is a tradition of thinking about fairy tales as both atemporal and ahistorical. Arguments that a fairy tale is infused with historical and geographical specificity are countered by the production of evidence that cites similar representations in entirely different places and times; the "once upon a time" framing, and the frequent use of tropes such as the castle and forest, speak against correlation to actual, real-world spaces (Campagnaro

2017: 10). This thinking is employed by the most notable theorist of fairy-tale spaces, W. F. H. Nicoliasen, and is rooted in the work of Max Lüthi, who posits a two-dimensional magical folktale or *Flächenhaftigkeit* (see Nicolaisen 1980: 14). In the traditional fairy tale "descriptions are exact, coherent and recognisable, yet outside the tale they lead nowhere because they contain no specific geographical names, topographical references, or points on a map. The spaces are entirely general" (Campagnaro 2017: 11–12).

An updated narrative does not mean the end of archetypal landscapes. Familiar motifs such as Angela Carter's isolated houses or the unnamed forest of the TV show *Grimm* (2011–17) evoke generic expectations. In Helen Oyeyemi's novel *Boy, Snow, Bird* (2014), for example, "Snow White" is transferred to contemporary America in the period 1930 to 1970. Despite the real-world setting, the area of Flax Hill, Connecticut, where the narrative takes place is also a classic fairy-tale space: "old, dark, thick-trunked trees ... Bearded men who carried axes and drove carthorses" (24), filled with mysterious houses that "you could start fanciful rumors about: 'Well a princess had been asleep there for hundreds of years'" (25). Yet when one character asks the question "Lost? Like in the woods?" this is answered with the corrective "Not just there. Anywhere" (92), an exchange that indicates that while forests and castles remain, there is a broader spatiality at work. Returning to our previous examples, while season one of *Grimm* centers on the forest, subsequent seasons relocate much of the magic to urban and suburban locations. Likewise, in the title story of Carter's *The Bloody Chamber* ([1979] 2006) Bluebeard's castle remains, yet is self-consciously identified—"that magic place, the fairy castle" (2)—against the quotidian reality of the narrator's mother with her walks from the grocer's shop. "Bluebeard" is well-suited to such adaption into identifiable space since the source tale has little magic within it, and Carter shares her approach with a number of other adaptations, namely Margaret Atwood's "Bluebeard's Egg" (1983), Jane Campion's *The Piano* (1993), and Oyeyemi's *Mr. Fox* (2011). Carter, however, extends this elsewhere. In "The Courtship of Mr. Lyon," based on "Beauty and the Beast," for example, Beauty is brought to a magical house due to an automobile breakdown and the promise of a garage with a 24-hour rescue service, yet the landscape is "of ivory with an inlay of silver" ([1979] 2006: 46).

As Carter notes, "the form of the fairy tale is not usually constructed so as to invite the audience to share a sense of lived experience" ([1990, 1992] 2005: xiii); it is designed with an excision of references to "denaturize its vision of everyday life" ([xix). The abstract construction of space serves these ends. So it is that in the contemporary, places not only depart from the archetype but they do so with unparalleled detail, an "extra-vivid materiality" (Simpson 2006: x) that reveals sensuous engagement with both natural and built space. Such difference is aligned with the movement to more expansive literary forms—

short stories and novels rather than "tales," with the influence of realism rather than or alongside the classical tale tradition. If contemporary spaces are thus more detailed, more evocative, and less archetypal than the traditions they draw from, they are also more specific.

As Nicolaisen outlines, in folktale places are rarely named, contributing to the sense of an acartographical space (2002: 5), which is implicated in the survival of stories across generations and in different geographies. Tellers of fairy tales, Nicolaisen argues, are deeply interested in place. A skilled teller will give the audience a strong sense of location. Yet this "sense of place" (Nicolaisen 1991: 4) can be distinctly differentiated from a particular place. According to Alfred Messerli:

> The European fairy tale creates two nonhomeomorphic worlds—a magical world of supernatural beings from the beyond, and a nonmagical one of normal human beings—worlds that are divided from one another through occasionally fluid but sometimes also inflexible boundaries and frontier regions. With this first structure a second coexists in that for the narrator and the listener both worlds belong in any case to the same "magic" virtual world of the fairy tale, which is clearly separated from their own real one.
> (2005: 274)

This clear separation from actuality means that places in traditional fairy tales do not act as coordinates for the real world, though they may be evocative of that world. A study of the versions of classic tales reveals that the variation that exists around the common "skeleton" of a tale relies upon a spatial difference which is historically and geographically constituted (Campagnaro 2017; Maitland 2012: 13), but that uniqueness is not the same as a specificity.

It is thus a departure of note that in "The Bloody Chamber" it is not just Bluebeard's business destination in New York that is referenced but also cafés in Montmartre, homes in Brittany, a music school in Paris. Likewise, *Grimm* is very specifically set in Portland, Oregon, a place that show creator David Greenwalt describes as "looking like a fairy tale" (Turnquist 2017); and Oyeyemi's *Boy, Snow, Bird* and *Mr. Fox* are both rooted in New York. Other examples include the television reworking of "Beauty and the Beast" and its reboot (1987, 2012–), and *Tell Me a Story* (2018–), a television psychological thriller loosely based on "The Three Little Pigs," "Little Red Riding Hood," and "Hansel and Gretel," which in all three cases locate the action in New York. In an interview, Carter recognized that while her landscapes are in keeping with fairy-tale tradition, their connection to the actual is also a departure:

> I was looking at it again last week. I read from it for the first time in ages the other night, and I thought, this is pretty cholesterol-rich because of the fact that they all take place in invented landscapes. Some of the landscapes

are reinvented ones. "The Bloody Chamber" story itself is set quite firmly in the Mont Saint Michel, which is this castle on an island off the coast of Brittany; and a lot of the most exotic landscapes in it, the Italian landscapes, were quite legit. "The Tiger's Bride" landscape, admittedly, is touristic, but it's one of the palaces in Mantua that has the most wonderful jewels, and that city is set in the Po Valley, which is very flat and very far out, so in the summer you can imagine the mist rolling over. The landscapes there [in *The Bloody Chamber*] are quite real. Even the werewolf stories are set in some horror-filled invented landscapes, but there's more a kind of down-to-earthness in those stories.

(Katsavos 1994: 14–15)

Carter's acknowledgment of her departure points neatly to its purpose; the landscapes, she tells us, are "quite real."

A SUBSTITUTE FOR THE GENUINE THING

As Nicolaisen notes, in contemporary tales "named locations are ... essential props in the establishment of their veracity" (2002: 7). Specificity, then, is synonymous with real-world correspondence. In this respect departures from traditional fairy-tale spatialities are also essential to a reconstructed relationship to the notion of the "real." Detailed description and specificity of locale are devices designed to entice particular audiences, assisting entry into the world via identifiable reference points. To this end, the contemporary tale is part of a broader trend that uses identifiable place to invite access into the fantastic, the use of identifiable places to root readers and act as counterpoint to the unreality of fantasy elements evident, for example, in the use of London in J. K. Rowling's *Harry Potter* series (1997–2007) and Oxford in Philip Pullman's *His Dark Materials* series (1995–2000). In film and television, in particular, globalized cultures and internet access means that spaces are simultaneously specific and abstractly identifiable; yet this is also true of many of the iconic spaces referenced in literature—Paris and New York, for example—are immediately identifiable due to a globalized culture where the majority of those with access to the texts carry with them a cultural imaginary of the Eiffel Tower or Empire State Building. The notion of landscapes being "potentially realizable in different locations" to produce spaces "recognizable but not knowable" (Nicolaisen 1980: 15) upon which the traditional tale relies is thus transformed, as there is no longer the need for audiences to have physically experienced spaces to feel intimately connected to them.

This transformation of magical place into "real" begins, ironically, with the marvelous, and more particularly, with J. R. R. Tolkien. For Tolkien, a fairy story "should be presented as 'true' ... it cannot tolerate any frame or machinery suggesting that the whole story ... is a figment or illusion" (1947: 5). This "true" relies upon what Tolkien refers to as secondary belief, a corrective to the willing suspension of disbelief which in its operation—"a substitute for the genuine thing" (12)—makes the acceptance of true fundamentally impossible. Secondary belief rests upon a detailed imagination of place, what Tolkien defines in his 1954 essay "Time and Tide" as "subcreation"—the development of a complete world "with its own theology, myths, geography, history, paleography, languages, and orders of beings" (Pearce 1998: 83). "Real" is thus cemented through the construction of a mythology of place—a world-building exercise complete with maps and relational landscapes.

The trajectory of Tolkien's own work unfolds this expansion into the real. For Tolkien, his *magnum opus* was not *The Lord of the Rings* (1955) or *The Hobbit* (1937) but rather *The Silmarillion* (1977), which traces the entire mythology of his imagined world of Middle-Earth and was published posthumously after Tolkien painstakingly worked on it for more than fifty years. The scale of *The Silmarillion* reduces place to its essential details, entirely in balance with the text's temporality and its evocation of both biblical and mythic form. Yet while *The Silmarillion* was for Tolkien his major work, it is far less well-known than his two earlier texts, which each expand a single reference point in *The Silmarillion* into an entire narrative. In these more famous works, place is sharply delineated, but also more familiar. For instance, the Shire is "based on rural England and not any other country in the world" (Tolkien, quoted in Pearce 1998: 154), while Mordor is a rendering of the industrial postwar urban landscape of heavy industry and manufacturing.

Tolkien's work establishes a marvelous tradition for complex world-building that is taken up by writers such as Terry Pratchett, Ursula Le Guin, and George R. R. Martin. A useful contemporary comparison can also be found in Zoe Gilbert's short-story cycle *Folk* (2018). Rooted in the folklore of the Isle of Man and transferring this to the imagined island of Neverness, Gilbert repeats Tolkien's strategy of rooting marvelous geography in familiar landscapes. Like Tolkien, Gilbert is concerned with subcreation first and foremost, tracing the contours of the single village on the island. Her scale exceeds a single generation, preferring snapshots to detailed character analyses, and privileging place and culture over individual lives, with descriptions of sea, wood, and field repeated so that while characters change, landscape endures as the rooting element. Neverness is not of the present—at least not of the present of our own world—and yet like Middle-Earth it is also not of a particular time in the past of our world either. There are no fairies; rather, there is the magic of the everyday to which Tolkien refers, declaring that "Oberon, Mab, and Pigwiggen may be diminutive elves or fairies, as Arthur, Guinevere, and Lancelot are not; but the good and evil story of Arthur's court is a 'fairy-story' rather than this tale of Oberon" (Tolkien 1947: 3). In the stories of *Folk* we encounter a man with a wing instead of an arm, the mythical threats of the gorse mother, and the prophecies of the water bull. Yet as Rowan Hisayo Buchanan notes in the book's inside cover endorsements "the villagers are neither Cinderellas nor wicked witches, they are weak and brave by turn with fluttery human hearts." The "real" of the space is enhanced by the text's self-conscious positioning of itself as contemporary post-fairy tale; characters tell fairy tales complete with "Once Upon a Time" (Gilbert 2018: 42), like the story of Jack Frost, to give the sense of the converse "reality" of the place in which the tale is told.

THIRDSPACE

Folk is distinct as a literary subcreation that is more common to fantasy writing. In contrast, the move in other texts to identifiable places reflects perhaps a contemporary response to the lack of respect given to marvelous literature, the deep awareness that the scorn poured on Tolkien whenever he is associated with the concept of "great literature" in part relates to the rooting of his narrative in a "nonexistent world" (Pearce 1998: 1). Yet immersion in the worlds Tolkien and Gilbert create, combined with readers' secondary belief, cements a reality that connects that world to our own. As Tolkien notes, simplistic escapism is impossible in such circumstances. For if actual spaces are escaped, then reading necessarily returns us to them because they are always woven into the terrain that is traveled through. Such associations draw attention to the closeness between marvelous subcreation and narratives that align themselves with particular real-world spaces.

Identifiable-world narratives, then, are not sharply delineated from Tolkien's subcreation but rather are a further extension into the "real" that his work pioneers. In this respect such spaces are less marvelous or fantastic, and more in keeping with magical realism (see Hegerfeldt 2005; Schwabe 2014). As I argue elsewhere, magical realism often employs what can be best described as a literary thirdspace in its evocation of place (Upstone 2009). Initially used by the geographer Edward Soja to define the very real and yet extraordinary spaces of postmodern Los Angeles, thirdspace rests upon an essential understanding of space as "simultaneously real and imagined," produced through the combination of physical space and its subjective interpretation by the individual (Soja 1996: 11; Teverson and Upstone 2011). Soja's theory of space addresses his perception of an imbalanced overreliance on temporality: precisely the same overreliance that Nicolaisen identifies in his early work on space and folk tale (Nicolaisen 1980).

To create an enchanted reality, these literary narratives of real-world spaces share with *Folk* a scorn of explicit magic for everyday enchantment, and the specific is combined with a subjectivity that emphasizes the imagined nature of space. In Lucy Wood's *Diving Belles* (2012), for example, which is set in modern Cornwall and based upon Cornish myths, a character asks, "Do you like castles?" (162). Yet this represents an ironic playing at magic, which has little to do with the mysterious power of the natural world, where sea and human merge in stories of mermen, people are turned to stone, and there are wishing trees and stray giants that wander the moors and cliffs. The conjunction of physical space with subjectivity in such enchantment is amply represented in Wood's story "Beachcombing," in which a young boy is the lens through which we view the life of an older woman, his grandmother, who has taken up residence on a Cornish beach. The "magic" lies in the interruption of reality by cows falling from the cliffs, and the woman's belief in Bucca, Cornish male sea spirits. She believes that the loss of her husband and son, both fishermen, was the result of her forgetting one day to leave an offering for the Bucca before they set out for the day's catch; she has lived on the beach ever since. Bucca are not visible but reveal themselves in their impact upon the landscape, throwing shells and sticks and seaweed across the beach, pouring rain into the woman's cave. This mystical belief means that when a door is washed up on the beach, the woman and her visiting grandson imagine it not as a piece of jetsam but, rather, as a door into the room from which it once came. Whether the "magic" the boy and the woman speak of here is "real" is less significant than how it facilitates a reimagining of the coastal space as one that exists as a fusion of its literal qualities and their subjective experiences. Bucca may not be real, yet their impact on the woman and her carrying this impact with her into her beach abode means that the space exists for both her and the boy only within this mystical context. And that reality is, for them, the space's signifying as a site of cultural and familial resonance, and its magic.

It is in this sense that psychic investment in ordinary spaces transforms them into spaces of enchantment, without the necessary presence of the supernatural. In Atwood's *The Robber Bride* ([1993] 2009b), a reworking of Grimm's "The Robber Bridegroom" set in 1980s Toronto, contemporary magic is more speculative and includes the reading of tarot cards, a comic suggestion of reincarnation, and a single dream sequence in a world where the rules of enchantment appear to have changed. As the unnamed narrator of Atwood's later short story "I Dream of Zenia with the Bright Red Teeth" ([1993] 2009a) that accompanies later printings of the *The Robber Bride* declares: "the vampires, you used to know where you stood with them … but now there are virtuous vampires and disreputable vampires, and sexy vampires and glittery vampires, and none of the old rules about them are true any more" (514). In *The Robber Bride*, out-of-body experiences are not magical at all, but rather dissociative events resulting from psychological trauma. The map, however, is a space of world creation into which individual experience is poured and the extraordinary ordinary is given permanent presence:

She gets up from the chair and pours herself a glass of water; then, on top of Europe in the thirteenth century, she spreads out a street map, a map of downtown Toronto. Here is the Toxique, here is Queen Street, here is Roz's renovated office building; here are the ferry docks, and the flat island where Charis's house still stands ... Here is McClung Hall, and, to the north, Tony's own house, with West in it, upstairs in bed, groaning gently in his sleep; with the cellar in it, with the sand-table in it, with the map on it, with the city in it, with the house in it, and the cellar in it, with the map in it. Maps, think Tony, contain the ground that contains them ... they help her to see, to visualize the topology, to remember.

(Atwood [1993] 2009b: 503)

Characters in these cases are caught in a psychogeographical investment, a self-consciousness regarding the subjective nature of space that is strikingly different from the objectivity and matter-of-fact description of the traditional tale. In her nonfiction wanderings around real-world forests in *Gossip from the Forest* (2012), Maitland suggests that spaces are explored with "a double map": the first a palimpsest in which can be located the fragments of the real history of forests, the second a magical map, "which relocates the forest in our imaginations and was drawn up when we were children" (53). This dual map-making is also the approach of many contemporary tellers. In Carter's short stories the queen of the vampires is "a cave full of echoes ... she herself is a haunted house" ([1979] 2006: 108, 119); when the young man awakes after his liaison with the queen of the vampires he finds a house that is "tawdry," stripped of its shine in the wake of her death. Likewise in "The Erl-King" the woods "enclose and then enclose again; the intimate perspective ... changed endlessly around the interloper" (97). Reading the story as a mediation on Romantic subjectivity, Harriet Kramer Linkin notes that "it is impossible for human beings to enter the wood without bringing their own sociocultural maps with them. Even as the narrator identifies the wood as an unmotivated sign, her cultural encoding functions as an interpretive screen through which she reads nature" (1994: 311).

It is in the context of this real and imagined thirdspace that we encounter disjunctive spaces, complete with multiple and parallel universes, or what Claudia Schwabe (2014) calls the "reality fairy tale" in comparison to the "one world fairy tale" of shows such as *Grimm*. It would be fallacious to say that traditional tales, even when limited to those written in the West, are without the kinds of spatial dislocations we see in contemporary rewritings. Marina Warner, for example, notes the "dislocations of time and space" (1994a: 144) common to classical fairy-tale fashions in France, and traditional tales abound with magical wells, caves, and ladders that transport individuals. At the same time, however, these spaces in traditional tales are largely discrete, and movement is often between a magical and non-magical space. One consequence of the move to the real is the increasing interweaving of these two spaces. Specificity of place determines that magic often becomes a matter of an enchanted or heightened sense of the "realness" of the space in which the narrative is set, rather than of two opposing if interwoven realms.

In *Folk*, for example, the final story, "Tether," gestures toward a world within the world, neither of which is our "actual" world. Returning to a frequent character in the book called Madden Lightfoot, it examines her involvement in a secret cult of magical kite flying, in which the flyer is transported to an alternative acorporeal plane of existence that can only be returned from via a tethering to the landscape. Madden is so consumed by this world that her own bodily existence becomes insignificant, and she chooses to be untethered and remain in this space forever. The declaration of Madden's lover, Hark, that "magic was dishonesty … It could not be real" serves, however, as a provocation to push against obvious allegorical readings and into the storyworld where such possibilities *are* real (Gilbert 2018: 225). Indeed, when Hark finally takes the kite ride himself, he discovers the whisper of Madden's voice and the understanding that the parallel existence she spoke of does exist. This ending foregrounds what is evident in the narratives elsewhere, namely the sense of a "real" actual world layered underneath a "real" imagined world, a palimpsest in which the fairy tale sits above the imagined world, which itself sits above an actual physical space.

Here the narrative operates neatly within the terms of magical realist spaces, as the contained world of fairy tale gives way to a structure that requires "a faculty for boundary-skipping between worlds" (Wilson 1995: 210). In his essay on magical realist space, Rawdon Wilson outlines three models: the first, associated with realism; the second with fantasy, the third with magical realism. While traditional fairy tale may conform to Wilson's second definition, based on imagined worlds with self-contained coherence and internal rules, the contemporary fairy tale has more in common with his third definition in which there exist "fictional worlds in which the indications of local place are sometimes those of the extratextual world but at other times those of another place, very different in its assumptions" (217):

> Think of it as copresence, as duality and mutual tolerance, as different geometries at work constructing a double space. Magical realism focuses the problem of fictional space. It does this by suggesting a model of how different geometries, inscribing boundaries that fold and refold like quicksilver, can superimpose themselves upon one another.
>
> (210)

In Wood's *Diving Belles* (2012) characters trace worn pathways "marked out by other people's feet" (52), space pulling them into rituals and magical occurrences, so that "once upon a time" is evoked not as recourse to fantasy, but to the deep meanings of the real (66). Elsewhere, the work of Neil Gaiman is marked by such multiple spatialities, exemplified by novels such as *American Gods* (2001) and *Anansi Boys* (2005) in which gritty urban locales in both Britain and the United States are combined with mythological spaces such as "the land of the dead" and "the beginning of the world." This is also the structure of Disney's first live-action fairy tale, *Enchanted* (2007), which employs the conventional vertical movement between non-magical and magical realms of traditional folktales, in which the ladder, well, hole, or cave marks the liminal boundary between worlds (see Nicolaisen 1980: 17); and of Oyeyemi's *Gingerbread* where Flax Hill is a town that "misbehaved ... collapsing ... and reassembling in the morning" (2018: 15). The novel's heroine, Perdita, falls into a trance, having consumed an ancient recipe for magical gingerbread that results in an appearance of death but is in fact an alternative state in which the mind leaves the body for an alternative world. *Gingerbread* reveals this world as "real" via an origins story complete with a magical well, teddy bears' picnic, and the original Grimms' tale characters, as readers are informed that "Wikipedia doesn't get to decide which places have actual geographical existence and which don't" (2018: 46–7).

In each of these cases the lines between worlds are blurred by the movement of not just characters but also of magic itself. Characters do not simply fall down wells and appear in magical places, magic also appears through these doorways and comes to influence actual space. The appearance of magic within both the "magical" and the "actual" world disrupts the discrete nature of such spaces. Thus while Tracie Lukasiewicz describes spatiality in the film *Pan's Labyrinth* (2006) for example as "neomagical realism" (2010: 61) because there is no incorporation of magic into the "real world," it is possible to maintain that even here within the harsh social realism of the film's setting in Falangist Spain there are subtle movements between spaces that disrupt seemingly discrete boundaries.

IF YOU GO DOWN TO THE WOODS

Pan's Labyrinth embodies a contemporary desire for stark social realism, but alongside this it deploys a strategic use of magic to open up a discourse around the horrors of war and its innocent victims. In the contemporary cultural moment, movements such as metamodernism, post-postmodernism, renewalism, and new sincerity emphasize the ethico-political import of cultural production. These movements focus on the radical reappraisal of conventional realism, particularly in relation to its patriarchal and imperialist connotations. Deeply influential both in literary and wider cultural terms, they invoke the capacity of non-realist, magical, or fantastic tropes to provoke social transformation. At the same time, however, they also emphasize connection to reality as a means to address real-world imperatives, most notably in the context of identity politics such as feminism, queer politics, and postcolonialism, but also broader ethical turns. It is in the context of this engagement with the "real" that fairy tale works to create spaces that affirm Carter's view that fiction conscious of its own difference to reality can nevertheless serve real-world transformations (Simpson 2006: ix). The conjunction of real place—the actual, the specific, the evocative—with magic constructs a range of provocative, speculative ethico-political interventions.

Tolkien's own preference in these terms was for what he refers to as applicability, as opposed to the didactic implications of allegory. The fluidity of such applicability exceeds the intention of the author, and rests upon the openness of the text to multiple sociopolitical usages. In his own work, applicability thus relates the landscape of Middle-Earth to the First World War, to fascism and—for later readers—to the environmentalist agenda. Equally, subcreation does not divorce the narrative in *Folk* from political imperative as the cycle is "a dark historical mirror to the harried face of modern Britain" (Myers 2018). The character Verlyn with his wing evokes contemporary debates around disability, sexuality, and the marginalization of otherness, a marginality spatialized as Verlyn finds expression of his desire only in the hidden spaces on the village outskirts. When his lover marries one of his brothers Verlyn discovers their relationship by observing them walking along the shore at the very center of Neverness's economic and social life, deeply interwoven with the culture's ableist hypermasculinity. Similarly, "Tether" contributes both to controversies surrounding assisted suicide and drug addiction. For Tolkien, a passionate philologist, subcreation was impossible without the naming of places, while in *Folk* the map (Figure 6.1) serves as a peritext that positions each member of the community spatially in relation to each other. Both narratives thus affirm an unofficial, grassroots making of place, enshrined in cartography. In his self-declared semi-retirement in Aberdeen, Nicolaisen devoted his time to compiling the alternative names of Northeast Scottish places, identifying localized and familial connections that for him "imply a kind of intimacy which even the most accurate official map would never achieve" (2002: 9) and which can be seen as part of a creation and contextualization of place via folklore, which affirms not major landscapes but minor landmarks and localized understandings (Nicolaisen 1976). This cartographical interest further connects political imperatives to notions of actuality.

While it is thus a misunderstanding of the political implications of subcreation, the movement to real-world spaces can be seen to be driven by an imperative to increase this relevance of fairy tale to real-world agendas. In Disney's *The Princess and the Frog* (2009), for example, the classic narrative is transferred to early twentieth-century New Orleans to reconstruct the classic

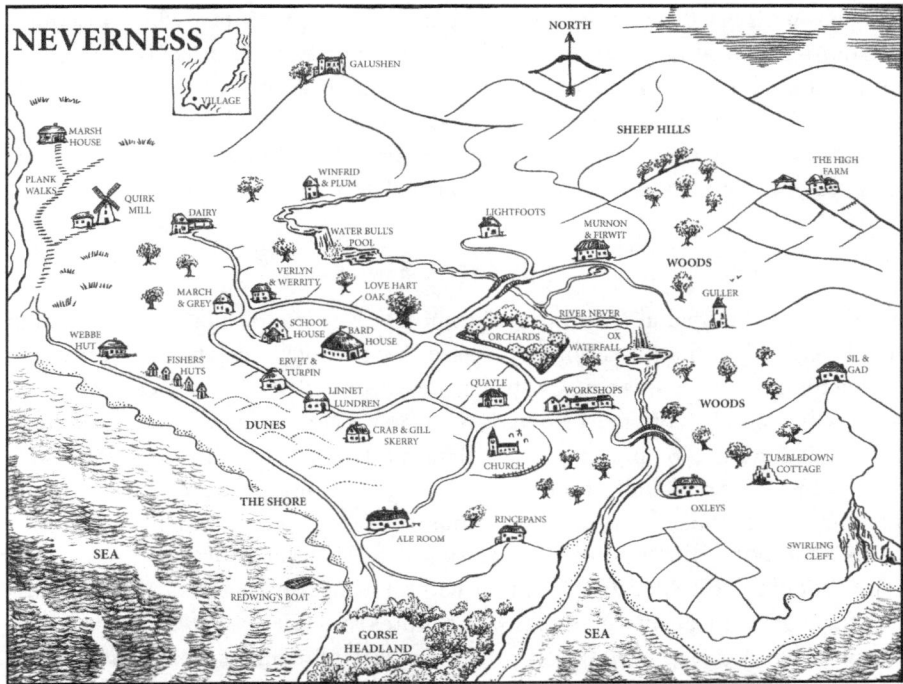

FIGURE 6.1: Map of Neverness by Isobel Simonds. © Isobel Simonds 2018, from *Folk* by Zoe Gilbert, used by permission of Bloomsbury Publishing Plc.

tale of transformation in the context of racial politics. The tale's origin story is an echo resting underneath the modern, declaring a radical subversion of the traditional whiteness of popular fairy tale. One might also argue, however, that the shift simultaneously protects the "classic" space as one of whiteness (see Breaux 2010), a social prejudice brought into starker relief in 2019 when Disney received public criticism for casting an African American actress as Ariel in their forthcoming live action adaption of *The Little Mermaid*. Much has been written elsewhere of the political agenda of *The Bloody Chamber* (see, for instance, Makinen 1992; Sheets 1991), but we can also cite more recent examples. Neil Jordan's reworking of Carter's story for the film *The Company of Wolves*, for instance, takes Carter's own universality and filters it through references that create a Northern Irish subtext (see McCann 2010). The other world in *Gingerbread* is a seedy underworld in which the gingerbread house is a place where "gingerbread girls" perform at "Breadcrumb balls" for the titillation of the adult community. In *Boy, Snow, Bird* we understand the wicked stepmother archetype as a myth perpetuated by patriarchy and through this examine the connection between physical abuse of women and male gaslighting. Snow herself—with her dark ebony hair and pale skin—represents a 1950s discourse surrounding racial passing; the revelation at the end of the novel of Boy's own immigrant heritage is related to her beginnings in a "mixed neighbourhood" (Oyeyemi 2014: 291). In such examples the setting of the tale exposes the limitations of the universal, as often in reality a *de facto* patriarchal whiteness; new spaces, in contrast, allow for the particularity of new voices.

TIME LAG

To think of this spatial politics invokes not merely a radicalized spatiality, but more explicitly a spatiotemporality. Space in traditional fairy tale is interwoven with a temporality that is equally straightforward; with "a preference for flatness and the linear. The fairy tale dispenses with an in-depth space *and* time structure" (Messerli 2005: 276; my emphasis). The modern reworking of the fairy tale is, in contrast, profoundly time lagged. Coined by postcolonial theorist Homi Bhabha to examine the disjunctive temporalities of postcolonial fiction, time lag is a temporal disruption that is always also "a spatial movement of cultural representation" (1992: 59). Encounter with time lag, Bhabha writes, "insists that any form of political emergence must encounter the *contingent place* from where its narrative *begins*" (1994a: 253). To be in different times, Bhabha is clear, is also to be in different spaces (256). Centered upon notions of what could be, or might have been (253), the alternative temporalities of time lag are also the possibilities for spaces that could emerge. As time moves forward and backward to disrupt teleological thinking and resonate past into present and future, so spaces are repeated, returned to, and rethought. Moreover, they are intimately entwined with the coterminous expression of historically separate events, as multiple spaces are put to work via a metonymic potentiality. This spatialized time lag is essential to those fictions that address the desire for simultaneously real and imagined spaces through the lens of multiple worlds, drawing attention to Nicolaisen's assertion that "past space makes past time possible" (1991: 13).

If Tolkien is the influential figure in terms of subcreation, then his literary nemesis C. S. Lewis is the master of time lag. Although there are earlier precedents for such disjunctive spatiotemporalities in science-fiction narratives such as H. G. Wells's *The Time Machine* (1895), it is Lewis who offers the most notable example in the context of fantasy. Unlike Wonderland, in which the "curious dream" explains why so little time passes during Alice's adventures, in *The Lion, the Witch and the Wardrobe* (1950) the shared experience of the Pevensie children instead reinforces the reality of the two worlds, and thus the existence of multiple spaces with different temporalities, where a whole lifetime in Narnia passes within a small passage of time in England. This differential is undoubtedly useful as a plot device, allowing Lewis's characters to live entire lives, and yet for them to remain children in England so that they can return again to Narnia at a much later date in *Prince Caspian* (1951), *The Horse and His Boy* (1954), and *The Last Battle* (1956). Yet beyond this Lewis's temporality serves to engage with real-world sociopolitical contexts. So it is that in *The Lion, the Witch and the Wardrobe* the Pevensie children can absorb the lessons of Narnia, yet return to enact these lessons with their wartime relevance in the real-world. Although we see little of what these lessons are in the children's subsequent appearances, nevertheless this "return" serves as provocation to apply the novel's explicit Christian values to British postwar society.

Contemporary tales employ time lag in a simultaneous rupturing of both spatiality and temporality, which does not merely update the tale and recreate its correlative space but also enacts a disrupted relationality. At the center of this interruption is the assertion that there is a difference between what space is and when it is, the boundary between the current moment and the moment inhabited being somehow severed. So it is in the penultimate story of Wood's *Diving Belles*, in which a discussion of the stars prompts the awareness that "they're not really there … they're in the past" (2012: 203). What can be seen, readers are told, is not what is now. Yet when the question in reply is to what those stars are like now, the answer is "Maybe the same" (203). It is not merely that the space we exist in may be a space of the past but also that the space we are in exists within a temporality the timeline of which is inherently unstable and outside definition. So in *Mr. Fox* the 1930s setting is accompanied by scenes in which emails are sent at a computer (Oyeyemi 2011: 156); in *Boy, Snow, Bird*, the space of Flax Hill, which endlessly rearranges itself, is also a space where the fairy-tale house of Snow is one where "there were no clocks, no real sense of time passing" (Oyeyemi 2014: 71). Likewise in the 2018 production of Massenet's *Cendrillon* by the British Opera House Glyndebourne, the temporal updating of "Cinderella" to a contemporary moment complete with mobile phones is destabilized by a dream structure that allows for recourse to timelessness. For its part, Grange Park Opera's 2019 production of the German composer Engelbert Humperdinck's *Hansel and Gretel* (1891–2), replaces the forest in its entirety with nineteenth-century Victorian London. Although the story is framed in conventional terms—the domestic space serving as a structural container that both begins and ends the narrative (Campagnaro 2017: 13)—what lies in between is a rejection of fairy tale's traditional abstract forest and cottage for the specificity of urban streetlamps and Dickensian sweet shops. Bhabha's example of time lag is Toni Morrison's *Beloved*, a text that itself plays on the concept of fairy tale with its own evocation of "once upon a time" ([1987] 2007: 119), and in which a metonymic substitution transforms a house into a slave ship. Likewise, in *Hansel and Gretel* the forest becomes a city, and the gingerbread house a sweet shop. Such metonymic substitution defies Nicolaisen's dictate that we must never forget that while folktale spaces exist metaphorically, they also exist precisely as what they are (1980: 16).

Time-lagged spatiality is essential to contemporary reworkings that use the fairy tale to interrogate existing dominant discursive positions. The ability in texts such as *The Bloody Chamber*, for example, to bring the gothic past into the present opens up the potential to interrogate politically laden spaces, particularly the domestic space and its conventional associations with unrecognized female labor. Equally, in Japanese artist Yanagi Miwa's photography cycle *Fairy Tale: Strange Stories of Women Young and Old* (2007), surrealist, black-and-white images reproduce classic fairy tales with an all-female cast of models. Each model is a child, often disguised as an old woman, placed into domestic spaces with their windows bricked up, crumbling walls, and decay. The temporal location of these spaces is unclear. Some look like seventeenth-century farmhouses, others like nineteenth-century gothic mansions, but in each case the women are contained and the outside is invisible. In her reading of Miwa's artistic reworking, Mayako Murai notes how in viewing Miwa's images "we are reminded that so many of the canonized fairy tales are set in either an enclosed domestic space or a complete wilderness, both separated from society" (2013: 248). Yet Miwa's unclear temporality is also a provocation to take such images into the present as much as to see them as a document on the past; our classical fairy-tale imaginaries as produced by canonical and dominant representations are an inheritance that we continue to live in contemporary gender relations.

MAGICAL COSMOPOLITANISM: ALL AT ONCE UPON A TIME

An ability to produce counter-discourse via space is implied by Bhabha's time lag, which is a variant of his own notion of the third space, his term for the space of hybridity in which there is no longer opposition but rather cultural translation. Bhabha's description of this space is of a political object "neither the one nor the other," which is importantly distinct from the notion of being both one and the other (1994a: 25). At the same time, Wilson's term for his own magical realist space is also the word hybrid, reflective of "the purely natural way in which abnormal, experientially impossible (and empirically unverifiable) events take place ... sudden folds crease the seemingly predictable, the illusive extratextual, surface" (1995: 220). This recognizes that although magical realism is a form of "in-betweenness" it is also a form of "all-at-onceness" (Zamora and Faris 1995: 6).

For Zamora and Faris, "all-at-onceness" produces a consequent "resistance to monological political and cultural structures" (Zamora and Faris 1995: 6). While much has been written on the counter-discursive potential of contemporary fairy tale, particularly in the context of feminism and queer theory, an awareness of spatial hybridity both adds to this criticism and takes it potentially into new territories. In particular, it suggests that to consider fairy-tale space in terms of an "other" is to create a no longer representative spatial binary between inside and outside. In *Grimm* the Wesen are associated with historic abuses of power, strikingly revealed when Nick watches archive footage of Hitler only to see him revealed as a Wesen on screen. While Nick has a standard police issue firearm, he battles Wesen via an arsenal of ancient weaponry and books of ancient lore found in his Aunt's trailer. The trailer exists thus in temporal flux, providing a space that connects Nick to a past in which he comes to understand the enchantments of the present. Yet what emerges from such understanding defies the spatial separation of monster and human. *Grimm* maintains the notion that the urban setting of the monstrous is crucial for its potential as a metaphorical other to be fully exploited, a strategy that show creator David Greenwalt repeats from his earlier production *Angel* (1999–2004), the *Buffy the Vampire Slayer* (1997–2003) spin-off. Unlike *Buffy*, *Angel* is set in contemporary Los Angeles, his explicit intention being to bring audiences into a world more "urban and gritty" rather than a space where "it's sunny and bright but bad terrible things happen" (Greenwalt n.d.). Yet whereas *Angel* might offer the "dark underside" (Upstone 2005: 102) of LA, in *Grimm* it is the entirety of Portland that is enchanted: Nick and his girlfriend live in a suburban housing estate while his nemesis, the police inspector, is pictured in a high-rise, downtown apartment. Thus as Juliana Lindsay notes, "the forest [in *Grimm*] is simply another setting. The majority of crimes and major occurrences of brutality through monsters are in cities, exposing a primal order to nature in *Grimm* in opposition to increased urban disorder in the Grimmverse" (2016: 5). Whilst *Buffy* has its Hellmouth, and *Angel* its downtown LA outside of the gaze of the glamour of West Hollywood, in *Grimm* the Wesen are hidden in plain sight, part of the fabric of everyday Portland life. The frequency with which Nick sees the Wesen emphasizes the undetected interweaving of human and monster. We move, therefore, away from the notion of marginal or liminal spaces, toward an intermingling where the conventional reading of the monster as a metaphorical other (Cohen 1996) is replaced with one in which a time-lagged sense of place is intrinsic to how such otherness is unraveled in favor of hybridity.

The role of temporality in such manipulations is further evidenced by the ABC show *Once Upon a Time* (2011–18), the epitome of Wilson's definition of magical realist space in which "there are two worlds, distinct and following dissimilar laws, that interpenetrate and interwind, all unpredictably but in a natural fashion" (1995: 222). *Once Upon a Time* begins from the premise that fairy-tale characters drawn from a wide range of both traditional tales and cinematic interpretations—particularly recent Disney animations—have been transplanted to the fictional location of Storybrooke, a picturesque small town in the actual world United States, but hidden by a magical border that, if crossed, strips inhabitants of their fairy-tale identities. The show follows the attempts of these characters firstly to uncover their pasts in a fairy-tale world, the Enchanted Forest, and then in subsequent seasons to battle various storybook villains who threaten the town not only in this world but also in others, including Oz and Neverland. Amidst the show's complex plotlines and convoluted story arcs, the unifying theme of the show—heavily influenced by revisionist narratives such as Gregory Maguire's *Wicked* (1995) and *Mirror, Mirror* (2003)—is the blurring of the traditional fairy tale's distinction between heroes and villains. The show's temporal manipulations create alternative spaces within each world in which characters are repeatedly relocated within the terms of these classic identifying tropes. In season five, episode one, for example, the show's heroine Emma Swan is transformed into "the Dark One" and dragged into the fairy-tale world. The episode begins in real-world Minneapolis in 1989, when a mysterious cinema usher warns a then-child Emma that when she is given the opportunity to remove Excalibur she must resist. The action then moves to the Enchanted Forest, in which the sword is removed by Arthur, and then to Storybrooke, where a stand-off under the town's clock (symbolic of the multiple timelines employed during the show) results in a portal that transports Snow White, the evil Queen Regina, Hook, dwarves, Robin Hood, and Prince Charming to the forest. This "transportation" involves Zelina (the wicked witch of the West) creating a cyclone that transports the inhabitants as passengers of the town restaurant, Granny's, literally bringing the two spaces together as the restaurant lands within the Enchanted Forest. In the forest, Emma meets an anthropomorphized version of the dark power she holds, but in the form of Rumpelstiltskin, the previous dark one who is at that moment also in a coma in Storybrooke. When these spaces and timelines align, Emma's turn to darkness is prevented by Hook's entreaty that "We can find another way, together. Look at us, heroes and villains together for you, because of you. And if we can overcome our demons, then so can you." The characters then enter Camelot, a further conflation as the mythological world now sits within that of the fairy tale. The episode then concludes with a scene "six weeks later" in which the inhabitants of Granny's land back in Storybrooke, with no memory of their time in Camelot or of Emma having been transformed into the Dark One.

The description of this single episode not only highlights the complex time lag involved in the show but also how the time lag serves the construction of a hybrid space that defies normative social constructs. Both the intermingling of hero and villain and the working together of those conventionally identified as heroes or as villains serves as a metaphor for the need to radically disrupt cultural identities, a correlative of Bhabha's reading of postcolonial discourse as a place where the writer enacts "translation of the meaning of time into the discourse of space" (1994b: 251). The same manipulation can be found in literary texts; in *Gingerbread*, for example, Druhástrana is a place where the history of England is studied, and the other world becomes a metaphor to examine migration discourse. In *Mr. Fox*, Mary and Mr. Fox produce the story of a Yoruba woman and an Englishman, set in Paris, and also a contemporary fairy tale—complete with traditional lack of specified location—in which there is no forest but rather a desert. The woman in the Paris story tells tales at the request of her ancestors, who remind her they are from "a different place and time" (Oyeyemi 2011: 89). In the time lag of *Mr. Fox*, Oyeyemi's Yoruba character indicates influence not only from Western fairy tales but also African Yoruba myth—the tradition that informs her work from her very first novel, *The Icarus Girl* (2005). In traditional African fairy tale, the division between worlds—particularly the world of the living and the world of the dead—is a common theme, seen in West African tales such as "The Girl who Stayed in the Fork of a Tree" and "The Market of the Dead" (Carter [1990, 1992] 2005). Oyeyemi's writing points in this regard to a conjunction of space with time in the service of a wider cultural politics: bringing together multiple traditions and thus through generic interventions, questioning discourses of cultural purity.

The Scottish writer Leila Aboulela captures such magical cosmopolitanism in her novel *Bird Summons* (2019). Set in the present day, the novel traces the interweaving stories of three women, Salma, Moni, and Iman, as they make a pilgrimage through the Scottish Highlands to the birthplace of a renowned Scottish Muslim woman, Lady Evelyn. On their journey, Iman is accompanied by the Hoopoe bird, who tells her a series of fairy-tale stories to guide her path, not only Middle Eastern stories but also Scottish myths. The Hoopoe serves as a metaphor for cultural translation—always there but "not entirely visible" (82), it is only in the "special place" of the Highlands that it emerges. In bringing these spaces together, Aboulela makes an explicit comment on the women's hybridity and opposes this to the notion of otherness. This is not limited to how they are seen by white British culture, but also is a questioning of their own self-othering, their conscious oppositions of real-world spaces as embodied in Iman's sense of the eastern crescent moon against the Scottish sky's pink twilight (81). Lady Evelyn, it is revealed, was raised in Algiers and Cairo and her childhood experience of "the sound of the azan" is carried back to Scotland to the "mauve mountains and glens ... all together, one and the same" (275). When Iman arrives at the women's hotel, she finds a cupboard full of costumes, and proceeds to spend the journey taking on different identities. So it is that a British Muslim woman—dressed at various points as the Little Mermaid, Princess Amidala from *Star Wars*, Cinderella, the White Witch, Cleopatra, and even a US army marine—wanders her way through an ecosystem where Scottish trees and lakes are the home of a Middle Eastern mythical bird. At the novel's dramatic climax, magic takes over and Moni is transformed into a human ball, Iman changed into a wild animal, and Salma consumed by a specter of her past lover, the three women finding themselves first in a fairy-tale forest and then in a fairy-tale house. When Salma's lover does not appear she observes the need to "back out, to search for him elsewhere, in another version of the past" (242). The past here is thus not a time but rather a place—a space to be moved out of, and an "elsewhere." In the wake of these transformations it is the Hoopoe who leads the women to Evelyn's home, drawing the women into a reworking of the mystic poem *Conference of the Birds* in which Farid ud din Attar leads the birds to the mythical Simurg. The nonlinear journey the women make thus represents Bhabha's time lag with a specifically cross-cultural emphasis, an enunciation of Bhabha's concept of the "black" space distinguished "from the Western sense of synchronous tradition" (1994a: 251).

Bird Summons reveals how the ancient nature of the natural landscape can be seen to evoke a time lag in which forest and sea are gateways between present and past, and thus construct a dialogue between both times and spaces with revelatory potential. The empowered landscape, with its strong pathetic fallacy, resists the easy psychological symbolism of the traditional tale in favor of something closer to Tolkien's sense that "Faerie contains many things besides elves and fays ... it holds the seas, the sun, the moon, the sky; and the earth, and all things that are in it: tree and bird, water and stone ... For the story-maker who allows himself to be 'free with' Nature can be her lover not her slave" (1947: 4. 20). In this way, the landscape becomes the originator of magic rather than a metaphor centered on the human. So it is that when one considers a magical cosmopolitanism, this concern exceeds the diversity of human subjects, in favor of an ecological matrix of posthuman hybridity. Such an approach is evident in *Folk*, where pathetic fallacy grants trees their own "held breath" (Gilbert 2018: 177) and where, in one story, a young fiddler is instructed to go out into the wild to undergo a rite of passage in which the song is to be drawn from the landscape. When the young girl finds her music, it comes from the sea cave she is drawn to during the ritual, and it "belongs to the cave" (136). Yet what is gained from the cave is not only the music it holds but also the revelation of her mother's murder. Like Friedrich Schlegel's "earth's colourful dream ... for the one who listens in secret" (1799) the cave offers a magical temporal relocation that is also a truth-telling.

This "truth" is emphasized equally by Maitland, whose *Gossip from the Forest* examines the recurring fairy-tale trope within the context of our contemporary understanding of deforestation; the forest, Maitland argues, is not merely the present space of our ecological investment, it is also the haunting of storytelling traditions that are protected within the natural spaces that hold their memories. Maitland's dislike of "modern technology" neglects dynamic digital storytelling cultures, and her work posits false oppositions between technology and ecosystem that repeat an anthropocentric imaginary of "nature." At the same time, her work also advances a powerful transformation of the scientific argument for conservation into a cultural argument: that what is protected is not merely the ancient woodland as connection to the past but that woodland as gateway to the voices of that past.

A more sensitive and self-conscious engagement is offered in Wood's *Diving Belles*. The stories in the cycle capture a time lag of place as gateway, in which there is "the memory of wind in the fraying edges of things" (Wood 2012: 193). In the final story of the collection a droll teller ruminates on his hatred of newcomers who talk of the place he has inhabited for hundreds of years. The teller is overwhelmed by the gentrification of the town, filled with new houses, local people leaving for places with cheaper rents. Whereas "he used to be able to locate exactly where he was," the overwhelming force of change has watered down the narrative: "The stories were embedded in the landscape and he followed them, from that cove to that hill to that ruin—it was all mapped out. When he looked around him now, he saw only flickers: in that stone shaped like a giant table, in that gnarled tree, nothing more than flickers" (219). Such associations are prevented from slipping into nostalgia, however, as the droll teller also finds that his "authentic" tales are drawn rather from television shows, and that the loss of the familiar landscape leaves him not only unsettled but also "relieved." Wood therefore identifies simultaneously with the ecocritical desire to affirm the value of the ecosystem, but also the problematic use of that ecosystem by conservative agendas in relation to nationalism and anti-immigration sentiment. When the story concludes with a utopian moment of renewal, it is associated not with an abstract of the Romantic sublime but rather with the very specific Cornish landmark of the mine, with its connections to working-class life: "He could hear the story creeping out of the mine towards him ... It was taking its time ... The bell tolled louder and louder and now here he was beginning again; somehow, despite everything, he was beginning again" (223). What is cosmopolitan here is not merely the incorporation of human subjects but also the landscapes into which those subjects have poured their stories.

CONCLUSION

In Kawabata Yasunari's novella *Nemureru Bijo* (1961) (*House of the Sleeping Beauties*, 1997), Charles Perrault's "Sleeping Beauty" is updated to the present day, the castle transformed into a house in which aging men pay to sleep with—but never sexually interfere with—young girls who have been drugged into unconsciousness to provide the service. Enchantment in this context is translated into the pleasure of men at the expense of nameless women, who exist only as bodies for the exploration not only of male desires but also of their subjectivity. Such narratives illustrate that reworkings of the archetypal spaces of traditional tales are not synonymous with the disruption of dominant discourse. Conversely, radical subversions via fairy tale may occur without a dramatic revision of their spatiality. Donoghue's *Kissing the Witch*, for example, maintains the traditional tale length and abstract spatiality in combination with a queer gender politics that asks readers to reconsider the signifying power of domestic space in particular.

Such examples remind us that no straightforward correlation is to be made between space and politics. Yet what is clear is that spaces are implicated in a rethinking of the nature of enchantment: a placement of the magical within the everyday landscape, but also a reappraisal of the forms such magic takes—from the presence of spirits, to the monstrosity of humans, to the untamed might of the sea, to the fake grass an island in Mallorca. Moreover, where form creates additional scope in the extended narrative of the novel, short-story cycle, opera, or television series, fairy tales are enfolded into a spatiality that offers at least the potential for spaces to contribute to new ways of thinking both about fairy tales themselves and about their signifying power.

If the fairy tale made real is a strategy in part for the incorporation of the other, it is also an operation that exists in part through the challenge to audiences to accept either multiple universes and/or thirdspace spatialities that question the existence of that other. To navigate the texts discussed here, readers must not only adopt Tolkien's mode of belief but also do the work required to make sense of multiple intersecting spatiotemporal disruptions. These are texts that not only create space for the other within the real but also take the reader through a process of material engagement with the text that challenges conventional modes of thinking. The "realness" of space in the texts discussed here contributes to the return of fairy tale to its traditional adult audience, to the correction of the "accident of our domestic history" (Tolkien 1947: 11) that resigned fairy tale to the nursery. In this "realness," writers and artists use fairy tale to create speculative realities rich with ethical and political provocations. In the climate of renewed environmental concerns, fairy-tale space argues for a landscape that must be protected for its cultural importance, for its relevance to a transformative practice of imagination, and for a resonance that defies market interests. As a space of hybridity and temporal disjunction, fairy-tale space equally represents intercultural dialogue, which challenges separations of race, gender, ethnicity, and ability. The space of fairy tale today is thus often radical, presenting an imagined world both real and unreal, which asks us to question our own relation to materiality, and which in its incitements presents a powerful argument for the form's continued creative power and cultural relevance.

CHAPTER SEVEN

Socialization

Traditional Wonder Tales and Other Guides for Growing Up

JILL TERRY RUDY

I remember that my Grandma Smith took me to see Disney's *Sleeping Beauty* (1959) at the new Fox Cottonwood Mall Theater, Holladay, Utah, re-released in 1970.[1] What comes to mind now are the songs and the bumbling, caring fairies. It's the only time I remember going to a movie with my grandmother, although I had been attending the Saturday matinee in my hometown almost every week with my Terry cousins for three years. With Disney's *Snow White* (1937) re-released the summer of 1967 when I was four, my cousin and I still remember that she took me out by the candy counter because I was so terrified by some early scenes that I couldn't stay in the movie. Maleficent was less scary, and I was older, so I survived *Sleeping Beauty*.

In *Tales of Innocence and Experience* (2003), Eva Figes writes lyrically about sharing fairy tales with her young granddaughter. In part, she accomplishes this by turning a picture book into a personal narrative:

> I am this child, her story is familiar as my own, seems to be my own. I know each tree, every sunlit clearing, the echo of birdsong high in the canopy, beyond it glimpses of blue sky. I tell her about finding pine cones, and soft patches of dark green moss, and how much the little girl and her grandmother loved each other.
>
> (Figes 2003: 7)

In this haunting memoir, Figes portrays the intergenerational sharing of knowledge, particularly how her innocent childhood and beautiful early experiences with her grandparents have been wrenched from her by the Holocaust. And yet, they remain. She surmises, "My life is not a fairy tale, and the child who escapes the forest cannot possibly be the unknowing child who was sent into it. But perhaps, the beloved dead do watch over us, as they so often do in Grimms' stories" (Figes 2003: 182–3). Figes's storytelling becomes a thoughtful walk among generations.

In the introduction to *Voices of Fire* (2014), her insightfully designed study of traditional knowledge, place, and literature, kuʻualoha hoʻomanawanui also shares a resounding experience of her grandmother's stories:

> I knew it was time to present my haʻi ʻōlelo to the group, here in Kaimū in the middle of the night under a bright Māhealani moon illuminating the shimmering sea misted by Pele's steam billowing off the ocean before us; the rumble of the ocean and the relentless hiss of lava pouring into it were deafening. I recalled the stories of my kūpuna who were kamaʻāina to this place, their land just beyond Kaimū in Kapaʻahu and Poupou, areas already reclaimed by Tūtū Pele. I remembered visiting Punaluʻu, a freshwater pond renamed "Queen's Bath" by settlers in the twentieth century. I retold the stories my tūtū told to me, about going upland on a donkey to the Poupou lands, a place renamed "Royal Gardens" by developers, where her tūtū pā (grandfather) tended their mala kalo (dryland taro gardens), and her tūtū mā (grandmother) sat beneath the shade of the hala trees and wove hats, "double-piko style" (with two centers on the crown), from the hala leaves she gathered there. I recounted the genealogical connections to other lines of her ʻohana (family). I told how it took them two days to walk to Hilo, first traveling ma uka (inland and uphill) to ʻŌlaʻa, where they spent the night with cousins, before walking to Hilo town on the sea the following morning. When I was pau (done), I felt a slight stirring of the cool breeze wafting the scent of limu (seaweed) and salt inland from the undulating sea, causing the leaves of the hala groves around us to chatter. Ke haʻa lā Puna i ka makani—Puna was dancing in the breeze. A soft light rain sprinkled my arms and face, as one of my classmates exclaimed with awe, "E nānā aʻe!" (Look up!). We all looked up. The Māhealani moon was full and bright, the stars sparkled and glistened, a shimmering night rainbow arched across the deep aubergine sky, and not a single cloud was anywhere in sight.
>
> (2014: xxviii–xxiv)

Opening her book with chants and prayers for permission, hoʻomanawanui frames the study by her relationship with her *tūtū wahine* (grandmother) Sarah Poniʻala Kakelaka, which also establishes a way she learned to connect land, ancestors, and stories: "Despite my tūtū's urban upbringing and fierce adherence to a Christian worldview, there were always the moʻolelo (stories and history) of our ʻāina, lovingly told, stories of our kūpuna, stories that were told so that we would remember them so they would continue to live within us" (hoʻomanawanui 2014: xiii). Context and wholeness, including place, matter in sharing such stories.

Figes's and hoʻomanawanui's perspectives and insights frame this overview of socialization and traditional stories because children's learning depends on these intergenerational, participatory relationships. Academically, socialization is a term related to initiation and education, such as inducting new teachers into the classroom or doctoral students into intellectual disciplines. In critical studies, it refers more to enforcing dominant behavioral and ideological norms. With literary and social science fields, conversely, socialization usually refers to preparing children for a place in society. Colloquial equivalents involve teaching, learning, and child-rearing. Tacking between academic and colloquial understanding, this chapter considers socialization in relation to the guidance offered through traditional stories—in particular, wonder tales—that reaffirms conventions and subversively posits different possibilities. This participatory socialization is significant because stories and storytellers lead children to find their place, navigate their way through this mortal world, and fulfill their (happily) ever afters.

WHAT IS AT STAKE WITH SOCIALIZATION, FAIRY TALES, AND WONDER TALES

Recently my niece and my dad asked me what I was working on, and when I mentioned writing about how fairy tales influence children, they enquired why that matters. I responded that if fairy tales teach children to expect to be princesses that's one thing, but if they teach them to solve thorny problems along the way to growing up, then that's something else.

Although rarely appearing in scholarly titles or indexes, socialization nonetheless remains a deep, even founding, concern of contemporary fairytales studies. As stories point children, and adults, toward their place in society, scholars register concern if those stories portray limiting social roles. Elizabeth Wanning Harries asserts that tales "have designs" at "defining proper behavior and enforcing codes of conduct" (2015: 1). This critique examines claims that children's stories and literature impose social codes as preset givens.

Many scholars explicitly attribute such socializing power to fairy tales. No one does this more boldly than Jack Zipes, who explains that when modern childhood emerged in the eighteenth century so too did stories that enforced rules and roles. "Socialization through fairy tales," Zipes argues, entails the "internalization of specific values and notions of gender" (2012a: 9). He examines how the collections of Charles Perrault, the Grimms, and Hans

Christian Andersen use stories to "operate ideologically to indoctrinate children so that they will conform to dominant social standards that are not necessarily established in their behalf" (33). Elaborating on this critical position, three additional US-German professors with research interests in folklore, fairy tales, and children's literature, Maria Tatar (1987), Ruth Bottigheimer (1987), and Donald Haase (1993), all produced books examining the Grimm brothers' editorial practices and socializing influence. The tales, they concluded, trained children by directing behaviors and mores related to sexuality, violence, and social status.

Fairy tales involve socialization primarily because the genre affiliates directly with growing up. Not only do people encounter tales in childhood, but fairy tales often are about youth setting out in life. David Buchan writes, "Centrally the genre is concerned with the maturation of the individual" (1990: 979). "The Story of a Boy Who Went Forth to Learn Fear" (ATU 326; see Chapter 8, this volume, for a discussion of the ATU Tale Type Index) comes to mind. Included in the 1819 version of the Grimms' *Kinder und-Hausmärchen*, and translated by D. L. Ashliman (2001), the tale follows a "stupid" youngest son who does not understand why people shudder in fear. When asked about earning his bread, he oddly mentions overcoming this shuddering deficiency as a way to provide. Sent away by his father, he ends up accepting the challenge to stay in a haunted castle for three nights, faces demon cats, dead men, and a monstrous old man, wins the princess in marriage, and only learns to shudder when his wife's maid throws minnows on him.

Jim Henson's *The StoryTeller* (1987) version, meanwhile, takes a more romantic turn when the youth only shudders in fear as his sweetheart revives from a coma (Figure 7.1). The fairy-tale protagonist faces challenges and reaps rewards, large and small. Other classic tales like "Cinderella" (ATU 510A), "Snow White" (ATU 709), "Sleeping Beauty" (ATU 410), and "Beauty and the Beast" (ATU 425) also feature young characters facing trials with family and society on the way to establishing their own happier futures—in various ways through various versions.

While the socializing power in fairy tales may seem obvious, however, the sociohistorical interest in tales told, written, and screened in discrete times and places also implies great variety in what wonder tales mean and do for the people who share them. As Pauline Greenhill and Sidney Eve Matrix wisely observe, "Each traditional fairy tale telling forms a copy for which there is no original" (2010: 1). On the one hand, it appears that fairy tales force children into normative social roles and behaviors, while on the other, no tale has a standard version, and thus stories and storytelling transform, and are transformed by, changing situations, values, and cultures. Considered as a European narrative form, especially in popularized versions, the fairy tale has participated in authoritarian processes. But, considered as traditional

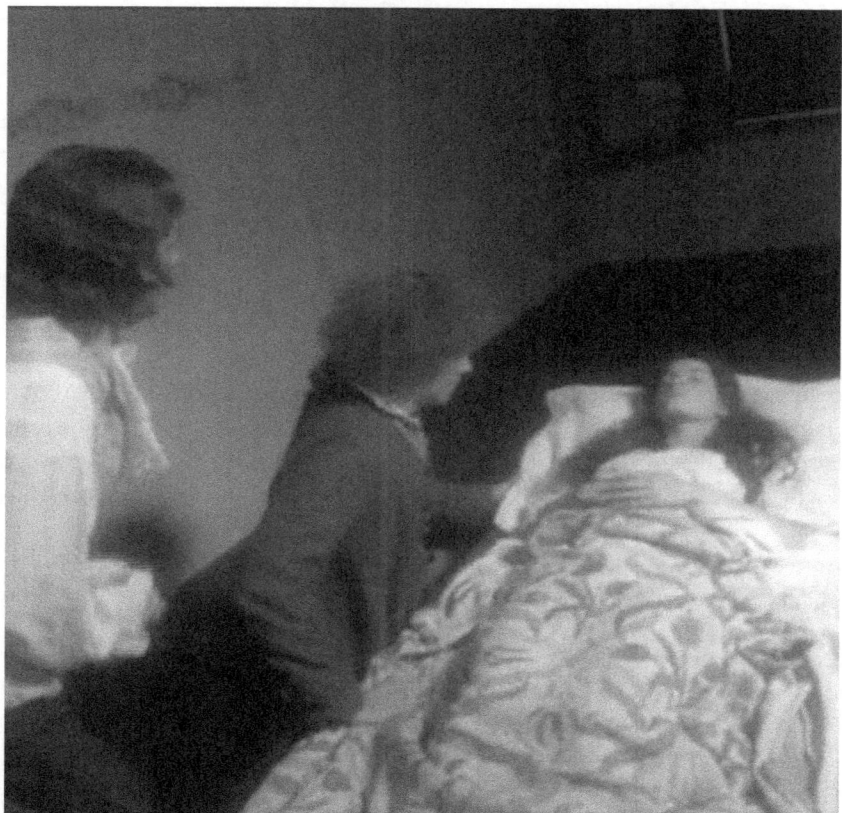

FIGURE 7.1: Still from "Fearnot" (1987), an episode of Jim Henson's television series *The StoryTeller*. Fearnot matures when he learns to shudder in fear of losing his sweetheart.

narratives developed and shared in distinctive cultures over time and space, these stories have more to contribute to the growth of human beings and the perpetuation of relationships extending from humans to other creatures, nature, and spirituality. Attentive scholarship adds communalist views to earlier discourses on fairy-tale socialization and places fairy tales in context with other wonder-tale traditions and cultures (Haase 2010; Teverson 2019). To distinguish from discourses privileging Western views and European history, furthermore, many scholars study the traditional narratives known as fairy tales by their local names and knowledge systems, such as moʻolelo, mytheuousi, skázki, while the terms wonder tale or Märchen serve for more general inclusivity (Teverson 2019: 10–12). Because of the ongoing popularity and import of wondrous stories, other narrative genres involving myths, legends, fantasy, and speculative fiction remain important to understand and expand fairy-tale socialization. These genre-mixing connections are crucial to seeing how wonder tales relate with children's and young adult (YA) literature and popular media.

Amidst these conversations and genre-mixing, I reiterate the intergenerational significance of storytelling as a performance accomplished with children, not only as indoctrination for them. I assert the relevance of traditional stories with the capacity to inculcate, perpetuate, and innovate children's knowledge, values, and competence in addition to demarcating capital and social hierarchies. For these reasons, I include wonder tales in the title of this section and refer to "fairy-tale socialization" when alluding to dominating discourses. This chapter considers canonical fairy tales such as "Little Red Riding Hood" (ATU 333) and Walt Disney's *Snow White and the Seven Dwarfs* (1937) along with lesser known stories. While tales at their domineering and commodified worst alienate and demean social relations, at their utopian best, and in the realities and potentialities of daily practices, wonder tales not only teach independence and autonomy but also validate collective knowledge and belonging in place.

PSYCHOANALYTIC APPROACHES AND FAIRY-TALE SOCIALIZATION OF CHILDREN'S DRIVES AND NEEDS

Psychoanalytic approaches undergird socialization conversations in fairy-tale studies not only because Sigmund Freud (1856–1939) and Carl Jung (1875–1961) find key concepts illustrated in traditional tales but also because their theories still influence an understanding of child development and family relations. Andrew Teverson explains primary perspectives on fairy tales and the unconscious:

> For the Freudian, the unconscious is concerned with the formation of the human subject as the locus of repressed forces and the latent meanings of fairy tales must therefore be sought in the repressed unconscious desires of particular human subjects. For the Jungian, the unconscious has a collective dimension, so the meaning of fairy tales must be discovered in the grand universal archetypes that have shaped the thinking of all humanity from the earliest stages of consciousness.
>
> (2013: 111)

Both Freudian and Jungian views involve symbolism where key objects mean more than outward appearance. Both views see tales as related to sublimated truths about individual and social needs and desires.

Because Freud attentively listened to clients and made intertextual connections with their reported dreams and problems, his work involves interpretive moves that find fairy tales explanatory. Freud schematizes human development into psychosexual stages and theorizes human motivations in relation with the pleasure and reality principles and the libido and death drives

(Reubins 2014: 16–21). A notable example involves a woman who dreams of a "curious manikin" who dances around a brown room. The woman associates the little man with her father-in-law and with Rumpelstiltskin. Freud interprets the dream as antithetically connecting the story with the woman's real concerns (Teverson 2013: 111–13). Freud's associates and followers often make universalizing claims for fairy-tale symbolism, which have affected greatly the public's awareness and understanding of the fairy tale's role in socialization by schematizing developmental benchmarks based on psychosexual assumptions, but in practice, Freud himself sought to understand dream symbolism in the context of his patients' experiences and upbringing.

Jung's views are applied most directly to fairy-tale socialization by the Swiss psychoanalyst Marie-Louise von Franz (1915–98). While relatable to individuals, von Franz argues that "the kind of fairy tale that expresses collective structures touches the emotions more deeply [and] stays better in one's memory" (1997: 16). In studies such as *Interpretation of Fairytales* (1970) and *Archetypal Patterns in Fairy Tales* (1997), von Franz reviews basic Jungian principles as they relate to the longevity and applicability of fairy tales, and promotes the view that while "Jung built up his concepts of shadow, animus and anima, and Self from looking at the single individual ... a fairy tale is not that. A fairy tale is not simply the tale of a personal experience ... It was something that had to fit the psyche of the whole collective" (1997: 14–15). In her analysis of the "Twelve Dancing Princesses" tale type (ATU 306), von Franz focuses on a Danish version that includes only one princess who wears out twelve shoes each night. Von Franz sees the task at hand as one that entails moving forward and taking opportunities, using valuable objects such as the stick of invisibility and the ball of autonomous movement (1997: 38). Additionally, motifs in the fairy tale such as the white woman, golden needle, three forests, princess, troll, dinner, and dancing receive analysis, with von Franz concluding that the tale shows how work with the unconscious relates to acknowledging one's true life situation. Unlike Freudian approaches that assume all important issues with which adults must grapple originate in childhood, von Franz's psychoanalytic approach suggests work with the unconscious also involves adults in fairy-tale socialization.

Influenced by Freud and Jung, Bruno Bettelheim produced the most popular theory of fairy-tale socialization in his highly influential *The Uses of Enchantment* (1976). Vanessa Joosen (2011) acknowledges the continuing international reach of Bettelheim's claims and analyzes how they are utilized and contested in contemporary creative works and scholarship. Astutely aimed at a general audience, Bettelheim takes the Grimm versions of classic tales as the originals that must not be altered, or even illustrated, because they innately speak to children's deepest Freudian conflicts such as sibling rivalry and oedipal desires. As more adults were finding fairy tales to be outdatedly dangerous, especially for young girls' development, Bettelheim's popular perspective on fairy-tale power to magically guide children through life's problems has proven stubbornly appealing.

Some lament Bettelheim's views on the grounds that they validate the behavior of authoritarian adults while blaming children for greedy, excessive behaviors and needs. While admiring these/his/psychoanalytic interpretations, Alan Dundes (1991) takes aim at Bettelheim's slapdash scholarly standards in "Bruno Bettelheim's Uses of Enchantment and Abuses of Scholarship." Tatar finds his interpretations remain popular because they view children as passive and justice as vengeful (1992: xxvii). *The Uses of Enchantment*, thus, engages adult readers with what Tatar recognizes as "our own culture's thinking about children" (1992: xxv) and fails to locate the tales in their social and historical context. The book's continuing positive reception indicates that fairy-tale socialization supports belief in story's power to magically dissipate evil and wrongs, address unconscious inner turmoil, all while affirming children's ability to meet the trials and tribulations of growing up if they read the right tales. At the same time, however, the universalizing tendencies of psychoanalytic scholarship decontextualize fairy tales from their social moorings and overlook the ideological and political implications of the tales' latent and manifest values.

IDEOLOGICAL CONCERNS, THE CIVILIZING PROCESS, AND SOCIOHISTORICAL APPROACHES

Where psychoanalytic approaches promote the therapeutic good that fairy tales accomplish for children's inner conflicts, feminists identify constricting messages in what these stories do (Joosen 2011). Zipes also highlights the importance of countercultural approaches of the 1960s when West German "writers and critics gradually came to regard" fairy tales as fictions that indoctrinate "children to learn fixed roles and functions within bourgeois society, thus curtailing their free development" (2012a: 58). These approaches recognize stories themselves as socializing agents that teach children their place and control their aspirations. The ideological debates about what fairy tales have taught children promote putting fairy tales into sociohistorical context while unearthing and critiquing their socializing messages. These approaches advocate individual and social transformation through tales more than just therapeutic effects.

Feminist approaches to fairy tales consider how tales may afford active, heroic role models or may reinforce more limiting views on female agency. An important exchange about the genre between Alison Lurie and Marcia K. Lieberman emblematizes these different approaches. In her seminal essay "Some Day My Prince Will Come: Female Acculturation through the Fairy Tale" (1972), published during widespread debates about how gender identity develops, Lieberman asserts that fairy-tale patterns "undoubtedly played a major role in forming the sexual role concept of children" (1972: 384). She rejects Lurie's optimistic claim, advanced in her essay "Fairy Tale Liberation" (1970), that folk and fairy tales offer plentiful examples of active heroines on the grounds that those alternative stories are found in academic collections and do not circulate widely, as Andrew Lang's anthologies and Disney's fairy-tale movies do. Ruth Bottigheimer's content analysis of the Grimms' collection in *Grimms' Bad Girls and Bold Boys* (1987) tends to confirm Lierberman's assessment; both find ample evidence that these fairy tales portray active male protagonists and dutiful females who wait for rescue. Other specialists in German literature and folklore also take up the issues of socialization to specify how Märchen create such powerful effects and provide context for these arguments.

The history of European fairy-tale anthologies becomes a crucial research area for nascent fairy-tale studies because scholars associate print collections with the emergence of childhood, children's literature, and shifting class structures—all implicated in what some refer to as the civilizing process, and others call modernity. Fairy tales also serve as a founding canonical genre in the earlier nineteenth-century emergence of folklore studies, where they were associated with romantic nationalism and philological knowledge more than with psychological, literary, and personal development (Bauman and Briggs 2003; Bendix 1997). In *National Dreams* (2003), Jennifer Schacker also studies how nineteenth-century tale collections after the Grimms create and perpetuate distinctions between oral, peasant cultures, on the one hand, and literate, modern ones, on the other. Thus, stagist cultural views come to correspond with folklore and early fairy-tale studies, relating peoples and cultures with a scale of savagery, barbarism, and civilization. This also applies to fairy-tale socialization because childhood historically emerges as a process of passing through these civilizing stages. Notably, indigenous and other alternative views of childhood and human development do not appear in this initial sociohistorical contextualizing of fairy-tale scholarship.

The civilizing process associated with fairy-tale socialization reinforces westernized values and practices of patriarchy and materialism, while also championing individualism and autonomy. Following Norbert Elias's formulation, Zipes argues that the civilizing process fosters stable political states because it encourages adherence to customs and mores, and self-restraint that supports the "power of ruling classes" (2012a: 19–20). Tales may intervene in the inculcation of civilizing values, as is the case in the work of the late seventeenth-century French salon writers, or they may promote bourgeois roles and behaviors, as Zipes sees happening with the Grimms (19, 58). In important areas of individual development and social organization, Zipes understands folk and fairy tales as always "concerned with sex roles, social class, and power" (21). Such concerns mirror ideological approaches of the late twentieth century.

Fairy tales contribute to this civilizing process as part of children's literature and education through the stories' content and through values emphasized by authors and editors. Since the 1980s, the prominent fairy-tale scholars have endeavored to show this by contextualizing collections and providing analytical readings of specific tales. Zipes's (1983) study of "Little Red Riding Hood," for example, charges Perrault with restricting the protagonist's ability to act for herself while reinforcing the wolf's violent, sexually domineering role. Comparably, the various editions of *Kinder und Hausmärchen* (*Children's and Household Tales*) provide ample material for examining how the Grimms collected tales are emended and altered to induce children's fear, increase female passivity, reduce sexual license, enhance violent punishments, and reward dutiful work (Bottigheimer 1987; Haase 1993; Tatar 1992; Zipes 2012a). Scholars start with the assumption that earlier collections, including Giambattista Basile's *Lo cunto de le cunti* (*The Tale of Tales*, 1634–6), retain the more bawdy, unrestricted, folk versions of canonical tales (Tatar 1992: 39–42; Zipes 2012a).[2] This scholarly work contextualizes the civilizing process as it emerges with a European interest in literary fairy tales and with concern for children's instruction, literacy, and bourgeois social standing.

Reception and reading practices also matter crucially in understanding how this civilizing process happens, though at present our knowledge concerning the formative influence of fairy tales on children and their futures needs more research and evidence. Reception theory, as a result, remains an underutilized approach in fairy-tale studies. Haase observes, "Although scholars can demonstrate how fairy tales have been intentionally manipulated to serve in the processes of socialization and constructing gender, we have a much more difficult time documenting personal responses of recipients and the genre's actual influence on their attitudes and behaviors" (2000: 36–8). To address this in part, Tatar's *Enchanted Hunters* (2009) shows how fairy tales and other children's literature help readers make meaning with stories and find their place in society. Autoethnographic methods also remain a vital way to understand how fairy tales actually inculcate attitudes and affect behaviors over a lifetime (Bacchilega and Rieder 2014; Sawin 2014; Stone 2008).

Psychoanalytic and ideological approaches to fairy-tale socialization assume that children absorb the messages about identity and life possibilities portrayed in bedtime stories, books, and other media, though how this civilizing process actually works is difficult to pinpoint. Fairy-tale studies has centered on big ideas related to the civilizing process and ideological messages, but analysis of the interactions of specific people and groups with specific tales have not received as much attention. Certainly, the ways wonder tales prepare children for their place in life will be understood better with more dialogic approaches. Scholarly and creative works, such as Figes's lyrical memoir discussed above or Cherie Dimaline's YA novel *The Marrow Thieves* (2017), portray situated interactions of people and tales, and such projects deserve more attention. Equally, engagements with popular culture, including fandoms, afford tantalizing possibilities for such study (Hay and Baxter 2014; Kustriz 2019). When some fairy-tale versions achieve wide distribution through mass-media channels and franchising, the socializing stakes feel electrically charged.

DISNEY, THE CULTURE INDUSTRY, AND FAIRY-TALE SOCIALIZATION THROUGH MARKETED CONTENT

Anyone who has taught Zipes's "Breaking the Disney Spell" (1999) quickly learns how attached many students are to the Disney version. Some students admit not knowing any other fairy tales; some profess their early self-promotion from Disney to canonical collections and bounteous YA adaptations found in classrooms, public libraries, Scholastic book sales, and Goodreads recommendations. Some acknowledge that their loved ones always provided them with books, usually lavishly illustrated. Some appreciate a new perspective on why Disney movies bother them. Many find Zipes's portrayal of Disney as narcissistic and his movies as manipulative to be disturbing and unconvincing. One of my graduate students admitted the essay's merits, and then went on to claim convincingly that after an apocalypse, the Disney version would emerge in oral storytelling because fairy tales would be needed and Disney "rules" (Dresden 2013). No one disputes Zipes's claim that Disney's American versions of tales by the Grimms and Perrault have become globally dominant in terms of shaping how fairy tales are conceived and received by children.

Critical concern about Disney's influence peaks at the turn of the twenty-first century in terms of socialization and also American cultural imperialism and late capitalism. This configuration of corporate conglomeration propels the Disney versions' global influence (Shickel 1997; Wasko 2001). As Zipes observes, Disney represents "American ideology—its populism, Puritanism, elitism, and consumerism—and he felt those values should be spread throughout the world by all his products" (2012a: 209). The premier of Disney's *Snow White and the Seven Dwarfs* (1937) indicates the early marketing machinery. The animated feature not only involves watching at a theater, with its premier at Radio City Music Hall adding Broadway cache to Hollywood glamor, but also purveying books, phonograph records, and toys.[3] Where some movie producers rejected television as a competitor, Disney recognized that TV could promote his films and other projects, especially Disneyland (Telotte 2004). Theme parks further corporatize and capitalize experience itself, and this is the socializing move that concerns the ideologically attuned. Discussing online parodies, Cristina Bacchilega notes that Disney Studios remains "key to the image of the fairy tale in popular cultural memory" that is now both pushed against and almost inescapable (2013: 11). Lynda Haas and Shaina Trapino report that Disney publishing alone reaches "eighty-five countries in seventy-five languages" (2018: 275). By sheer popularity, Disney serves as a synecdoche for all the ways the culture industry packages and pervades contemporary experience, especially growing up.[4]

Mass communication involves capital in ways that industrialize culture, increasing distribution and audiences while altering social relations in favor of making money. As I've stated, people are communicative omnivores who share tales, and other messages, in old and new technologies (2018b: 17). Telling tales and reading books does not disappear with portraying fairy tales in movies, on television, in toys, games, and across the internet; though, as is indicated by Zipes's use of the term, "culture industry," rather than "popular culture," these acts of tale telling are increasingly the outcome of organized production that recreates and disseminates fairy tales for money. More specifically, many children now access fairy tales through an adaptation industry that recasts tales in multiple media, products, and venues (Murray 2012). Zipes describes what is at stake, "Each time we think we come close to recognizing who we are and what we can do with our immense talents and imagination, we are blocked because, as [Walter] Benjamin suggests, we stumble against those market forces that make commodities out of our lives" (1997: 138). Rather than being socialized for sharing talents and imagination, commercialized societies, through Disney fairy tales and other myriad products, merely provide children with "a sense of how to consume and be consumed by enchanting commodities" (127). Although commoditized, popular fairy tales still provide more than consumerist messages especially because tales circulate in various versions and link people and ideas over time and space (Hamer 2018; Yoshinaga 2018). And yet, the alienating dissociations circulate far, and industrialized culture rarely satisfies needs for creativity and belonging—capacities not slaked by purchased belongings or experiences.

Producers of the myriad fairy-tale products aimed at children and family audiences demonstrate some creativity by sheer magnitude, while the consumerist impulses also proliferate. The overall concern about princess culture and how girls grow up is articulated in Peggy Orenstein's study *Cinderella Ate My Daughter: Dispatches from the Front Lines of the New Girlie-Girl Culture* (2011), in which the marketing of princess iconography to young girls is analyzed. A representative example of this may be found in the 2006 animated film *Barbie in the 12 Dancing Princesses* directed by Greg Richardson and produced by Mattel Entertainment. A doll shaped like a woman rather than a baby, since her launch in 1959, Barbie epitomizes consumerist socialization because the product itself images how girls could, and should, grow up. Attempting to address feminist backlash over the doll's impossible measurements by introducing over 100 different career Barbies, racial concerns with various plastic hues, and consumerist charges with tag lines about helping girls achieve potential, Barbie serves as a harbinger of socializing concerns that stretch from the United States across the globe.

Making movies to connect dolls with story worlds further directs the marketer's message and highlights the contemporary need for storytelling. Popular stories with the cache of tradition resonate widely (Foster and Tolbert 2016). The Barbie movies indicate that a toy company such as Mattel must participate in media production and storytelling to promote sales. Facing competition from the sexualized Bratz dolls, and two years after the Disney Princess line launched,[5] the first Barbie direct-to-video movie appeared. According to Lisa Orr, adding "content" with the doll "meant relying less on the girls' own imaginations and more on telling them how to play" and showing their parents and relatives what to buy (2009: 13). Given market pressures, Barbie's becoming a computer-generated imagery (CGI)-animated actress in direct-to-video fairy-tale ballets seems somehow a more inevitable career move than her 2004 US presidential run.

The content of *Barbie in the Twelve Dancing Princesses* adeptly confronts the civilizing process while making consumerist demands. Product developers and marketers have a great deal of material to work with since there are twelve protagonists along with Barbie/Genevieve's love interest Ken/Derek the cobbler. Each character comes branded with a special hobby or skill, which requires accessories, along with a unique gem stone. Where von Franz invests several characters and objects in "The Dancing Princess" story with archetypal meaning (1997: 38), the Barbie movie focuses on promoting new products. And yet, the plotline and dialogue of the movie directly refute the propriety and confining social roles of the civilizing process. The widowed king brings in his cousin, the villain, to make his daughters "proper princesses." To take over the kingdom, Duchess Rowena slowly administers poison to the king and restricts the girls' activities in the name of giving them "proper guidance." Fostered by memories of their dead mother, eventually the girls discover a magical kingdom where they dance and enjoy themselves until Rowena tries to trap them and complete her rule over the kingdom. The evil plot is thwarted when Genevieve uses the proper skills taught by Rowena to send her dancing curse back on her and her henchman. Finally, the king states the takeaway message that rather than being proper ladies, "You are each special, beautiful princesses, and you'll do great things in your own way." Linda Dégh has shown how magic is latently for sale with contemporary fairy-tale advertising and discourse (Dégh 1994); in this case, too, the manifest content of the Barbie movie links beauty and autonomy with the necessary magical playthings for growing up to achieve unique potential. The empowering message seems intended to mask the consumerist agenda.

Other discourses such as parental teachings, religious values, academic anthologies, and fandoms attempt to compete with the pervasive culture industry messages of individualism and monetized success. Anne Kustriz discusses a continuum of fan activity from "as is" connoisseurship that venerates the popular culture object to "creative fandom" that sees the object as open-ended and seeks to build community (2018: 343). Sandra Beckett's thoughtful studies of "Little Red Riding Hood" introduce English-speaking readers to hundreds of international versions of the story, revealing that the production of picture books (Basu 2018), YA and adult retellings (Kérchy 2018), and university or small press imprints also participates in, or alongside, the culture industry (Beckett 2002). Beckett's work also speaks to changing perspectives on the tale because her organizing categories focus on the interaction of Red Riding Hood with the wolf, or on the wolf primarily (Beckett 2014). Beckett observes that "the marked attempt to rehabilitate the wolf in public opinion has had a profound influence on the wolf's literary image" (2014: 8). Such moves relate to shifting attitudes toward justice that reach past retribution to what Marek C. Oziewicz calls restorative or Open Justice, "balanced between the claims of community and those of the individual—with the individual now seen as an actual, gendered, situated person with particular traits" (2015: 25–6). A common twenty-first-century culture industry move emphasizes the dark side of fairy tales and disassociates them from children. At the same time, many adaptations for adults, and for children, provide villains' backstories, or rehabilitate their bad behaviors. This is exemplified in Disney's *Maleficent* (2014) and *Maleficent: Mistress of Evil* (2019), which provide insight into the supposedly evil fairy's behavior in "Sleeping Beauty" by relating her story of rape and betrayal. Adapting fairy tales keeps them culturally relevant while suggesting their sociohistorical contexts for those inclined to remember or research them.

The promise, and need, for each child to engage fairy tales, and life, on their own terms appears in many contemporary narratives produced by the culture industry, with some echoes and amendments in late twentieth-century fairy-tale studies as well. Tatar advocates for stories where children "figure as heroes and heroines" (1992: xxvii). Haase reminds readers that enchantment, or "being spellbound and powerless," is a "curse" and that rather than being bound by the "external authority" of tales and cultural systems, children should be "helped to discover their individual ownership of fairy tales" (1999: 363). He advocates sharing multiple versions of tales and historicizing them in ways that allow adults and children to "reread and interpret the tales in new ways" (363). Zipes also proposes better storytelling as an antidote, "showing children, through interaction, the diverse forms and strategies of narrative and story and how specific genres are used to address social situations" (1995: 224). Marina Warner holds out for "stories that try to find the truth and give us glimpses of the greater things" (2014: 178).

This form of interaction involves listening, instructing, and being physically present, however, and is not enabled by the commodifiable version of interactivity proffered by the culture industry. Orr affirms that the Disney princess line and Barbie fairy-tale movies occur within monetizing systems where interactivity still is controlled by product designers and marketers who appeal to nostalgia and a "have it all" attitude (2009: 21). Being a Disney or Barbie princess happens in a culture industry where "the very idea that we may purchase, for ourselves or our children, a liberatory identity [should be] suspect" (26). Bacchilega's formulation of a fairy-tale web with multiple entry points of production and reception encourages wariness about consumerist enchantments and points toward "a disillusionment with the reality of the social conditions that canonized tales of magic idealize" (2013: 5). According to Bacchilega, dealings of tellers, readers, and viewers within the web may afford recognition of wonder and mutually engaged social relations amidst the magic-laden constraints of marketed fairy-tale commodities and prescribed identities.

STORY CAPACITIES, COGNITIVE-AFFECTIVE APPROACHES, AND HOW FAIRY TALES SOCIALIZE

Psychoanalytic approaches that focus on inner drives along with sociohistorical approaches that critique ideological constraints of the civilizing process and culture industry all assume that fairy tales socialize children as *stories* portraying how the world works and where children fit within it. Consumerist fairy-tale magic fuels behaviorist plots. Discussions of the civilizing process and the culture industry often see that advertising and other cultural messages condition children's desires for proper actions in terms set by restrictive mores and purchased products. All this works because fairy tales send powerful, practically irresistible messages about what life is about that resonate with children and adults.

Narratological and cognitive-affective approaches seek to understand how and why stories and literature have such dynamic aptitudes. Arthur Frank's socionarratology provides keen insights into story's capacities to engage minds and influence relationships and lives. He offers thirteen capacities that afford understanding of "how stories do their work for people and on people" (Frank 2010: 28). Although Frank does not mention fairy tales specifically, his enumeration of story capacities relates directly to the structural and thematic elements associated with tales. "Trouble" is Frank's first capacity because stories "deal with human troubles" and "make trouble" as well (28). Trouble ties closely with the capacities for character, point of view, and suspense because response to trouble often "declares what sort of person [a character] is," leading participants to attend to point of view and be in suspense about how the trouble could possibly be resolved (29–31). Although fairy tales are associated with happy endings, retellings and adaptations present many different possibilities. Knowing how the story should end actually builds suspense as adaptations tweak or drastically refigure familiar characters and plots.

Other story capacities relate to interpretive possibilities and morals that apply directly to how fairy tales speak to individuals and societies through versions that enact value judgments. Frank refers specifically to Disney's version of "The Sorcerer's Apprentice" (ATU 325) to discuss how stories can depict situations that are "out of control" and that stories may "act in ways their tellers did not anticipate" (35). This relates to the interpretive openness, resonance, symbiotic, shape-shifting, and performative capacities through which stories resist one fixed meaning (Frank 2010). Additionally, stories relate to values, "what counts as good and bad, of how to act and not to act," which corresponds with a capacity to "enact" truths and, "perhaps most significant" to Frank, to "arouse people's imaginations" (40–1). This capacity certainly relates to fairy tales as stories specializing in how the past and future may be conceived differently. Rather than mandating one conditioned response to stories, Frank sees that story capacities work best, and are understood most usefully, in dialogic relationships—"analysis is always about the relationship between *at least two* and most often three elements: a story, a storyteller, and a listener" (16; emphasis in the original). Cognitive literary criticism and changing views of child development also attend, more than previous theories, to the dialogical and reciprocal learning that happens through stories and children's literature.

These theories emphasize a child's need for human nurture and for cognitive and behavioral models that help the child to navigate the world. Albert Bandura's social learning theory posits that these models can come from books and movies as well as face-to-face encounters (Bandura 1977), which relates to Frank's claims about what stories do with people. Frank calls stories "a *selection/evaluation* guidance system" that "makes certain aspects of the world seem worth attending to and suggests default evaluations of what is accepted" (2010: 46–7; my emphasis). Stories, especially fairy tales, package experience not only for commodities but also with bundles of navigable information that relate aesthetically pleasing figurative language with characters in compelling scenarios.

Cognitive-affective approaches are important because they ask questions about how literature and stories help human minds learn from actual and vicarious experiences. Maria Nikolajeva turns to cognitive criticism to "acknowledge the value of literature and reading in educating and socialising young people" (2014: 3). Concepts of scripts and theory of mind address how people realize their place in the world through patterned exchanges and attentive observations with other people. Frank mentions theory of mind in connection with making interpretations. More directly, Oziewicz identifies it with the ability to "attribute mental states to the self and others so that their behavior can be predicted and explained" (2015: 62). For example, Nikolajeva considers that "fiction represents fictional character's emotions as well as their interpretation of each other's emotions" (2014: 79). This vicarious examination of others' mental states, afforded by stories and literature, mitigates harsh consequences since it enables people to negotiate challenge and conflict in the stories without directly confronting actual angry giants or ravenous witches.

The dialogue exchanges between the wolf and Red Riding Hood exemplify this testing out of mental states, ostensibly through discussions about planned tasks and physical attributes. Nikolajeva points out the benefits when attention is so focused: "We want to understand (or are for survival, compelled to understand) our own and others' ways of feeling and thinking, views, beliefs, intentions, desires, motivations, and decisions" (2014: 77). Stories also portray the actions characters take based on how they interpret others' mental states and see events through to a conclusion. In my study of fourteen televised "Little Red Riding Hood" episodes, all but a few include the woodland dialogue where Red Riding Hood misreads Wolf's ill-intent and tells him where she is going (Rudy and Greenhill 2020). Showing how words may contradict actualities, the exchange in the version made for the series *Hello Kitty's Furry Tale Theatre*, titled "Little Red Bunny Hood" (1987), involves subtle deceit and literal thinking. When Little Bunny Hood says, "I don't talk to strangers," she already contradicts herself because she hasn't met the wolf before; knowingly, he replies, "We're not strangers. We've already met" because they are already in conversation (Maliani 1987). Child viewers, like Red Riding Hood and other youthful fairy-tale characters, are novices at social interaction. When the wolf eventually turns on Red Riding Hood, novices learn to interpret not only what characters literally say but their intentions as well.

The playfully repeated dialogue about Grandmother/Wolf's appearance in bed with big eyes, ears, hands, and teeth also suggests that appearances and verbal answers need to be correlated with actions expressing desires and intentions. A few of the televised Little Red Riding Hood versions include a misreading of the wolf as Grandma and then show a gaping mouth and black screen to indicate that Red Riding Hood has been swallowed. Other versions, though, have the girl correctly assess the wolf's identity and intentions and challenge his planned murderous act. The Cartoonito UK version, for example, has the protagonists chide the female-identified wolf for her evil plan and throw cookies at her, then the children convince the grandma to accept the wolf's apology by inviting her to help make cookies to appease hunger ("Little Red Riding Hood" 2011) (Figure 7.2).

As Nikolajeva emphasizes, there is a difference between novice, expert, and professional readers that children's literature works to address (2014: 10–20). In this case, the off-screen narrator provides some scaffolding clues about what the children should have known or recognized about the wolf's initial deceit and about the restorative justice resolution.

Learning by observing and interpreting others' mindsets confirms that often stories' cognitive and affective work happens indirectly. Theory of mind

FIGURE 7.2: Still from "Little Red Riding Hood" (2011), television episode, Cartoonito's *Fairy Tales for Kids*. Justice is restored when the wolf's apology is accepted and new friends bake cookies.

productively helps us study how interpreting others' emotions and designs occurring in oral, print, and electronic storytelling guides better evaluations in real life. Cognitive criticism not only sees fairy-tale socialization as putting children in identity-based social roles or a consumerist marketplace but also allows that stories and literature model and afford assessment of actions and attitudes in ongoing social situations, helping novices achieve more expert social skills and knowledge to navigate their worlds.

The concept of scripting also relates to ways that literature tells children about their place in life, and may help them assess cultural messaging. Oziewicz writes extensively of cognitive scripting because "complex ideas such as justice are stored and processed by the human mind as scripts—standardized sequences of causally linked events" that become "actualized" as stories (2015: 4). Scripting also relates to ideological concerns about fairy-tale socialization because dominating discourses involving sexual, racial, and other oppressed or monetized identities can be naturalized in fairy-tale scripts, leading people to restrict opportunities for themselves or for others. Equally, however, fairy tales may serve as the taproots for other speculative fictions that, through their association with possibility, all become "essential to our humanness" (4). Although many folklorists associate folk tales with optimism and rising to new opportunity, Oziewicz associates traditional tales with a poetic justice that tolerates unfairness, or even expects it to prevail (107). He sees that adaptations update fairy-tale scripts toward a more satisfying retributive justice that punishes perpetrators or works toward the restorative justice that redeems villains, like Cartoonito's cookie-baking wolf (107, 148). Cognitive approaches see that scripts link powerful concepts such as justice with the ways that stories and literature involve figurative language, allowing readers to think through the crucial situations we confront while growing up.

INDIGENOUS STUDIES AND SHARING WONDER STORIES TO GROW UP AND LIVE AS A PEOPLE

Fairy tales constitute one type of traditional wonder story whose functions are not limited to serving as the latent manifestations of the unconscious or to fueling desire for commodifiable products. And socialization may be realized through these tales as a result of the teaching and learning involved in growing up as a member of a family, kindred, and cultural group, or part of a religious community, not only as a result of a civilizing process that trains children for rigid identity roles and bourgeois status reinforced by a global cultural industry that commodifies objects and lives. More expansive views of fairy tales and socialization can arise from more relational approaches to scholarship and living.

Such expansive views need to include indigenous knowledge systems and claims to land and relationships because these systems depend on storytelling and afford well-being. Current fairy-tale studies works "to understand the fairy tale from multiple cultural locations across the globe" and to revise the canon of Perrault-Grimm-Andersen-Disney by involving more scholars and more perspectives (Teverson 2019: 11). Teverson recognizes that the term "fairy tale" remains useful when put under a "sentence": "showing that the fairy tales of Europe have their roots in a complex of international intersections" (12). Still, hoʻomanawanui solely refers to "wonder tale" because it is the more "apt description of the characteristics of traditional oral stories from non-European cultures" (2018: 123). Postcoloniality and decolonization also inform these crucial conversations in fairy-tale studies, with decolonization preferred because it emphasizes overturning the effects of colonization through indigenous self-determination (Bacchilega and Naithani 2018).

Indigenous studies, therefore, specifically represents the relationship of stories, lands, and people that remains vital to the teaching, or socializing, of children despite the losses, threats, and damage of colonial impositions (Aikau and Gonzalez 2019; Bacchilega 2007; Justice 2018; Kuwada and Yamashiro 2016; McDougall 2016; Weaver 1997). As hoʻomanawanui asserts, "modern media genres are simply new ways for us to tell and represent our traditional stories, including wonder tales" (2018: 123). An awareness of traditional wonder stories in sociocultural contexts that include lands, indigeneity, and contemporary communicative technologies portray deeper realities that literally help children find their place in the world.

Storytelling and other traditional expressive performances remain crucial acts and components of indigenous knowledge systems (IKS), which stem from and support given cultures and societies. Therese Mungah Shalo Tchombe and Tani Emmanuel Lukong define indigenous people as those "grouped under the criteria of ancestral territory, collective cultural configurations, and historical location," and they see indigenous socialization as offering "utility value in indigenous communities" (2016: 94). Their study considers how proverbs guide early adolescents in northwestern Cameroon in attaining emotional regulation within the Nso knowledge system and its cosmovision that "dictates the way land, water, plants, humans and animals are to be used" and sees that "the human world, the natural world, and the spiritual world are linked" (90). They assert that indigenous expressive forms "prepare adolescents to take up their adult roles in appropriate emotional dispensation guided and accepted by cultural values," values specific to their rural society and place (93). These values are not promoted by state-sponsored school systems or English media available on "emerging technological devices" that divert attention from traditional languages, sayings, and games (92). Indigenous knowledge, though, may be supported by such technologies.

Removing indigenous societies from the socialization that occurs through communicative technologies perpetuates false dichotomies about indigenous peoples, oral traditions, history, and contemporary life. And yet, associating all indigenous storytelling with fairy tales also undermines the truth value of wonder tales. As hoʻomanawanui declares, "mass media culture often relegates the Indigenous to the margins, stereotyped as pre-industrial, pre-technological people with little, if any, capability" (2018: 123–4). This leads to cultural appropriation, which occurs in Disney's *Moana* (2016). Yet, contrary to this, hoʻomanawanui proclaims, "Using digital media to disseminate ancient, traditional tales offers acts of cultural resurgence" (2018: 184). Joanna Hearne studies how indigenous stories shared digitally on Canadian television keep

"Indigenous concerns visible even as the stories travel into new circumstances" (2017: 126). Additionally, the storytelling scene emphasizes "oral-to-electronic" transmission with groups of listeners portrayed on-screen in the outdoors gathering around a storyteller (136) (Figure 7.3).

The oral-to-electronic transmission, however, does not erase important ways of reading, writing, and the literature, and literary criticism, that historically and currently affect socialization and the perpetuation of indigenous knowledge (Brooks 2008). Because each indigenous culture retains distinctive knowledge related with land, stories, and people, pedagogies that depend on intergenerational sharing permeate indigenous societies. This relates directly with fairy-tale socialization if fairy tales remain linked to traditional stories that teach how to confront problems in culturally sanctioned ways.

Young adult literature portraying such situated problem-solving through wonder tales speaks to and benefits indigenous and settler youth when

FIGURE 7.3: Still from television series *Raven Tales* (2006–). *Raven Tales* portrays oral-to-electronic indigenous storytelling transmission.

recognized and engaged truthfully. Such literatures matter in relation to socialization because they relate with place- and culture-based knowledge and traditional storytelling genres and customs. Caryn Lesuma studies specifically how young adult literatures of Oceania (YALO) have an important "role in shaping the cultural knowledges, attitudes, and purposes of the youth tasked with the future of determining our region" (2018: 2). For example, YALO "adapts the oral literature of Oceania into print in ways that are distinct" and understands wonder tales not as fiction but as history, because story and history "often mean the same thing from an Indigenous perspective" (7). For these reasons, the study of indigenous literatures will never correlate neatly with fairy-tale studies; nevertheless, the uses of international wonder tales for the purpose of socialization, especially when considered as learning for an encultured way of living, allow for the consideration of European fairy tales in parallel with localized storytelling traditions and literatures aimed at novices.

Wonder tales involve crucial developmental problems as well as nurturing the intellectual and affective tools and resources for resolving them, culturally customized when shared with children in caregiving situations such as those mentioned at the beginning of this chapter. The process of teaching children and guiding their learning often depends on popular, valued traditional stories such as fairy tales and other wonder stories. Tchombe and Lukong cite the developmental theories of Lev Vygotsky and Barbara Rogoff as a means to emphasize the "fact that children are active participants in their own socialization" (2016: 94). Rogoff is known for a "guided participation" approach to child development that works best when children are "rooted in the specific historical and cultural activities" of their close communities through interactions with adults and peers (1990: 3, 183). Such interactions involve sharing stories and sayings as well as other tasks of play and work, and serve to develop "interdependent goal-directed activity" in which children and their caregivers come "to find, understand and handle particular problems, building on the intellectual tools from previous generations and the social resources provided by other people" (190). Caregivers, teachers, even marketers, know that these stories resonate with young minds far into the future. Conducted in dialogical terms in situated cultural settings, further study of fairy-tale socialization through traditional stories and children's and YA literatures in various media merits the utmost attention and care.

CHAPTER EIGHT

Power

The Archaeology of a Genre

KIMBERLY J. LAU

Power is arguably the dominant analytic of our time. It has animated virtually all critical inquiry in the humanities and humanistic social sciences since the late twentieth century, and it continues to drive a great deal of contemporary scholarly, artistic, and cultural production. If such claims about power's reach and influence seem overly bold, that may be due to lingering traces of power's earlier conceptualizations, its tight articulation with sovereignty, mastery, control,[1] understandings of power that predate Michel Foucault's paradigm-shifting lectures and writings of the 1960s and 1970s. For Foucault, power is diffuse, enacted in social and cultural practices; as such, "power must be analysed as something which circulates … never localized here or there, never in anybody's hands, never appropriated as a commodity or a piece of wealth" (1980: 98). Power thus conceived—and now widely accepted, although not without decades of critical engagement, challenge, and revision[2]—often accompanies, complements, undergirds other modes of analysis. Indeed, it is nearly impossible to imagine undertaking studies of race, gender, sexuality, and/or class without addressing questions of power; same, too, for studies of empire, history, and anthropology as well as economics, politics, and literature. Any such list—like power itself—is boundless, contingent, and ever-changing.

Foucault's theorization of power as discursively constituted emerges out of three of his early works, *Madness and Civilization* ([1961] 1988), *Birth of the Clinic* ([1963] 1973), and *The Order of Things* ([1966] 1970), a series of nuanced and layered case studies that read across disciplinary archives to establish, respectively, the discursive formations critical to the birth of psychiatry and deviancy, the invention of the medical gaze and the attendant professional knowledges that dehumanize patients, and the development of the concept of the episteme. Foucault returns to these three studies in *Archaeology of Knowledge* ([1969] 1972) to cull from them a coherent method for the "enterprise"—archaeology—that he finds only loosely developed in his earlier works:[3]

> An enterprise by which one tries to measure the mutations that operate in general in the field of history; an enterprise in which the methods, limits, and themes proper to the history of ideas are questioned; an enterprise by which one tries to throw off the last anthropological constraints; an enterprise that wishes, in return, to reveal how these constraints could come about.
> ([1969] 1972: 15)

As a method of analysis, archaeology thus articulates previously unidentified "domains" through an analysis of the conditions, forms, and rules of "things said" within a given archive ([1969] 1972). Insofar as Foucault's archaeology seeks to make intelligible the implicit workings of power in naturalized historical formations, it also resonates with his conceptualization of genealogy as an analytic or method (Koopman and Matza 2013: 824). With genealogy, Foucault is even more explicit in identifying the relationship to power and knowledge: "a genealogy should be seen as a kind of attempt to emancipate historical knowledges from that subjection, to render them, that is, capable of opposition and of struggle against the coercion of a theoretical, unitary, formal and scientific discourse" (1980: 85).

While Foucault is perhaps best known for his application of these archaeological and genealogical methods in his studies of surveillance and discipline (*Discipline and Punish*, 1975) and of sexuality (*History of Sexuality, Volume 1*, 1976), I want to consider them here as they relate to genre formations and scholarly disciplines—specifically, the discipline of fairy-tale studies. In *Archaeology of Knowledge*, Foucault emphasizes the point that divisions such as those distinguishing science from literature or literature from history are "always themselves reflexive categories, principles of classification, normative rules, institutional types ... but they are not intrinsic, autochthonous, and universally recognizable characteristics" ([1969] 1972: 22). As with any social domain, scholarly disciplines are thus subject to historical conditions, forms, and rules that participate in the creation and maintenance of disciplinary knowledge claims and the naturalization of disciplinary authority; consequently, revealing the specific discursive constellations underlying such disciplinary formations necessarily involves an analysis of power. Inspired by (but not limited to) Foucault's theories of power and his archaeological method, this chapter seeks to articulate the normalized logics at the heart of fairy-tale studies to explore what other(ed)—and thereby marginalized and overlooked—discourses reveal about genres, geopolitics, and the possibility for productive literary disruptions and cultural subversions.

Of course, considerations of power are by no means new to fairy-tale studies. Indeed, the critical literature is rich with analyses of power as it relates to class, gender, and/or sexuality in individual tales, tale types, collections, performances, and adaptations; moreover, such readings represent a wide range of theoretical perspectives, including Marxist, psychoanalytic, feminist, and queer. And yet, despite this abundant literature from varied interpretive and theoretical frameworks, an archaeology of fairy-tale studies still makes a double intervention: first, by focusing not on fairy tales themselves but, rather, on fairy-tale studies as a scholarly discipline based on a single genre and, second, by exploring how disciplinary discourses enable the troubling and almost complete absence of race as a topic in fairy-tale studies, both as a discipline and as the body of critical literature that the discipline has generated. Against this archaeology of the genre and its disciplinary power, I read Helen Oyeyemi's fairy-tale novels as examples of how racially inflected contemporary fairy tales might highlight, as well as attend to, such critical absences.

THE MASTER'S HOUSE: UNIVERSALIZING THE EUROPEAN FAIRY TALE

Canons tend to be self-validating; that is, the qualities they possess become the qualities that we look for in our reading and praise all over again when we find them.
     —Elizabeth Wanning Harries, *Twice Upon a Time* (2001: 45)

The earliest European literary fairy tales appeared in the mid-sixteenth century with Giovanni Straparola's *The Pleasant Nights* (*Le piacevoli notti*, 1550–5), a collection of stories—including several fairy tales—in the style of Giovanni Boccaccio's *Decameron* (*c.* 1353). Not quite a century later, Giambattista Basile's *The Tale of Tales* (*Lo cunto de li cunti*, 1634–6) similarly imagines a multiday storytelling event as the basis for its frame tale; in Basile's collection, each of the five days features ten fairy tales, and the storytelling event culminates with the true bride's personal story, which simultaneously provides the fiftieth fairy tale and closes the frame. While many of Straparola's and Basile's fairy tales heavily influenced those authored and performed for salon and courtly audiences in late seventeenth-century France,[4] it wasn't until then that the fairy tale emerged with any real cultural significance. When it did, it inspired deeply gendered discourses concerning its "proper" form.

The vast majority of French fairy-tale writers of the period were aristocratic women, and their tales were generally long, complex, and ornate. Stylistically, their fairy tales challenged the idea of—and, among some, the ideological desire for—the fairy tale as a simple narrative, conveyed in the plain language of its supposedly naïve peasant storyteller, typically represented as a spinner or children's "nurse." Charles Perrault, whose *Mother Goose Tales* (*Contes de ma mere l'oye. Histoires ou contes du temps passé*, 1697) eventually came to represent *the* French fairy tale, ventriloquized this imagined storyteller to great effect, both in his manuscript, which he gifted to the niece of Louis XIV, and in his later published versions. Although Perrault and well-known *conteuses* and *salonnières*, such as Marie-Catherine d'Aulnoy and Henriette-Julie de Murat, never seem to have publicly or directly debated the fairy tale's "proper" form with respect to their own tales, they were certainly considered together—and generally pitted against each other—in the cultural and literary criticism of the day, perhaps best exemplified by the Abbé de Villiers's scathing and misogynistic attack on the genre.

In his 1699 *Dialogues on Fairy Tales and Some Other Works of Our Time, to Act as an Antidote Against Bad Taste* (*Entretiens sur les contes des fées et sur quelques autres ouvrages du temps, pour server comme préservatif contre le mauvais goût*), dedicated to the members of the Académie française (including Perrault), Villiers stages a dialogue between a Parisian and a Provincial concerning the contemporary vogue for fairy tales. The Parisian, clearly voicing Villiers' own perspective, derides the characteristic style of the *conteuses*' tales—their length, convoluted plots, and ornate details, often rendered in precious language—while also impugning the *conteuses* for what he sees as their ignorance, laziness, and interest in writing for profit as opposed to literary quality. Against this portrayal of the female fairy-tale writers, he celebrates Perrault for so masterfully imitating the simplicity of the naïve peasant woman, the uneducated "nurse" who epitomizes the traditional storyteller. For Villiers, Perrault's ability to reproduce the supposedly "authentic" language and style of the fairy tale requires a certain intellectual keenness: "one must be clever to imitate their ignorant simplicity so well" (quoted in Harries 2001: 24). By equating the "authentic" fairy-tale form with the intelligence of its literary creator, Villiers effectively dismisses the *conteuses* as well as their style of fairy tales, thereby contributing his authority and cultural capital to the development of a very specific idea of the fairy tale.[5]

Despite the fact that some of the *conteuses*' tales were included in seventeenth- and eighteenth-century worldly canons,[6] the prevailing sense of the fairy tale was the one animated in Perrault's collection and advanced by Villiers. This definition of the fairy tale as a simple narrative associated with old women telling stories to children by the fireside was reiterated, and thus further consolidated, a little over a century later when Jacob and Wilhelm Grimm (and, following them, other nineteenth-century critics) reproduced the gendered debate about the "proper" form of the genre in the introduction to their *Children's and Household Tales* (*Kinder- und Hausmärchen* [KHM], 1812). In her analysis of the gendered dimensions of fairy-tale canon formation, Elizabeth Wanning Harries (2001) calls attention to the ways the Grimms' assessment of Perrault's tales—particularly as compared to those of well-known *conteuses*—echoes the language and perspective of Villiers. In addition to admiring Perrault's "naïve and simple manner," the Grimms distinguish his tales from those of "his inferior imitators, Aulnoy, Murat" (quoted in Harries 2001: 22).[7] The persistence of these gendered discourses over more than a century lends insight into the process by which the boundaries of the fairy tale—as a genre—were not only determined but also enforced.

Beyond the introduction to *Children's and Household Tales*, the Grimms' collection is significant to the definition of the fairy tale in several fundamental ways, including the fact that it was widely translated and, in the process, frequently abridged, which effectively created a condensed canon of the tales typically associated with the genre in the popular imagination.[8] In addition, *Children's and Household Tales*, both a scholarly edition and a popular book, provides titles and numbers for each of its tales and originates in the context of nineteenth-century romantic nationalism. While numbering tales in a collection may seem straightforward, perhaps even essential, such a practice was idiosyncratic and suggested a nascent typology. At the same time, the spirit of romantic nationalism, so pervasive across Western Europe and Scandinavia during the nineteenth century, provided a rich ideological environment for the collection and editing of fairy tales, assumed to reflect the genuine voice of "the people"; within this cultural and political milieu, *Children's and Household Tales* was taken as the paradigmatic collection.[9] That status—together with the Grimms' academic framing, extensive notes, and numerous annotations—established the format for the national collections that would follow, and as these collections proliferated, their compilers generally used the Grimms' numberings to cross-reference their tales with the Grimms' collection (Georges 1983).

For these reasons, Robert Georges (1983) argues that the tale type—the folkloristic term for a set of narratives believed to share a plot—originates with the Grimms' *Children's and Household Tales*, although he also recognizes the more explicit scholarly methods and typological undertakings through which the tale type was fully consolidated as an academic concept: Antti Aarne's foundational tale type index (*Verzeichnis der Märchentypen*, 1910) classified tales according to their recurring motifs and drew from Finnish, Danish, and German collections. Closely aligned with this version of the tale type index, Kaarle Krohn's historic-geographic method (*Die folkloristische arbeitsmethode*, 1926), also known as the Finnish method, sought to map a given tale type's motifs to trace its history of transmission backward so as to determine its geographic and cultural origin, as well as to reconstruct its *ur* form. Georges's intellectual history of the tale type ultimately leads into his argument for its underlying biological basis and what that might suggest about the nature of narrative and narrating; as such, he is not concerned with the ways this particular set of disciplinary practices and precepts contributed to the very definition of the fairy tale and its study. Nonetheless, the concept of the tale type—along with its extension of the Grimms' early numbering system and its widespread applications in folk narrative research—has essentially determined the boundaries of the genre.

The tale type index, now in its third edition (*The Types of International Folktales: A Classification and Bibliography*; Uther 2004), is the definitive classification system for fairy-tale studies, and the scholarly literature—regardless of linguistic or geographical origin—essentially requires that tales be identified by their "ATU" (Aarne-Thompson-Uther, for the three main editors of the different editions) numbers. Not surprisingly, perhaps, even more than a century after the publication of Aarne's index, the European tales underlying his typology still constitute the primary focus of the definitive international classification system. When Stith Thompson translated Aarne's index into English in 1928, he also sought to expand its geographical and cultural range (Thompson 1928); nonetheless, by his second revision in 1961, Thompson still lamented its largely Eurocentric scope, writing in the preface that "the work might be called 'The Types of the Folk-Tale of Europe, West Asia, and the Lands Settled by These People'" (Thompson 1961). Thus, regardless of Thompson's efforts to extend the reach of the tale type index, it remains, as he himself concedes, decidedly European in its emphasis, especially for the narratives we conventionally associate with the fairy tale (ATU numbers 300–749). As a result, the tale type index puts into global circulation a purportedly "universal" definition of the fairy tale that remains, in reality, anchored to the European tradition. Although Hans-Jörg Uther's introduction to the ambitiously and optimistically titled *The Types of International Folktales* (2004) acknowledges such criticisms of the index and claims to have "eliminated or mitigated these faults" (8), the index's shortcomings in terms of geographical and cultural breadth are impossible to truly mitigate since they are fundamental to its entire structure.

The exclusionary nature of the tale type index's Indo-European foundation has not gone unnoticed, and quite a few scholars working in folk narrative traditions that fall outside the scope of the Aarne-Thompson version of the tale type index have produced their own cultural and/or regional indexes.[10] Uther and his editorial team worked to incorporate material from these regional indexes into the third edition of the tale type index, but they failed to expand the numbering system to accommodate tale types that fall outside of the original classificatory system; consequently, their good intentions have had only limited effect. In addition, because *The Types of International Folktales* draws on a wide variety of sources, including scholarly research, and because the vast majority of the scholarship is devoted to the European tale tradition, the tale type index remains highly Eurocentric. Even more, despite the proliferation of these tale type indexes, ATU numbers continue to prevail in the critical literature, thereby diminishing the power of non-European indexes to challenge the normative classification and conceptual systems (see, e.g., Haase 2010). As such, the Aarne-Thompson-Uther Tale Type Index exerts a doubled disciplinary power: first, in terms of its power to dictate how the fairy tale is defined and compared within fairy-tale studies as a scholarly discipline and, second, in terms of its power to encourage a self-disciplining that ensures the naturalization of the European fairy tale as *the* fairy tale.

Of course, the tale type index is not exceptional in its disciplinary power. Nineteenth-century fairy-tale collections from colonized cultural groups, for instance, generally reflect European understandings of the genre, not because the European fairy tale is universal and thus common to these traditions but, rather, because the tales in such collections were typically selected by missionaries, colonial officials, and/or their wives and daughters, who frequently recorded stories from the local and indigenous peoples with whom they worked and sometimes lived. In an effort to disarticulate white setler and indigenous cultures in discourses of the "Australian" fairy tale, Rebecca-Anne Do Rozario (2011) offers several trenchant examples from Andrew Lang's *Brown Fairy Book* (1904), which contains only one tale from Australia's indigenous cultures. Here, the opening to "The Bunyip" echoes the formulaic opening of classic European fairy tales—"Long, long ago, far, far away on the other side of the world" (quoted in Do Rozario 2011: 20)—and privileges Lang's presumed English-reading audience. Without access to the recorded version of this tale, it is impossible to know whether Lang altered its opening so as to make it conform to the European model, but he himself suggests as much when he praises his wife's translations of many of the tales in the *Brown Fairy Book* for precisely such alterations, noting that she "does not give them exactly as they are told by all sorts of outlandish natives, but makes them up in the hope white people will like them, skipping the pieces which they will not like" (quoted in Do Rozario 2011: 20). Clearly, the process of selecting and editing tales from European colonies and other non-European cultural regions was largely driven by dominant ideas about the fairy tale's genre conventions; as a result, the published collections that purport to represent dramatically different cultures through their tales often simply reproduce the European fairy tale—with local color—thereby further entrenching the sense of the genre's "universality."

Although the self-referentiality implicit in fairy-tale studies may seem like a relic of nineteenth-century investments in both nation-building and the authority of "science," bolstered by European imperialism and assumptions of cultural superiority, such disciplinary discourses and practices continue throughout the twentieth century and well into our contemporary moment. Even scholarly attempts to define the fairy tale privilege the European style and structure of the genre. For instance, Stith Thompson's 1946 definition of the märchen—the frequent use of which, to refer to the fairy tale, already underscores this point—essentially describes the form and plot of canonical European tales: "a tale of some length involving a succession of motifs or episodes. It moves in an unreal world, without definite locality or definite characters and is filled with the marvelous. In this never-never land humble heroes kill adversaries, succeed to kingdoms, and marry princesses" (quoted in Haase 2007: 323). Half a century later, leading fairy-tale scholars Marina Warner and Jack Zipes both refer to magical transformation—"shape-shifting," "metamorphosis" (Warner 2004a: xv), "wondrous change" (Zipes 2000: xviii)—as a defining quality of the genre, and yet such observations clearly derive from the canonical European fairy tale and are not necessarily reflective of other traditions. Such tautological attempts to define the fairy tale obviously normalize and universalize a very specifically European genre.

I provide this relatively lengthy—yet paradoxically truncated—archaeology of "the fairy tale" and its bearing on fairy-tale studies as an academic discipline to call attention to the ways power often exerts itself through seemingly "neutral" scholarly discourses. More than simply identifying "biases" or blindspots in the critical scholarship, I hope this archaeology foregrounds the processes and practices by which the fairy tale's ongoing production as a "universal" genre occludes the discourses—both historical and contemporary—of imperialism, colonialism, ethnic chauvinism, and racialized thinking so critical in eliding the distinction between the European fairy tale and *the* fairy tale.

POWERHOUSE: DWELLING IN HELEN OYEYEMI'S FAIRY-TALE WORLDS

But if this house could speak,
It would tell a different story.

—Aeschylus, *Agamemnon* (36–8)[11]

If the fairy tale's universality is a European illusion propped up by patriarchal and Eurocentric structures of power, contemporary fairy-tale fiction might very well be its undoing, its decentering and deconstruction. As early as the mid-nineteenth century, white women writers such as Christina Rossetti (1862) and Anne Thackery Ritchie ([1868–74] 2010) began reimagining classic European fairy tales as a way of interrogating and critiquing dominant gender expectations. Later feminist authors, also white, built on this tradition with similarly trenchant fairy tales that not only challenged hegemonic understandings of gender but also exposed the naturalized sexual violence implicit in so many canonical tales, thereby calling attention to the patriarchal and misogynist logics driving many of the classic tales as well as, in some cases, women's own complicity in such systems of oppression. Angela Carter's 1979 collection, *The Bloody*

Chamber, is perhaps emblematic of the twentieth-century feminist reinvention of the fairy tale, but she is certainly not a unique voice in this tradition. Anne Sexton ([1971] 2016), Tanith Lee (1983), Margaret Atwood (1983, [1993] 2009), Olga Broumas (1977), Francesca Lia Block (2000), and Emma Donoghue ([1993] 1997)—to name just a few—published feminist fairy tales in novels, short stories, and poetry collections. While the last few decades of the twentieth century were particularly generative for feminist fairy-tale writers, the practice of challenging dominant gender expectations in contemporary fairy-tale storytelling continues well into the current moment (see, e.g., Bernheimer 2007; Bernheimer and Giménez Smith 2010; Cunningham 2015). Even more, just as predominantly white feminist writers have long crafted fairy tales that reinterpret the canon, transnational authors are beginning to create fairy tales that contest the Eurocentric assumptions and ideologies at the heart of the genre itself (see, e.g., Bail 1998; King-Aribisala 2007; Somtow 2003). Relatedly, American authors such as Catharynne Valente (2015) and Bill Willingham (2006) have produced contemporary fairy tales that critique settler colonialism and European Orientalism and imperialism, respectively. Among such transnational works, Helen Oyeyemi's fairy-tale novels—*White Is for Witching* (2009), *Mr. Fox* (2011), *Boy, Snow, Bird* (2014), and *Gingerbread* (2019)[12]—stand out as a *collection* of tales whose themes and structures wend their way through a shifting textual labyrinth of European fairy tales as well as tales, both traditional and newly invented, from Africa, the Caribbean, the Middle East, and imaginary countries of her own invention. While Oyeyemi's fascination with disrupting Western mythologies and extending Western literary genres—"the doppelganger story" in *The Icarus Girl* (2005), the gothic vampire story in *White Is for Witching*, for instance (Hoggard 2014)—is foundational to her fiction more generally, European fairy tales are the most frequently recurring trope and the most common source of allusion in this set of novels; *Gingerbread*, *Mr. Fox*, and *Boy, Snow, Bird* represent sustained engagements with "Hansel and Gretel," "Bluebeard," and "Snow White," respectively. Even *White Is for Witching*, on the surface a gothic haunted-house narrative, opens with a reference to "Snow White"—"Her throat is blocked with a slice of apple / (to stop her speaking words that may betray her)" (Oyeyemi 2009: 1)—and continues to invoke that tale in a series of touchpoints throughout the novel. Toward the end of the novel, Miranda's observation that "we're in a fairy tale ... I knew it" (226; ellipsis in original) provides a meta-commentary on the overall significance of the European fairy tale to the novel's meaning, even as her remark refers to an incident with her twin brother Eliot, an incident she playfully likens to the "Hansel and Gretel" plot.

Oyeyemi's efforts to disrupt genre expectations by racializing the European fairy tale and foregrounding the presence of nonwhite characters have sometimes led to her work being misread in reductive and essentializing ways.

In one interview, for example, journalist Liz Hoggard (2014) suggests that Oyeyemi's books all "seem to be about migration and the need to belong," an idea that Oyeyemi vehemently resists: "No, no! This is a thing people always talk to me about ... people get a bit excited if there's a black person and say, 'Oh this is about that thing' when actually it's about expanding the genre of haunted house stories." Clearly, Oyeyemi's novels cannot be reduced to narratives of migration and assimilation. At the same time, however, the ways she expands traditional literary genres by normalizing blackness call attention to the unmarked whiteness of these traditions as well as to the related Eurocentrism, colonial and racist histories, and ethnic chauvinisms that sustain them in often invisible ways. Reading these novels as a collection of fairy tales thus encourages a reconsideration of the genre as constituted by long histories of European imperial and scholarly power, powers shaped by the undeniable force of racial thinking.

Across these novels, Oyeyemi exploits European fairy-tale conventions in ways that simultaneously make strange the familiar and normalize the unexpected. In the process, typically inanimate objects become living, active, narrating agents, characters that far exceed the usual fairy-tale magic of enchanted objects, while ethnically and racially diverse human characters are entirely normalized as part of Oyeyemi's fairy-tale landscapes. As a result, when the novels specifically call attention to race, it is to make visible the operative racisms of the stories—both the implicit racisms of the European tales and the diegetic racisms at play in Oyeyemi's narratives. *White Is for Witching*, whose gothic house is one of the novel's four primary narrators, exemplifies the critical interventions at play when such elements converge. Situated at the nexus of the gothic haunted-house story, the vampire narrative (including the Caribbean soucouyant tradition),[13] and "Snow White," *White Is for Witching* revolves around a haunted—or, perhaps more accurately, living and conscious—house ("29 Barton Road") in Dover and the four generations of white Silver women (Anna, Jennifer, Lily, and Miranda) who inhabit it. Focalized through Miranda in the aftermath of the death of her mother, Lily, the novel follows Miranda's attempts to escape the house and Dover as well as the afflictions that beset her there: the eating compulsion pica, the visitations from her ancestors, the threat of the "goodlady," the bloody murders of local Kosovan boys, and the house's desire to keep her there, transformed into a ghostly vampire together with the other Silver women. When Miranda's black lover, Ore, comes to visit her in Dover, the family's racist legacy surfaces in violent ways, and it is through this plot twist that the novel interrogates the racist dimensions of "Snow White."

The struggle between Miranda and the house forms the central tension in *White Is for Witching*, and it is this tension, together with the house's frequent association with the goodlady, that casts house and goodlady as evil stepmother. Indeed, as Lily makes clear in her entreaty to Miranda that she eat real food, the goodlady functions as a surrogate mother: "She's what I had instead of a mother, much stricter than any mother. She's like tradition, it's very serious when she's disobeyed ... You must eat real food, and you must eat as much as you can manage, or you might end up with the goodlady for your mother. Wouldn't you rather have me?" (Oyeyemi 2009: 77). Here, Lily's reference to tradition and the serious consequences of defying the goodlady make clear that she is not only stepmother but evil stepmother—and one perennially available for the role. Even more, the house's own self-representation as witch, especially a witch with the power to generate poisoned apples, furthers the association with Snow White's evil stepmother: "It was an all-season apple. I can make them grow. Do you know the all-season apples? They have a strange, dual colouring. If you pitied Snow White, then you know. One side of such an apple is always coma-white, and the other side is the waxiest red" (160).

More significant than the simple association between house/goodlady and evil stepmother in "Snow White," however, is the book's refrain, echoed in its title: "white is for witching." While the first reference to the phrase is ambiguous—"White is for witching, a colour to be worn so that all other colours can enter you, so that you may use them" (136)—there is no doubt that the second reference, in which the house addresses Sade, the "African" cook and cleaning woman working at the Silver bed-and-breakfast, is an explicitly racial, indeed racist, one: "Juju is not enough to protect you. Everything you have I will turn against you. I'll turn sugar bitter for you. I'll take your very shield and crack it on your head. White is for witching, *so ti gbo*? Do you understand now? *White* is for witching, Sade goodbye" (201; emphasis in original). Here, the house's use of Hausa—"*so ti gbo*" ("have you heard")—and its follow-up question ("Do you understand now?") assert the dominance of its white witching over Sade's African folk knowledge and potential power of resistance in a move that recalls the imperial use of both local vernacular phrases and patronizing traditions of "education" as part of colonial discursive power and rule. Emphasizing "*White*" in the second case simply makes explicit the house's claims to racial superiority. By equating witching with whiteness—and with outright racism—the novel draws out the same racial superiority implicit in "Snow White," where the eponymous character is valued above all else for her whiteness, naturalized as beauty when she is identified as "fairest in the land."

While the racism implicit in normalizing the equation between beauty and whiteness may seem an obvious point, the tale's overriding attention to female rivalry—here, the *evil* in the evil stepmother trope—essentially elides the racism altogether. *White Is for Witching* works against this elision, however, by reframing the tale's female rivalry. No longer rooted in intergenerational familial rivalry, the female competition is here imagined as a struggle between the house and Ore for Miranda, and this recasting animates the racist dimensions of "Snow White." Haunted into returning home—"'I can't stay here ... I'm to go home. The house wants me,'" Miranda tells Ore after Ore wakes her from a nocturnal trance (203)—Miranda finally gives voice to her feelings for Ore, to the house's racist abhorrence:

> "I'm in love," Miranda whispered, once she was hidden.
> We saw who she meant. The squashed nose, the pillow lips, the fist-sized breasts, the reek of fluids from the seam between her legs. The skin. The skin.
> (is it alright to say how much I like this
> the way our skin looks together)
> Anna was shocked. Jennifer was shocked. Lily was impassive.
> Disgusting. These are the things that happen while you're not looking, when you're not keeping careful watch. When clear water moves unseen a taint creeps into it—moss, or algae, salt, even. It becomes foul, undrinkable. It joins the sea.
>
> (223)

Driven by its investment in white racial purity, the house follows the stepmother-witch's fairy-tale lead and attempts to destroy Ore with one of its poisoned all-season apples: "There was an apple on my pillow. / It was white" (237). Here, the novel makes explicit the toxic and dangerous implications of the ways white is for witching.

When the ploy to dispatch Ore with the poisoned apple fails, the house resorts to a much more hostile and literal ethnic cleansing. Toweling off after a shower during her visit, Ore is alarmed by what she sees in the mirror:

> The towel the girl in the mirror was drying herself with—I frowned and looked at my towel. Where it had touched me it was striped with
> black liquid, as dense as paint
> (don't scream)
> there were shreds of hard skin in it. There was hair suspended in it
> "The black's coming off," someone outside the bathroom door comments. Then
> they whistled "Rule Britannia!" and laughed.
> *Bri-tons never-never-never, shall be slaves.*
>
> (246–7; emphasis in the original)

Ore's disturbingly fantastic toweling literalizes the interlocking nature of white racist supremacy, nationalism, imperialism, and ethnic cleansing (further alluded to in the novel's subplot concerning the gruesome murders of young Kosovan men). While ethnic cleansing per se is not thematized in "Snow White," the novel productively links the European fairy tale to the real material histories and racialized practices derived from, rationalized by, and sustained in racist ideologies such as those manifest in the ways "Snow White" naturalizes whiteness as the hegemonic conflation of beauty and goodness.

The malevolent and racist house at the heart of *White Is for Witching* is only one of Oyeyemi's enchanted houses, and situating it within the broader context of her other fanciful structures lends further insight into the ways that her contemporary fairy tales challenge the genre and the discipline, in the process exposing the various powers—scholarly, imperial, cultural—that have contributed to the European fairy tale's universalization.[14] Although rooted more in transnational folklore than European fairy tale, *The Opposite House* (2007) interweaves, blends, perhaps even collapses the lives of two women— Maja, an Afro-Cuban singer living in London, and Yemaya, a somewhat fantastic Nigerian Santeria practitioner—and their relationship to the *somewherehouse*. Technically the domain of Yemaya, the somewherehouse's most notable characteristic is its twin doors: "One door takes Yemaya straight out into London and the ragged hum of a city after dark. The other door opens out onto the striped flag and cooking-smell cheer of that tattered jester, Lagos—always, this door leads to a place that is floridly day" (Oyeyemi 2007: 1).

Oyeyemi's use of the somewherehouse to thematize the transmission and transformation of cultural practices as affected by histories of migration (forced, elective, and sometimes elected under essentially forced circumstances) provides an apt metaphor for the structures that contain and constrain tradition while also enabling opportunities for renovation and rebuilding by transnationally positioned others. Specifically related to the European fairy-tale tradition and read alongside the somewherehouse, *White Is for Witching* thus offers a metacommentary about the ways the European fairy tale entraps white women in its racist inheritance. While the grand matriarch, Anna, chooses to stay in the Silver house, the next three generations of Silver women—especially Miranda— all seek to escape before being interred in the racist house's toxic interior: "She was just some girl on a bench on a train station platform, crying because something stood between her and another girl and said, no. The goodlady said it couldn't be. Who was the goodlady to say that? How did she dare? / If she could get free, if she could get well—" (Oyeyemi 2009: 269). Significantly, Ore manages to escape the racist house (and the tradition it represents) by relying on the knowledge she has learned from her favorite Afro-Caribbean tale of the girl who kills the soucouyant. Sade, too, overcomes the house's assaults and deadly taunts by keeping faith in her juju, by refusing to speak aloud the house's evil machinations, and by sharing her wisdom with Ore. These escapes from a racist structure are particularly telling when read alongside the somewherehouse, with its two structurally connected doors; together, the two novels and their escape routes metaphorize, map, and mobilize the narrative traditions of a global south—Cuba, Nigeria, the Caribbean, "Africa"—and their power to disrupt and challenge the monolithic authority of the European fairy tale as a universal genre.

Given the ideological power of stories to affect material realities, it can be little surprise that Oyeyemi's novels convey a certain urgency to contest, defy, and expand the European fairy-tale tradition, often compelled by an ancestral call to narrate, tell stories, testify. In *Mr. Fox*, for instance, the story of Brown and Blue ("Like This") features a woman, Brown, who finds herself in a new home with a room in which she is clearly intended to write something, although she is at a loss as to what she is to write. Shortly after her arrival, a note appears under the door: "*Write the stories*" (Oyeymi 2011: 96). She begins with *Once upon a time*, but abandons that effort and begins making a list of things she has lost. Another note slides under the door: "*WRITE THE STORIES*" (96). This pattern ensues for days until she encounters a strange man, made up as a harlequin, who introduces himself as Reynardine before quickly channeling a coterie of her ancestors: "'Can you see us?' And for a moment she saw and felt them all, crowding her. Faces she recognized from family photo albums, some she had never seen before, old ones leaning on walking sticks. They were all familiar" (103). In the ensuing conversation, they demand that she narrate from her Yoruba identity, regardless of the fact that she doesn't know the language and is living in Paris: "'Tell the stories. Tell them to us. We want to know all the ways you're still like us, and all the ways you've changed. Talk to us. We're from a different place and time ...'" (104); when she claims she can't, they reply that she can and must, that the stories belong to them: "'It doesn't matter what language they're in, or what they're about; they belong to us. And we gave them to you without looking at them first. So now it's time to see what we've done'" (104). While at first Brown can only conceive of stories that begin with *Once upon a time*, can only equate story with the dominance of the European fairy tale, her Yoruba ancestors reorient her very definition of story by inserting themselves into the narrative legacy. In turn, Brown writes the stories, story upon story upon story. In exchange, Reynardine returns what she has lost, the lover she walked away from and immediately mourned, but the happy ending requires that she join him in death, albeit a death in which they have the consciousness to appreciate that they can spend an eternity waltzing in their stone house under Père Lachaise.

For Oyeyemi, such ancestral stories are obviously entangled with the European fairy-tale tradition—the initial impulse to start with *Once upon a time*, the slightly twisted happily ever after—but they also push against the boundaries of the genre, exemplified by the fact that Brown's stories include personal narratives, memories of stories she told herself as a child, inventions about imaginary cities (including one that "men were forbidden to enter," 107), tales set in specific locations such as the Okitipupa village. In contrast to this rich cache of stories compelled by Brown's Yoruba ancestors, Miranda's ancestral demands simply make her emotionally and physically sick. As Sade helps Miranda understand that her "old ones" are calling her, Miranda is pushed beyond herself: "Then she saw herself on the floor. Water makes a mirror of any surface ... Miranda wanted to say, *That is not my face*. No, it wasn't hers, she had to get away from it, peel it back. Or she had to leave and take this face with her, defuse it somewhere else" (113). Later, away from the house, Miranda's request that Ore tell her a story makes clear the association between the destructive power of her "old ones" and the imprisoning power of the European fairy tale:

> Please tell a story about a girl who gets away.
>
> I would, even if I had to adapt one, even if I had to make one up just for her. "Gets away from what, though?"
>
> From her fairy godmother. From the happy ending that isn't really happy at all. Please have her get out and run off the page altogether, to somewhere secret where words like "happy" and "good" will never find her.
>
> You don't want her to be happy and good?
>
> I'm not sure what's really meant by happy and good. I would like her to be free. Now. Please begin.
>
> I was silent. I couldn't think of a single story she would want to hear.
>
> (190)

Despite her familiarity with the legend of the soucouyant and her single book of Caribbean folktales, Ore, too, remains steeped in European fairy tales and Western literature, evidenced in her assessment of Miranda's library: "Her bookshelf was quite good—*Grimm's Fairy Tales*, Perrault, Andersen, LeFanu, Wilkie Collins, E. T. A. Hoffmann" (185). As such, she can't satisfy Miranda's request for a story "about a girl who gets away." Indeed, it is only in her life-or-death struggle with the racist Silver house that Ore summons her knowledge of how to defeat the soucouyant to prevail over Miranda's ancestral legacy. For Miranda, meanwhile, there is no freedom, no escape, from the power of the European fairy tale in which she is trapped.[15]

The American writer Audre Lorde famously claimed that "the master's tools will never dismantle the master's house" (Lorde [1984] 2010), and Toni Morrison built on Lorde's influential proclamation in her opening address for the 1994 Race Matters conference at Princeton University:

> If I had to live in a racial house, it was important, at the least, to rebuild it so that it was not a windowless prison into which I was forced, a thick-walled, impenetrable container from which no cry could be heard, but rather an open house, grounded, yet generous in its supply of windows and doors. Or, at the most, it became imperative for me to transform this house completely.
>
> (Morrison 1998: 4)

Morrison goes on to discuss how her fiction has facilitated this commitment to a complete transformation of the "house that race built," the phrase that became the title of the published proceedings from that conference.

I refer to Lorde and Morrison in closing because their entwined evocation of house metaphors to conceptualize power and dominance—particularly racial dominance—seems like an apt inheritance for Oyeyemi, whose fantastic and horrifying houses animate oppressive narrative structures while also suggesting possibilities for radical reconstruction and renewal. In her most recent novel, *Gingerbread*, Oyeyemi introduces a fanciful house on the move, a house that appears "as if it stands on chicken legs and keeps running away" (2018: 249), one that leads the real estate agent on "a merry dance" (250), and that "seems to have moods" (257). With its wonderfully charming history—built of magical materials by thousands of fireflies in a single night, reminiscent of a classic gingerbread house "straight out of a story," according to a German hiker who caught a glimpse of it (although a group of Japanese tourists argued that it was not made of gingerbread but "thinner, crisper stuff … *yatsuhashi*," 257)—this house continually escapes attempts to approach it, attempts to possess it. A sign posted out front reads, in the perhaps make-believe language of Druhástranian: *Only those who have nothing can enter this place* (257).

If, as I have been arguing, Oyeyemi's enchanted houses endeavor to dismantle the master's house—the house that European ideas and ideologies of race built with the help of a set of fairy-tale power tools—*Gingerbread*'s delightfully escapist, trickster-like house begins to lay the foundation for a new narrative structure. In *White Is for Witching*, when Miranda's heart is broken by the racist house's violent disruption of her love for Ore, Oyeyemi seems to suggest that the power of the European fairy tale is yet too tight, that the desire for alternative stories—like the one of a girl's escape that Miranda requests of Ore—is still too reliant on the master's tools. In *Gingerbread*, by contrast, the enchanted house provides a site for the reunion of two friends—one worldly (Harriet), one otherworldly (Gretel)—separated for the greater part of their lives but unknowingly (for Harriet) connected through Gretel's caring watch, her desire for Harriet's joy, and her narration of their story as it unfolds: "Harriet Lee, you're right about the house being a last last last last chance for you and Gretel. That it is and that it will be, and a long time from now, when you have nothing left, we'll meet at the house and pass through it … Let's talk when we get to the house, that third unhaunted house" (258). This house can only be built of other tools. It is a celebration. A homecoming. An entirely different happy ending.

NOTES

Chapter 1

1. Though our focus here must be geographically narrow, we recognize the profound importance of decolonizing fairy-tale studies and acknowledge the wealth of materials to be found around the world (see Bacchilega 2013; Haase 2010; and Teverson 2019).

Chapter 2

1. Significant research on film adaptations of fairy tales has appeared in the past few decades; book-length studies include Walter Rankin's *Grimm Pictures: Fairy Tale Archetypes in Eight Horror and Suspense Films* (2007), Pauline Greenhill and Sydney Eve Matrix's *Fairy Tale Films: Visions of Ambiguity* (2010), Jack Zipes's *The Enchanted Screen: The Unknown History of Fairy-Tale Films* (2011), Anne E. Duggan's *Queer Enchantments: Gender, Sexuality, and Class in the Fairy-Tale Cinema of Jacques Demy* (2013), and Qinna Shen's *The Politics of Magic: DEFA Fairy-Tale Films* (2015).
2. As Jennifer Schacker (2018) has discussed, musical theatre also drew from fairy tales, as in the case of nineteenth-century British pantomimes based on tales by d'Aulnoy and Perrault, and fairy-tale "extravaganzas" were very popular in nineteenth-century France and England.
3. My discussion of photographic adaptations of fairy tales in this chapter is based partly on my article "Photographic" (2018).
4. I would like to thank Anne E. Duggan for raising this critical issue.
5. I would like to thank Anne E. Duggan for alerting me to this point.
6. Similar kinds of tourism-oriented uses of canonical fairy tales can be found not only in Germany—Hamelin is another famous example—but also in other countries including tourism related to Hans Christian Andersen's life and work in Denmark and China (the Andersen-themed amusement park Shanghai Andersen Paradise, opened in 2017, is planned to be replicated in thirty more places throughout China with the help of the Danish government).

7   My analysis of *The Old Animals' Forest Band* in this chapter is based partly on my article "'The Tongue-Cut Sparrow' and the Art of Translating Animals in Fairy Tales" (2019b).
8   This information was provided by the editors of Tara Books in a personal email communication with the author on June 4, 2019.
9   This idea of speech balloons, like that of color coding, was first suggested by Rathna Ramanathan, the book designer of this picturebook, to the artist. This information was provided by the editors of Tara Books in a personal email communication with the author on June 4, 2019.

Chapter 7

1   The movie theater and the mall were torn down around 2008 due to low occupancy; the land remains open because of the developer's bankruptcy and neighborhood debates.
2   Earlier collections—such as those by Giambattista Basile or the earliest editions of the Grimms—contain more bawdy and sexually explicit tales that get edited out of what will become the canonical tales of Perrault and the Grimms. The 1690s tale tellers read Basile and Giovanni Francesco Straparola, and toned down the sexual and scatological elements of the tales when they adapted them. Perrault changes Straparola's and Basile's female cats into a male one for his "Puss in Boots," and Basile's language would have been viewed as "vulgar" by Perrault and his cohort.
3   When I went to Disneyland with my Terry cousins in 1969, the evil witch and her cauldron were waiting to terrorize me again, but this time in the Snow White ride's 3D manifestation.
4   Eerily, and this is true, as I wrote this sentence at my house in August 2019, I could hear "It's a Small World" humming out from some approaching ice cream truck.
5   The first dolls in the Disney Princess line were licensed to be made by Barbie's maker, Mattel, although the license now belongs to its rival Hasbro. Claire Suddath reports that the Disney Princess line is a $5.5 billion business (2015). Barbie movies are reported to bring in over $300 million through 2016 in DVD sales alone, with *12 Dancing Princesses* registering over $28 million in US domestic DVD sales (The Numbers 1997–2020).

Chapter 8

1   See, for example, Hobbes ([1651] 1982); Locke ([1689] 1988); Marx ([1867] 1977); Weber ([1922] 1978).
2   See, for example, Butler (1997); Diamond and Quinby (1988); de Lauretis (1987); Legg (2007); Said (1993, 2000); Spivak ([1988] 2000).
3   Although "archaeology" figures in the subtitle to *Birth of the Clinic*, Foucault never makes clear in any systematic way in that work what he means by the term.
4   Indeed, several tales from Straparola's and Basile's collections reappear with only the slightest variation in the French *contes des fées*.
5   Many feminist fairy-tale scholars have provided excellent analyses of Villiers's *Dialogues on Fairy Tales* and the gendered politics of authorship, literary production, and social critique in relation to the French fairy-tale vogue. See, for example, Duggan (2005); Harries (2001); Jones (2003); and Seifert (1996).
6   See Duggan (2005) for a detailed discussion of Madame d'Aulnoy's fairy tales and the politics of canonicity. As Duggan points out, d'Aulnoy was frequently included

in "worldly" canons—unofficial canons for aristocratic salon participants—until such canons were marginalized by eighteenth-century "pedagogical canons," which laid the foundation for the twentieth-century "classical canon" (13–15).

7   See Harries (2001: 19–45) for an in-depth discussion of fairy-tale canon formation and the marginalization of the *conteuses*, including her compelling reading of C. A. Walckenaer's 1926 *Letters about Fairy Tales* (*Lettres sur les contes des fées*).

8   See Dollerup (1999) for a discussion of translation of the Grimms' *Kinder- und Hausmärchen* and the creation of an international canon that generally revolves around tales with feminine heroines and happy endings.

9   For more on *Kinder und Hausmärchen* in relation to romantic nationalism, see, for example, Abrahams (1993); Haase (1999); Harries (2001); Snyder (1951); Stewart (1991).

10 Here, I refer specifically to the Aarne-Thompson Tale Type Index—and not to the Aarne-Thompson-Uther Index—because the best compilation of other cultural/regional indexes, David Azzolina's *Tale Type and Motif Indexes: An Annotated Bibliography*, was published in 1987. It is difficult to track all of the indexes published since then and to cross-reference them with Uther's *The Types of International Folktales*, although Uther claims to have done so.

11 Translation in Rush Rehm's *The Play of Space* (2002: 79).

12 While space considerations make a comprehensive analysis of all of Oyeyemi's fairy-tale novels impossible, I would argue that it is nonetheless productive to consider them as a collection here, where I focus most fully on *White Is for Witching*. I have published elsewhere on *Boy, Snow, Bird* in relation to "Snow White" and the African folktale tradition (Lau 2016).

13 See Stephanou (2014) for an extended and insightful reading of the soucouyant and the vampire in relation to British imperialism, nationalism, and consumption.

14 For an alternative reading of Oyeyemi's enchanted houses in *The Opposite House* and *White Is for Witching* as related to European and Yoruba underworlds, see Harris Satkunananthan (2018).

15 See Porter (2013) for a discussion of how the combination of European and Yoruba narrative traditions constitutes a "transatlantic gothic hybridity" that reveals "affirmative" cultural resonances and continuities.

REFERENCES

The 10th Kingdom (2000), [Television Program] Dir. D. Carson and Herbert Wise, written by S. Moore, USA: NBC.

Aarne, Antti (1910), *Verzeichnis der Märchentypen*, Folklore Fellows Communications 3, Helsinki: Academia Scientiarum Fennica.

Aboulela, Leila (2019), *Bird Summons*, London: Weidenfeld and Nicolson.

Abrahams, Roger D. (1993), "Phantoms of Romantic Nationalism," *Journal of American Folklore*, 106 (419): 3–37.

Abram, David (2010), *Becoming Animal: An Earthly Cosmology*, New York: Pantheon Books.

The Adventures of Prince Achmed (1926), [Film] Dir. Lotte Reiniger, Germany: Comenius-Film.

Aikau, Hōkūlani K. and Vernadette Vicuña Gonzalez, eds. (2019), *Detours: A Decolonial Guide to Hawai'i*, Durham, NC: Duke University Press.

Aladdin (1992), [Film] Dir. Ron Clements and John Musker, Burbank: Buena Vista Pictures.

Aladdin (2019), [Film] Dir. Guy Ritchie, Burbank: Walt Disney Studios Motion Pictures.

Aldred, B. Grantham (2016), "Music and Musical Instruments," in Anne E. Duggan and Donald Haase, with H. J. Callow (eds.), *Folktales and Fairy Tales: Traditions and Texts from around the World*, 2nd edn., vol. 2, 678–9, Santa Barbara, CA: Greenwood.

Ali, Agha Shahid (1987), "'The Wolf's Postscript to 'Little Red Riding Hood'," in *A Walk Through the Yellow Pages*, Tucson, AZ: SUN-Gemini Press. Available online: https://poets.org/poem/wolfs-postscript-little-red-riding-hood (accessed July 29, 2019).

Alice (1988), [Film] Dir. Jan Švankmajer, Czechoslovakia: Four Film International and Condor Films.

American McGee's Alice (2000), [Video Game] Dir. American McGee, USA: Electronic Arts.

Angel (1999–2004), [TV Series] created by David Greenwalt, and Joss Whedon, USA: Mutant Enemy, Warner Bros Television.

REFERENCES

An Archive of Our Own (2007–), The Organization for Transformative Works. Available online: https://archiveofourown.org/ (accessed July 20, 2019).
Ashliman, D. L. (1996–2020), *Folktexts: A Library of Folktales, Folklore, Fairy Tales, and Mythology*. Available online: http://www.pitt.edu/~dash/folktexts.html (accessed July 20, 2019).
Ashliman, D. L., trans. (2001), "The Story of a Boy Who Went Forth to Learn Fear," Grimms' Brothers Home Page. Available online: https://www.pitt.edu/~dash/grimm004.html (accessed July 14, 2019).
Ashwin, Kate and Kel McDonald (2016–), *Cautionary Fables and Fairytales Series*. Available online: http://cationaryfables.com/index.html (accessed July 20, 2019).
Atwood, Margaret (1983), *Bluebeard's Egg*, Toronto: McClelland & Stewart.
Atwood, Margaret ([1993] 2009a), "I Dream of Zenia with Bright Red Teeth," in *The Robber Bride*, 512–23, London: Hachette Digital.
Atwood, Margaret ([1993] 2009b), *The Robber Bride*, London: Hachette Digital.
Auden, W. H. (1944), "In Praise of the Brothers Grimm," *The New York Times*, November 12: BR, P. 1.
Auden, W. H. (1973), "Grimm and Andersen," in Edward Mendelson (ed.), *Forewords and Afterwords*, 198–208, London: Faber and Faber.
Autumn, Emilie (2003a), "Rapunzel," track 4 on *Enchant*, Traitor Records/Trisol Music Group, MP3.
Autumn, Emilie (2003b), "Rose Red," track 9 on *Enchant*, Traitor Records/Trisol Music Group, MP3.
Aymé, Marcel (1939), *Les contes du chat perché*, Paris: Éditions Gallimard.
Azzolina, David S. (1987), *Tale Types and Motif Indexes: An Annotated Bibliography*, Shrewsbury: Garland.
Bacchilega, Cristina (1997), *Postmodern Fairy Tales: Gender and Narrative Strategies*, Philadelphia: University of Pennsylvania Press.
Bacchilega Cristina (2007), *Legendary Hawai'i and the Politics of Place: Tradition, Translation, and Tourism*, Philadelphia: University of Pennsylvania Press.
Bacchilega, Cristina (2008), "Extrapolating from Nalo Hopkinson's *Skin Folk*: Reflections on Transformation and Recent English-Language Fairy-Tale Fiction by Women," in Stephen Benson (ed.), *Contemporary Fiction and the Fairy Tale*, 178–203, Detroit, MI: Wayne State University Press.
Bacchilega, Cristina (2013), *Fairy Tales Transformed?: Twenty-First-Century Adaptations and the Politics of Wonder*, Detroit, MI: Wayne State University Press.
Bacchilega, Cristina (2018a), "Adaptation and the Fairy-Tale Web," in Pauline Greenhill, Jill Terry Rudy, Naomi Hamer, and Lauren Bosc (eds.), *The Routledge Companion to Media and Fairy-Tale Cultures*, 145–53, New York: Routledge.
Bacchilega, Cristina (2018b), "Postmodernism," in Pauline Greenhill, Jill Terry Rudy, Naomi Hamer, and Lauren Bosc (eds.), *The Routledge Companion to Media and Fairy-Tale Cultures*, 74–82, New York: Routledge.
Bacchilega, Cristina (2019), "'Decolonizing' the Canon: Critical Challenges to Eurocentrism," in Andrew Teverson (ed.), *The Fairy Tale World*, 33–44, London: Routledge.
Bacchilega, Cristina and Sadhana Naithani (2018), "Colonialism, Postcolonialism, Decolonization," in Pauline Greenhill, Jill Terry Rudy, Naomi Hamer, and Lauren Bosc (eds.), *The Routledge Companion to Media and Fairy-Tale Cultures*, 129–40, New York: Routledge.

Bacchilega, Cristina and John Rieder (2014), "The Fairy Tale and the Commercial in *Carosello* and *Fractured Fairy Tales*," in Pauline Greenhill and Jill Terry Rudy (eds.), *Channeling Wonder: Fairy Tales on Television*, 336–61, Detroit, MI: Wayne State University Press.

Baena, Rosalía (2001), "Telling a Bath-Time Story: *Haroun and the Sea of Stories* as a Modern Literary Fairy Tale," *Journal of Commonwealth Literature*, 36 (2): 65–76.

Bail, Murray (1998), *Eucalyptus*, London: Harvill Press.

Bandura, Albert (1977), *Social Learning Theory*, Upper Saddle River, NJ: Prentice Hall.

Barad, Karen (2002), *Meeting the Universe Halfway: Quantum Physics and the Entanglement of Matter and Meaning*, Durham, NC: Duke University Press.

Barbe bleue (2009), [Film] Dir. Catherine Breillat, France: Flach Film/CB Films/Arte France.

Barbie in the 12 Dancing Princesses (2006), [Film Transcript], Barbie Movies Wiki. Available online: https://barbiemovies.fandom.com/wiki/Barbie_in_The_12_Dancing_Princesses/Transcript (accessed August 12, 2019).

Bareilles, Sara (2004), "Fairytale," track 6 on *Careful Confessions*, Tiny Bear Publishing, MP3.

Barnes, Djuna ([1936] 2007), *Nightwood*, London: Faber and Faber.

Barron, Steve, dir. (1987), [Television Episode] *The StoryTeller*, season 1, episode 2, "Fearnot," aired May 22, 1988, UK: Jim Henson Productions.

Barthelme, Donald (1967), *Snow White*, New York: Scribner.

Barthes, Roland ([1957] 1972), *Mythologies*, trans. Annette Lavers, New York: Hill and Wang.

Basile, Giambattista (1634–6), *Lo cunto de le cunti overo lo trattenemiento de peccerille*, 5 vols, Naples: Ottavio Beltrano.

Basu, Balaka (2018), "Children's Picture Books and Illustrations," in Pauline Greenhill, Jill Terry Rudy, N. Hamer, and Lauren Bosc (eds.), *The Routledge Companion to Media and Fairy-Tale Cultures*, 612–22, New York: Routledge.

Baum, L. Frank (1900), *The Wonderful Wizard of Oz*, Chicago: George M. Hill Company.

Bauman, Richard and Charles L. Briggs (2003), *Voices of Modernity: Language Ideologies and the Politics of Inequality*, New York: Cambridge University Press.

Beauty and the Beast (1987–90), [TV Series] created by Ron Koslow, written by Alex Gansa, Howard Gordon, D. Peckinpah, and George R. R. Martin, USA: CBS.

Beauty and the Beast (1991), [Film] Dir. Gary Trousdale and Kirk Wise, Burbank: Buena Vista Pictures.

Beauty and the Beast (1994), [Stage Musical] Music by Alan Menken, lyrics by Howard Ashman and Tim Rice, book by Linda Wollverton, Broadway. USA.

Beauty and the Beast (2012–16), [Television Series] Dir. G. Felder, USA: CBS, CW Television Network.

Beauty and the Beast (2017), [Film] Dir. Bill Condon, Burbank: Walt Disney Studios Motion Pictures.

Beckett, Sandra (2002), *Recycling Red Riding Hood*, New York: Routledge.

Beckett, Sandra, ed. (2014), *Revisioning Red Riding Hood around the World: An Anthology of International Retellings*, Detroit, MI: Wayne State University Press.

Bell, Elizabeth, Lynda Haas, and Laura Sells, eds. (1995), *From Mouse to Mermaid: The Politics of Film, Gender, and Culture*, Bloomington: Indiana University Press.

La Belle et la Bête [*Beauty and the Beast*] (1946), [Film] Dir. Jean Cocteau, France: DisCina.

La Belle et la Bête [*Beauty and the Beast*] (2014), [Film] Dir. Christophe Gans, France/Germany/Spain: Eskwad, Pathé, TF1 Film Production, Studio Babelsberg.

Bells Does Tumblr (n.d.), Available online: https://bellsabub.tumblr.com/post/139243155462/lierdumoa-garrottduroque-joeybarriero-yo/amp (accessed December 18, 2020).

Bendix, Regina (1997), *In Search of Authenticity: The Formation of Folklore Studies*, Madison: University of Wisconsin.

Benjamin, Walter (1999), *Illuminations*, trans. Harry Zohn, ed. Hannah Arendt, London: Pimlico.

Bennett, Jane (2010), *Vibrant Matter: A Political Ecology of Things*, Durham, NC: Duke University Press.

Benson, Stephen (2003), *Cycles of Influence: Fiction, Folktale, Theory*, Detroit, MI: Wayne State University Press.

Benson, Stephen (2008), "Introduction: Fiction and the Contemporaneity of the Fairy Tale," in Stephen Benson (ed.), *Contemporary Fiction and the Fairy Tale*, 1–19, Detroit, MI: Wayne State University Press.

Bernheimer, Kate (2001), *The Complete Tales of Ketzia Gold*, Tallahassee, FL: FC2.

Bernheimer, Kate (2007), *Brothers and Beasts: An Anthology of Men on Fairy Tales*, Detroit, MI: Wayne State University Press.

Bernheimer, Kate (2009), "Fairy Tale Is Form, Form Is Fairy Tale," in *The Writer's Notebook: Craft Essays from Tin House*, 61–73, Portland, OR: Tin House Books.

Bernheimer, Kate (2010), *Horse, Flower, Bird*, Minneapolis, MN: Coffee House Press.

Bernheimer, Kate and Camren Giménez Smith, eds. (2010), *My Mother She Killed Me, My Father He Ate Me*, London: Penguin.

Bettelheim, Bruno (1976), *The Uses of Enchantment: The Meaning and Importance of Fairy Tales*, New York: Knopf.

Bhabha, Homi K. (1992), "Postcolonial Authority and Postmodern Guilt," in Lawrence Grossberg, Cary Nelson, and Paula Treichler (eds.), *Cultural Studies*, 56–68, New York: Routledge.

Bhabha, Homi K. (1994a), "The Commitment to Theory," in *The Location of Culture*, 19–39, London: Routledge.

Bhabha, Homi K. (1994b), "Conclusion: 'Race', Time and the Revision of Modernity," in *The Location of Culture*, 236–56, London: Routledge.

Birke, Lynda (1999), "Bodies and Biology," in Janet Price and Margrit Shildrick (eds.), *Feminist Theory and the Body*, 42–9, Edinburgh: Edinburgh University Press.

Blackwell, Jeannine and Shawn C. Jarvis (2001), *The Queen's Mirror: Fairy Tales by German Women, 1780–1900*, Lincoln: University of Nebraska Press.

Blank, Hanne (2012), *Straight: The Surprisingly Short History of Heterosexuality*, Boston: Beacon Press.

Bloch, Ernst (1988), *The Utopian Function of Art and Literature: Selected Essays*, trans. Jack Zipes and Frank Mecklenburg, Cambridge, MA: MIT Press.

Block, Francesca Lia (2000), *The Rose and the Beast*, New York City: HarperCollins Publishers.

Bluebeard (2009), [Film] Dir. Catherine Breillat, Strasbourg: Arte.

Bluebeard's Bride (2017), [Board Game] created by Whitney Beltrán, Marissa Kelly, and Sarah Richardson, Albuquerque, NM: Magpie Games.

Bodden, Valerie (2009), *The Story of Disney*, Mankato, MN: Creative Education.

Bonner, Sarah (2019), "Tales Retold: Fairy Tales in Contemporary European Visual Art," in Andrew Teverson (ed.), *The Fairy Tale World*, 438–50, London: Routledge.

Borges, Jorge Luis (1998), "The House of Asterion," in *Collected Fictions*, trans. Andrew Hurley, 220–2, New York: Viking.
Borja-Villel, Manuel (2018), "Foreword," in Alyce Mahon, Ann Coxon, and I. M. Castro (eds.), *Dorothea Tanning*, 9–11, London: Tate.
Bottigheimer, Ruth B. (1987), *Grimms' Good Girls and Bold Boys: The Moral and Social Vision of the Tales*, New Haven, CT: Yale University Press.
Bottigheimer, Ruth B. (2004), "Fairy Tales and Folk-Tales," in Peter Hunt (ed.), *The International Companion Encyclopaedia of Children's Literature*, 159, London: Routledge.
Braidotti, Rosi (1994), *Nomadic Subjects*, New York: Columbia University Press.
Braidotti, Rosi (2002), *Metamorphoses: Towards a Materialist Theory of Becoming*, Cambridge and Malden: Polity Press.
Braidotti, Rosi (2007), "Bio-Power and Necro-Politics," published as "Biomacht und nekro- Politik: Uberlegungen zu einer Ethik der Nachhaltigkeit," in *Springerin, Hefte fur Gegenwartskunst*, 13 (2) (Spring): 18–23.
Braidotti, Rosi (2013), *The Posthuman*, Cambridge: Polity Press.
Breaux, Richard M. (2010), "After 75 Years of Magic: Disney Answers Its Critics, Rewrites African American History, and Cashes in on Its Racist Past," *Journal of African American Studies*, 14 (4): 398.
Bremen (2020), "Bremen Town Musicians." Available online: https://www.bremen.eu/tourism/attractions/bremen-town-musicians (accessed May 1, 2020).
Breton, André (1972), *Manifestoes of Surrealism*, trans. Richard Seaver and Helen R. Lane, Ann Arbor: University of Michigan Press.
Brooks, Lisa (2008), "Digging at the Roots: Locating an Ethical, Native Criticism," in Craig S. Womack, Daniel Heath Justice, and Christopher B. Teuton (eds.), *Reasoning Together: The Native Critics Collective*, 234–64, Norman: University of Oklahoma.
Broumas, Olga (1977), *Beginning with O*, New Haven, CT: Yale University Press.
Brown, Bill (2001), "Thing Theory," *Critical Inquiry*, 28 (1): 1–22.
Buchan, David D. (1990), "Folk Literature," in Martin Coyle, Peter Garside, Malcolm Kelsall, and John Peck (eds.), *Encyclopedia of Literature and Criticism*, 976–90, London: Routledge.
Buffy the Vampire Slayer (1997–2003), [Television Series] created by Joss Whedon, USA: Mutant Enemy, Warner Brothers/UPN.
Burgin, Richard and Jorge Luis Borges (1969), *Conversations with Jorge Luis Borges*, New York: Holt, Rinehard and Winston.
Butler, Judith ([1990] 1999), *Gender Trouble: Feminism and the Subversion of Identity*, New York: Routledge.
Butler, Judith (1997), *The Psychic Life of Power: Theories in Subjection*, Stanford, CA: Stanford University Press.
Byatt, A. S. (1995), *The Djinn in the Nightingale's Eye*, London: Vintage.
Byatt, A. S. ([1998] 1999), *Elementals: Stories of Fire and Ice*, London: Vintage.
Byatt, A. S. ([2000] 2001), *On Histories and Stories*, London: Vintage.
Byatt, A. S. ([2003] 2004), *The Little Black Book of Stories*, London: Vintage.
Byatt, A. S. (2004), "Happy Ever After," *The Guardian*, January 3. Available online: https://www.theguardian.com/books/2004/jan/03/sciencefictionfantasyandhorror.fiction (accessed June 11, 2019).
Calvino, Italo (1988), *Six Memos for the Next Millennium: The Charles Eliot Norton Lectures*, Cambridge, MA: Harvard University Press.

Campagnaro, Marnie (2017), "From Palace to House. The Changing Domestic Settings of Fairy Tales," *Encyclopaedia*, 21 (49): 8–30.
Campbell, Joseph (1949), *The Hero with a Thousand Faces*, Princeton, NJ: Bollingen Foundation.
Carastathis, Anna (2016), *Intersectionality: Origins, Contestations, Horizons*, Lincoln: University of Nebraska Press.
Cardcaptor Sakura (1998–2000), [Film] Dir. Morio Asaka, written by Nanase Ohkawa, Japan: NKH BS2.
Carrington, Leonora (1989), "The Debutante," in *The House of Fear: Notes from Down Below*, ed. M. Warner, trans. K. Talbot, 27–33, London: Virago.
Carroll, Emily (2014), *Through the Woods*, New York: Margaret K. McElderry Books.
Carroll, Lewis (1865), *Alice's Adventures in Wonderland*, Oxford: Macmillan.
Carter, Angela, trans. (1977a), *The Fairy Tales of Charles Perrault*, London: Victor Gollancz.
Carter, Angela (1977b), *The Passions of New Eve*, London: Victor Gollancz.
Carter, Angela ([1979] 2006), *The Bloody Chamber and Other Stories*, London: Vintage.
Carter, Angela ([1984] 2006), *Nights at the Circus*, London: Oberon.
Carter, Angela (1985), *Come Unto These Yellow Sands: Four Radio Plays*, Hexham: Bloodaxe Books.
Carter, Angela, ed. (1990), *The Virago Book of Fairy Tales*, London: Virago Press.
Carter, Angela, ed. ([1990, 1992] 2005), *Angela Carter's Book of Fairy Tales*, London: Virago.
Carter, Angela (1998), *Shaking a Leg: Collected Journalism and Writings*, London: Vintage.
Césaire, Aimé ([1947] 1995) *Notebook of a Return to my Native Land*, trans. Mirelle Rosello and Annie Pritchard, Tarset: Bloodaxe.
Césaire, Aimé and René Ménil (1942), "Introduction au folklore Martiniquais," *Tropiques*, 4: 7–11.
Chamoiseau, Patrick ([1988] 1994), *Strange Words*, trans. Linda Coverdale, London: Granta.
Cinderella (1922), [Film] Dir. Lotte Reiniger, Germany: Institut für Kulturforschung.
Cinderella ([1950] 1997), [Film] Dir. Clyde Geronimi, Hamilton Kuske, and Wilfred Jackson, New York: RKO Radio Pictures.
Cinderella (1957), [TV Film] Dir. Ralph Nelson, written by Oscar Hammerstein II, USA: CBS.
Cinderella (1965), [TV Film] Dir. Charles S. Dubin, written by Joseph Schrank, USA: CBS.
Cinderella (1997), [TV Film] Dir. Robert Iscove, written by Robert L. Freeman, USA: CBS.
Cinderella (1997), [Ballet] Dir. Matthew Bourne, music by Sergei Prokofiev, Plymouth: Theatre Royal.
Cinderella (2015), [Film] Dir. Kenneth Branagh, Burbank: Walt Disney Studios Motion Pictures.
Cinders (2012), [Video Game] Des. Tom Grochowiak, USA: MoaCube.
Clark, Timothy (2011), *The Cambridge Introduction to Literature and the Environment*, Cambridge: Cambridge University Press.
Cleto, Sara and Erin Kathleen Bahl (2016), "Becoming the Labyrinth: Negotiating Magical Space and Identity in *Puella Magi Madoka Magica*," *Humanities*, 5 (2): 20. https://doi.org/10.3390/h5020020.

Climent, James (2013), "Women's Rights," in Christopher G. Bates (ed.), *Global Social Issues: An Encyclopedia*, London: Routledge.
Cohen, Jeffrey Jerome, ed. (1996), *Monster Theory: Reading Culture*, Minneapolis: University of Minnesota Press.
Cole, Babette (1987), *Princess Smartypants*, New York: Putnam.
Colebrook, Claire (2002), *Gilles Deleuze*, London: Routledge.
The Company of Wolves (1984), [Film] Dir. Neil Jordan, London: ITC Entertainment.
Cool School (2014–), YouTube. Available online: https://www.youtube.com/user/coolschool/ (accessed July 20, 2019).
Coole, Diane (2010), "The Inertia of Matter and the Generativity of Flesh," in Diane Coole and Samantha Frost (eds.), *New Materialisms: Ontology, Agency, and Politics*, 92–115, Durham, NC: Duke University Press.
Coole, Diane and Samantha Frost (2010), "Introducing the New Materialisms," in Diane Coole and Samantha Frost (eds.), *New Materialisms: Ontology, Agency, and Politics*, 1–43, Durham, NC: Duke University Press.
Coover, Robert (1969), *Pricksongs & Descants*, New York: Dutton.
Crofts, Charlotte (2003), *"Anagrams of Desire": Angela Carter's Writing for Radio, Film and Television*, Manchester: Manchester University Press.
Cunningham, Michael (2015), *A Wild Swan and Other Tales*, London: Harper Collins.
D'Amore, Laura M. (2017), "Vigilante Feminism: Revising Trauma, Abduction, and Assault in American Fairy-Tale Revisions," *Marvels & Tales*, 31 (2): 386–405.
d'Aulnoy, Marie-Catherine Le Jumel de Barneville, Baronne (1697), *Les contes de fées*, 4 vols, 1st edn., Paris: Claude Barbin.
d'Aulnoy, Marie-Catherine Le Jumel de Barneville, Baronne (1698), *Les contes nouveaux ou les fées à la mode*, 2 vols, Paris: Veuve de Théodore Girard.
Dahl, Roald ([1964] 1995), *Charlie and the Chocolate Factory*, New York: Puffin Books.
Dahl, Roald ([1982] 2009), *Revolting Rhymes*, New York: Puffin Books.
Dahl, Roald (1988), *Matilda*, New York: Penguin Books USA.
Dancehall Queen (1997), Dir. Rick Elgood and Don Letts, Jamaica: Hawk's Nest Productions.
Darrieussecq, Marie (1996), *Truismes*, Paris: P.O.L. éditeur.
Darrieussecq, Marie (1997), *Pig Tales: A Novel of Lust and Transformation*, trans. Linda Coverdale, New York: The New Press.
Datlow, Ellen and Terri Windling, eds. (1995), *Snow White, Blood Red*, New York: HarperCollins Publishers.
Day, Aidan (1998), *Angela Carter: The Rational Glass*, Manchester: Manchester Univeristy Press.
de Beauvoir, Simone ([1949] 2011) *The Second Sex*, trans. Constance Borde and Sheila Malovany-Chevallier, London: Vintage.
De Lauretis, Teresa (1987), *Technologies of Gender: Essays on Theory, Film, and Fiction*, Bloomington: Indiana University Press.
Dea, Shannon (2016), *Beyond the Binary: Thinking about Sex and Gender*, Peterborough, ONT: Broadview Press.
Degh, Linda (1994), *American Folklore and the Mass Media*, Bloomington: Indiana University Press.
Desblache, Lucile (2005), "Beauties and Beasts: Contrasting Visions of Animal Representation in Women's Contemporary Fiction," *Comparative Critical Studies*, 2 (3): 381–95.

Diamond, Irene and Lee Quinby, eds. (1988), *Feminism and Foucault: Reflections on Resistance*, Lebanon, NH: Northeastern University Press.
Dicker, Rory C. (2008), *A History of U.S. Feminisms*, Berkeley, CA: Seal Press.
Die unendliche Geschichte [*The NeverEnding Story*] (1984), [Film] Dir. Wolfgang Peterson, USA/West Germany: Westdeutscher Rundfunk (WDR).
Dimaline, Cherie (2017), *The Marrow Thieves*, Toronto: Cormorant Books.
Disch, L. J. (1993), "More Truth than Fact: Storytelling as Critical Understanding in the Writings of Hannah Arendt," *Political Theory*, 21 (4): 665–94.
Disenchantment (2018–), [Television Series] created by Matt Groening. Netflix.
Do Rozario, Rebecca-Anne (2011), "Australia's Fairy Tales Illustrated in Print: Instances of Indigeneity, Colonization, and Suburbanization," *Marvels & Tales*, 25 (1): 13–32.
Dollerup, Cay (1999), *Tales and Translation: The Grimm Tales from Pan-Germanic Narratives to Shared International Fairytales*, Benjamin's Translation Library 30, Amsterdam: J. Benjamins.
Donkeyskin (1970), [Film] Dir. Jacques Demy, Los Angeles: Entertainment One Films.
Donoghue, Emma ([1993] 1997), *Kissing the Witch: Old Tales in New Skins*, New York: Harper Collins.
DragonHeart (1996), [Film] Dir. Rob Cohen, USA: Universal Pictures.
Dread and Delight: Fairy Tales in an Anxious World (2018), [Exhibition], August 25–December 9, Weatherspoon Art Museum of the University of North Carolina at Greensboro, Greensboro, NC.
Dresden, Madeleine (2013), class paper for English 640: Studies in Folklore, Brigham Young University Press.
Duggan, Anne E. (2005), *Salonnières, Furies, and Fairies: The Politics of Gender and Cultural Change in Absolutist France*, Newark: University of Delaware Press.
Duggan, Anne E. (2013), *Queer Enchantments: Gender, Sexuality, and Class in the Fairy-Tale Cinema of Jacques Demy*, Detroit, MI: Wayne State University Press.
Dundes, Alan (1968), "Introduction to the Second Edition," in Vladimir Propp, *Morphology of the Folktale*, 1–6, Bloomington: Indiana University Press.
Dundes, Alan (1991), "Bruno Bettelheim's Uses of Enchantment and Abuses of Scholarship," *Journal of American Folklore*, 104 (411): 74–83.
Dworkin, Andrea (1974), *Woman Hating*, New York: E. P. Dutton.
The Elephant Man (1980), [Film] Dir. David Lynch, USA/UK: Brooksfilms.
Eliot, T. S. (1923), "Ulysses, Order, and Myth," *The Dial*, 75 (5): 480–3.
Ellis, B. (2016), "The Fairy-Telling Craft of *Princess Tutu*: Metacommentary and the Folkloresque," in Michael Dylan Foster and Jeffrey A. Tolbert (eds.), *The Folkloresque: Reframing Folklore in a Popular Culture World*, 221–40, Logan: Utah State University Press.
Enchanted (2007), [Film] Dir. Kevin Lima, Burbank: Walt Disney Studios Motion Pictures.
Eragon (2006), [Film] Dir. Stefen Fangmeier, UK/Hungary/USA: Dune Entertainment/Davis Entertainment.
Erb, Cynthia (1995), "Another World or the World of an Other? The Space of Romance in Recent Versions of 'Beauty and the Beast'," *Cinema Journal*, 34 (4): 50–70.
Estés, Clarissa Pinkola (1992), *Women Who Run with the Wolves: Myths and Stories of the Wild Woman Archetype*, New York: Ballantine.
Ever After (1998), [Film] Dir. Andy Tennant, Los Angeles: Twentieth Century Fox.

Ex Machina (2014), [Film] Dir. Alex Garland, UK/USA: Film4/DNA Films.
Faerie Tale Theatre (1982–7), [Television Series] created by Shelley Duvall, USA: Gaylord.
Fairy Tale Fashion (2016), [Exhibition], January 15–April 16, Fashion Institute of Technology, New York.
Fairytale Gloom (2015), [Board Game] Des. Keith Baker, St. Paul, MN: Atlas Games.
Fanfiction (1998–). Available online: https://www.fanfiction.net/ (accessed July 20, 2019).
Fantasies and Fairy Tales (2018–19), [Exhibition] September 8–February 3, Los Angeles County Museum of Art, Los Angeles.
Figes, Eva (2003), *Tales of Innocence and Experience: An Exploration*, New York: Bloomsbury.
Florence + the Machine (2009a), "Blinding," written by Florence Welch and Paul Epworth, track 12 on *Lungs*, Island, MP3.
Florence + the Machine (2009b), "Rabbit Heart," written by Florence Welch and Paul Epworth, track 2 on *Lungs*, Island, MP3.
Foster, Michael Dylan and Jeffrey A. Tolbert (2016), *The Folkloresque: Reframing Folklore in a Popular Culture World*, Logan: Utah State University Press.
Foucault, Michel ([1961] 1988), *Madness and Civilization*, trans. Richard Howard, London: Vintage Books.
Foucault, Michel ([1963] 1973) *Birth of the Clinic*, trans. Alan Sheridan, London: Pantheon.
Foucault, Michel ([1966] 1970), *The Order of Things*, trans. Alan Sheridan, London: Pantheon.
Foucault, Michel ([1969] 1972), *Archaeology of Knowledge*, trans. Alan Sheridan, London: Pantheon.
Foucault, Michel (1980), "Two Lectures," in Colin Gordon (ed.), *Power/Knowledge: Selected Interviews & Other Writings 1972–1977*, 78–109, London: Vintage Books.
The Four Musicians of Bremen (1922), [Film] Dir. Walt Disney, USA: Laugh-O-Gram Films.
"Fractured Fairy Tales" (1959–64), [Television] *The Adventures of Rocky and Bullwinkle and Friends*, created by Jay Ward, Alex Anderson, and Bill Scott, written by Bill Scott, C. Hayward, and Allan Burns, USA: ABC.
Frank, Arthur W. (2010), *Letting Stories Breathe: A Socio-Narratology*, Chicago: University of Chicago Press.
Franz, Marie-Louise von (1974), *Shadow and Evil in Fairy Tales*, Zurich: Spring Publications.
Fraser, Lucy (2017), *The Pleasures of Metamorphosis: Japanese and English Fairy Tale Transformations of "The Little Mermaid,"* Detroit, MI: Wayne State University Press.
Freud, Sigmund ([1918] 2002), "From the History of an Infantile Neurosis [The 'Wolfman']," in *The "Wolfman" and Other Cases*, trans. David McLintock, 203–320, London: Penguin.
Freud, Sigmund ([1919] 2003), "The Uncanny," in *The Uncanny*, trans. David McLintock, 123–62, London: Penguin.
Frozen (2013), [Film] Dir. Chris Buck and Jennifer Lee, Burbank: Walt Disney Studios Motion Pictures.
Futurama (1999–2013), [Television Series] created by Matt Groening, USA: Fox.

Gaiman, Neil (1997), *Stardust*, New York City: HarperCollins.
Gaiman, Neil (2002), *Coraline*, New York City: HarperCollins.
Galef, David (1984), "A Sense of Magic: Reality and Illusion in Cocteau's *Beauty and the Beast*," *Literature Film Quarterly*, 12 (1): 96–106.
Garner, Alan ([1960] 2017), *The Weirdstone of Brisingamen*, New York: HarperCollins.
Gaur, Suchi (2014), "Durga Bai: Telling Women's Stories with Gond Art," *Women's Web*, May 26. Available online: https://www.womensweb.in/2014/05/durga-bai-gond-artist/ (accessed May 1, 2019).
Georges, Robert A. (1983), "The Universality of the Tale-Type as Concept and Construct," *Western Folklore*, 42 (1): 21–8.
Germon, Jennifer E. (2008), "Kinsey and the Politics of Bisexual Authenticity," *Journal of Bisexuality*, 8: 243–58.
Gilbert, Sandra and Susan Gubar (1979), *The Madwoman in the Attic: The Woman Writer and the Nineteenth-Century Literary Imagination*, New Haven, CT: Yale University Press.
Gilbert, Zoe (2018), *Folk*, London: Bloomsbury.
Giroux, Henry A. (1999), *The Mouse that Roared: Disney and the End of Innocence*, Lanham, MD: Rowman & Littlefield Publishers.
Goldman, William ([1973] 2007), *The Princess Bride: S. Morgenstern's Classic Tale of True Love and High Adventure*, Orlando, FL: Houghton Mifflin Harcourt.
Goldstein, Dina (2007–9), *Fallen Princesses* [Photograph Series]. Available online: https://www.dinagoldstein.com/dina-goldsteins-fallen-princesses/ (accessed May 1, 2020)
Greenhill, Pauline (2018), "Cinematic," in Pauline Greenhill, Jill Terry Rudy, Naomi Hamer, and Lauren Bosc (eds.), *The Routledge Companion to Media and Fairy-Tale Cultures*, 357–66, New York: Routledge.
Greenhill, Pauline (2019), "Sexes, Sexualities, and Gender in Cinematic North and South American Fairy Tales: Transforming Cinderellas," in Andrew Teverson (ed.), *The Fairy Tale World*, 248–59, London: Routledge.
Greenhill, Pauline and Emilie Anderson-Grégoire (2014), "'If Thou Be Woman, Be Now Man!': 'The Shift of Sex' as Transsexual Imagination," in Pauline Greenhill and Diane Tye (eds.), *Unsettling Assumptions: Tradition, Gender, Drag*, 56–73, Boulder: University Press of Colorado.
Greenhill, Pauline and Sidney Eve Matrix, eds. (2010), *Fairy Tale Films: Visions of Ambiguity*, Logan: Utah State University Press.
Greenhill, Pauline, Jill Terry Rudy, Naomi Hamer, and Lauren Bosc, eds. (2018), *The Routledge Companion to Media and Fairy-Tale Cultures*, New York: Routledge.
Greenwalt, David (n.d.), "Interview," *BBC Online*. Available online: http://bbc.co.uk/cult/buffy/angel/interviews/greenwalt/page4.shtml (accessed May 8, 2020).
Grimm (2011–17), [Television Series] created by Stephen Carpenter, Jim Kouf, and David Greenwalt, USA: NBC.
Grimm, Jacob and Wilhelm Grimm (1812), *Kinder- und Hausmärchen*, Berlin: Realschulbuchhandlung.
Grinfas, J. and Amélie Nothomb (2015), "Interview Exclusive," in Amélie Nothomb (ed.), *Barbe bleue*, 149–51, Paris: Éditions Magnard.
Gripari, Pierre ([1967] 1988), *Le gentil petit diable et autres contes de la rue Broca*, Paris: Éditions Gallimard.

Gripari, Pierre (2013), *The Good Little Devil and Other Tales*, London: Pushkin Children's Books.
Gunawan, Michelle (2018), "Navigating Human and Non-Human Animal Relations: *Okja*, Foucault and Animal Welfare Laws," *Alternative Law Journal*, 43: 263–8.
Gupfinger, Reinhard and Martin Kaltenbrunner (2018), "Animals Make Music: A Look at Non-Human Musical Expression," *Multimodal Technologies and Interaction*, 2 (51): 1–14. https://doi.org/10.3390/mti2030051.
Guran, Paula, ed. (2016), *Beyond the Woods: Fairy Tales Retold*, Jersey City, NJ: Night Shade Books.
Gurimu meisaku gekijou [Grimm's Fairy Tale Classics] (1987–9), [Television Series] Dir. Hiroshi Saito, Japan: TV Asahi.
Haas, Lynda and Shaina Trapino (2018), "Disney Corporation," in Pauline Greenhill, Jill Terry Rudy, Naomi Hamer, and Lauren Bosc (eds.), *The Routledge Companion to Media and Fairy-Tale Cultures*, 257–69, New York: Routledge.
Haase, Donald, ed. (1993), *The Reception of Grimms' Fairy Tales: Responses, Reactions, Revisions*, Detroit, MI: Wayne State University Press.
Haase, Donald (1999), "Yours, Mine, or Ours?: Perrault, the Brothers Grimm, and the Ownership of Fairy Tales," in Maria Tatar (ed.), *The Classic Fairy Tales*, 353–64, New York: Norton.
Haase, Donald (2000), "Feminist Fairy-Tale Scholarship: A Critical Survey and Bibliography," *Marvels & Tales*, 14 (1): 15–63.
Haase, Donald (2007), "Fairy Tale," in Donald Haase (ed.), *The Greenwood Encyclopedia of Folktales and Fairy Tales*, 322–5, Santa Barbara, CA: Greenwood.
Haase, Donald (2010), "Decolonizing Fairy-Tale Studies," *Marvels & Tales*, 24 (1): 17–38.
Haase, Donald (2015), "The Bremen Town Musicians," in Jack Zipes (ed.), *The Oxford Companion to Fairy Tales*, 2nd edn., 72, Oxford: Oxford University Press.
Haase, Donald (2019), "Global or Local? Where Do Fairy Tales Belong?," in Andrew Teverson (ed.), *The Fairy Tale World*, 17–32, London: Routledge.
Hadestown (2016), [Stage Musical] music, lyrics, and book by Anaïs Mitchell, Broadway, USA.
Haffenden, John (1985), *Novelists in Interview*, London: Methuen.
Hall, Sarah ([2013] 2017), "Mrs Fox," *Toast Magazine*, December 14. Available online: https://www.toa.st/magazine/mrs-fox-short-story-sarah-hall.htm (accessed June 20, 2019).
Hall, Todrick (2013), "Disney Dudez by Todrick Hall," YouTube, June 25. Available online: https://www.youtube.com/watch?v=MWdFrw5DoJU (accessed July 20, 2019).
Hall, Todrick (2014), "'CinderFella' by Todrick Hall," YouTube, July 24. Available online: https://www.youtube.com/watch?v=F9ZA7bn5ujk (accessed July 20, 2019).
Hallett, Martin and Barbara Karasek, eds. (2014), *Fairy Tales in Popular Culture*, Ontario: Broadview Press.
Halsey, Mark (2006), *Deleuze and Environmental Damage: Violence of the Text*, Aldershot: Ashgate.
Hamer, Naomi (2018), "Children's Museums," in Pauline Greenhill, Jill Terry Rudy, Naomi Hamer, and Lauren Bosc (eds.), *The Routledge Companion to Media and Fairy-Tale Cultures*, 601–11, New York: Routledge.
Hansel and Gretel: Witch Hunters (2013), [Film] Dir. Tommy Wirkola, Hollywood: Paramount Pictures/Metro-Goldwyn-Mayer.

Haraway, Donna J. ([1984] 2016), "A Cyborg Manifesto: Science, Technology, and Socialist-Feminism in the Late Twentieth Century," in Donna J. Haraway (ed.), *Manifestly Haraway*, 3–90, Minneapolis: University of Minnesota Press.

Harries, Elizabeth Wanning (2001), *Twice Upon a Time: Women Writers and the History of the Fairy Tale*, Princeton, NJ: Princeton University Press.

Harries, Elizabeth Wanning (2015), "Socialization and Fairy Tales," in Jack Zipes (ed.), *The Oxford Companion to Fairy Tales*, 480–1, Oxford: Oxford University Press.

Harris, Dylan M. (2017), "Telling the Story of Climate Change: Geologic Imagination, Praxis, and Policy," *Energy Research & Social Science*, 31: 179–83. https://doi.org/10.1016/j.erss.2017.05.027.

Harris Satkunananthan, Anita (2018), "Otherworlds, Doubles, Houses: H. Oyeyemi's *The Opposite House* and *White Is for Witching*," *GEMA Online Journal of Language Studies*, 18 (4): 201–15.

Harry Potter and the Philosopher's Stone (*Harry Potter and the Sorcerer's Stone*) (2001), [Film] Dir. C. Columbus, UK/USA: 1492 Pictures.

Hay, Rebecca and Christa Baxter (2014), "Happily Never After: The Commodification and Critique of Fairy Tale in ABC's *Once Upon a Time*," in Pauline Greenhill and Jill Terry Rudy (eds.), *Channeling Wonder: Fairy Tales on Television*, 316–35, Detroit, MI: Wayne State University Press.

Hearne, Joanna (2017), "'I Am Not a Fairy Tale': Indigenous Storytelling on Canadian Television," *Marvels & Tales*, 31 (1): 126–46.

Hegerfeldt, Anne C. (2005), *Lies that Tell the Truth: Magical Realism Seen Through Contemporary Fiction from Britain*, Amsterdam: Rodopi.

Heiner, Heidi Anne (1998), *SurLaLune Fairy Tales*. Available online: http://www.surlalunefairytales.com/ (accessed July 20, 2019).

Heise, Ursula K. (2006), "The Hitchhiker's Guide to Ecocriticism," *Modern Language Association*, 121 (2): 503–16. Available online: http://www.jstor.org/stable/25486328 (accessed July 1, 2019).

Hennard Dutheil de la Rochère, Martine (2013), *Reading, Translating, Rewriting: Angela Carter's Translational Poetics*, Detroit, MI: Wayne State University Press.

Hernández, Isabel and Nieves Martín-Rogero (2014), "The Grimms' Fairy Tales in Spain: Translation, Reception, and Ideology," in Vanessa Joosen and Gillian Lathey (eds.), *Grimms' Tales Around the Globe: The Dynamics of Their International Reception*, 59–79, Detroit, MI: Wayne State University Press.

Herzogenrath, Bernd (2008), "Introduction," in Bernd Herzogenrath (ed.), *An [Un]likely Alliance: Thinking Environment[s] with Deleuze and Guattari*, 1–22, Newcastle: Cambridge Scholars Publishing.

Hillier, Jean ([2007] 2017), *Stretching Beyond the Horizon: A Multiplanar Theory of Spatial Planning and Governance*, London: Ashgate.

hoʻomanawanui, kuʻualoha (2014), *Voices of Fire: Reweaving the Literary Lei of Pele and Hiʻiaka*, Minneapolis: University of Minnesota.

hoʻomanawanui, kuʻualoha (2018), "Indigeneity: E Hoʻokikohoʻe i Peʻapeʻamakawalu (Digitizing the Eight-Eyed Bat): Indigenous Wonder Tales, Culture, and Media," in Pauline Greenhill, Jill Terry Rudy, Naomi Hamer, and Lauren Bosc (eds.), *The Routledge Companion to Media and Fairy-Tale Cultures*, 122–32, New York: Routledge.

Hobbes, Thomas ([1651] 1982), *Leviathan: Or the Matter, Form, and Power of a Commonwealth, Ecclesiastical and Civil*, London: Penguin.

The Hobbit: An Unexpected Journey (2012), [Film] Dir. Peter Jackson, New Zealand/USA: WingNut Films.

Hoggard, Liz (2014), "Interview: Helen Oyeyemi," *The Guardian*, March 2. Available online: https://www.theguardian.com/books/2014/mar/02/helen-oyeyemi-women-disappoint-one-another (accessed December 10, 2020).

Holbek, Bengt (1998), *Interpretation of Fairy Tales*, Folklore Fellows Communications, Helsinki: Academia Scientiarum Fennica.

Hopkinson, Nalo (2001), *Skin Folk*, New York: Warner Books.

How to Train Your Dragon (2010), [Film] Dir. Dean DeBlois and Chris Sanders, USA: Dreamworks.

Hutcheon, Linda, with Siobhan O'Flynn (2013), *A Theory of Adaptation*, 2nd edn., New York: Routledge.

Into the Woods (1987), [Stage Musical] music and lyrics by Stephen Sondheim, book by James Lapine, USA: Broadway.

Into the Woods (2014), [Film] Dir. Rob Marshall, Burbank: Walt Disney Pictures.

Isaac, Mike (2016), "Times Reporter Descends Into Pokémania," *The New York Times*, July 12. Available online: https://www.nytimes.com/2016/07/12/insider/how-pokemon-go-augmented-a-reporters-reality.html?_r=0 (accessed March 1, 2019).

James, Marlon (2019), *Black Leopard, Red Wolf*, New York: Riverhead Books.

Jenkins, Henry (2006), *Fans, Bloggers, and Gamers: Exploring Participatory Culture*, New York: New York University Press.

Jones, Christine A. (2003), "Poetics of Enchantment (1690–1715)," *Marvels & Tales*, 17 (1): 55–74.

Jones, Christine A. and Jennifer Schacker (2012), *Marvelous Transformations: An Anthology of Fairy Tales and Contemporary Critical Perspectives*, Peterborough, ONT: Broadview Press.

Joosen, Vanessa (2007), "Disenchanting the Fairy Tale: Retellings of 'Snow White' Between Magic and Realism," *Marvels & Tales*, 21 (1): 228–39.

Joosen, Vanessa (2011), *Critical and Creative Perspectives on Fairy Tales: An Intertextual Dialogue between Fairy-Tale Scholarship and Postmodern Retellings*, Detroit, MI: Wayne State University Press.

Jorgensen, Jeana (2008), "Innocent Initiations: Female Agency in Eroticized Fairy Tales," *Marvels & Tales*, 22 (1): 27–37.

Jorgensen, Jeana (2019), "Gender, Sexuality and the Fairy Tale in Contemporary American Literature," in Andrew Teverson (ed.), *The Fairy Tale World*, 260–72, London: Routledge.

Jorgensen, Jeana (2020), "Voiceless Yet Vocal: Speaking Desire in *The Shape of Water*," in Amanda Firestone and Leisa A. Clark (eds.), *Resist and Persist: Essays on Social Revolution in 21st Century Narratives*, 87–97, Jefferson, NC: McFarland.

Jorgensen, Jeana and Brittany Warman (2014), "Molding Messages: Analyzing the Reworking of 'Sleeping Beauty' in *Grimm's Fairy Tale Classics* and *Dollhouse*," in Pauline Greenhill and Jill Terry Rudy (eds.), *Channeling Wonder: Fairy Tales on Television*, 144–62, Detroit, MI: Wayne State University Press.

Joyce, James ([1922] 1993), *Ulysses*, Oxford: Oxford University Press.

Joyce, James ([1939] 1992), *Finnegans Wake*, London: Penguin.

The Juniper Tree (1990), [Film] Dir. Nietzchka Keene, Iceland: Keene Productions.

Justice, Daniel Heath (2018), *Why Indigenous Literatures Matter*, Waterloo, ONT: Wilfrid Laurier University Press.

Kamenetsky, Christa (1984), *Children's Literature in Hitler's Germany*, Athens: Ohio University Press.

Katsavos, Anna (1994), "Interview with Angela Carter," *Review of Contemporary Fiction*, 14: 11–17.

Kawai, Hayao (1988), *The Japanese Psyche: Major Motifs in the Fairy Tales of Japan*, trans. Kawai Hayao and Sachiko Reece, Zurich: Spring Publications.

Kelley, Robin D. G. (1999), "A Poetics of Anticolonialism," *Monthly Review*, 51 (6). Available online: https://monthlyreview.org/1999/11/01/a-poetics-of-anticolonialism/ (accessed May 1, 2020).

Kérchy, Anna (2018), "Children's and Young Adult (YA) Literature," in Pauline Greenhill, Jill Terry Rudy, Naomi Hamer, and Lauren Bosc (eds.), *The Routledge Companion to Media and Fairy-Tale Cultures*, 327–39, New York: Routledge.

Kill, Natalia (2011), "Wonderland," written by Natalia Kills, Michael Warren, and Theron Feemster, track 2 on *Perfectionist*, will.i.am, Cherrytree, KonLive, and Interscope, MP3.

King-Aribisala, Karen (2007), *The Hangman's Game*, Leeds: Peepal Tree Press.

Kingdom Hearts (2002–19), [Video Game] Dir. Tetsuya Nomura, Japan: Square Enix.

King's Ears, The (2016), [Mobile App], USA: Rascal Media.

Kōnoike, Tomoko (2006), *The Planet is Covered by Silvery Sleep*, [Sculpture] Mizuma Art Gallery, Toyko.

Kōnoike, Tomoko (2013), *Donning Animal Skins and Braided Grass*, [Sculpture] Gallery Hyundai, Seoul.

Koopman, Colin and Tomas Matza (2013), "Putting Foucault to Work: Analytic and Concept in Foucaultian Inquiry," *Critical Inquiry*, 39: 817–40.

Kurahashi, Yumiko (2008), "Two Tales from *Cruel Fairy Tales for Adults*," *Marvels & Tales*, 22 (1): 171–82.

Kustritz, Anne (2018), "Fandom/Fan Cultures," in Pauline Greenhill, Jill Terry Rudy, Naomi Hamer, and Lauren Bosc (eds.), *The Routledge Companion to Media and Fairy-Tale Cultures*, 340–9, New York: Routledge.

Kustritz, Anne (2019), "Fairy Tale, Fan Fiction, and Popular Media," in Andrew Teverson (ed.), *The Fairy Tale World*, 284–95, New York: Routledge.

Kuwada, Bryan Kamaoli and Aiko Yamashiro, eds. (2016), "Rooted in Wonder: Tales of Indigenous Activism and Community Organizing," *Marvels & Tales*, 30 (1): 17–21.

Lang, Andrew (1893), "Modern Fairy Tales," *The Illustrated London News*, December 3: 714.

Lau, Kimberly J. (2015), *Erotic Infidelities: Love and Enchantment in Angela Carter's The Bloody Chamber*, Detroit, MI: Wayne State University Press.

Lau, Kimberly J. (2016), "Snow White and the Trickster: Race and Genre in H. Oyeyemi's *Boy, Snow, Bird*," *Western Folklore*, 75 (3/4): 371–96.

Lebeau, Suzanne (1997), *L'Ogrelet*, Paris: Éditions Théâtrales.

Lee, Sung-Ae (2019), "Memory, Trauma, and History: Fairy-Tale Film in Korea," in Andrew Teverson (ed.), *The Fairy Tale World*, 356–67, London: Routledge.

Lee, Tanith (1983), *Red as Blood or Tales from the Sisters Grimmer*, New York: DAW.

The Legend of Zelda (1986), [Video Game] Des. Shigeru Miyamoto and Takashi Tezuka, Japan: Nintendo.

Legg, Stephen (2007), "Beyond the European Province: Foucault and Postcolonialism," in Jeremy W. Crampton and Stuart Elden (eds.), *Space, Knowledge, and Power: Foucault and Geography*, 265–89, Aldershot: Ashgate,

Leprince, Chloé (2016), "Marie Darrieussecq: Le féminin, j'ai beaucoup à en écrire, mais rien à en dire," *France Culture*, July 18. Available online: https://www.franceculture.fr/litterature/marie-darrieussecq-le-feminin-j-ai-beaucoup-en-ecrire-mais-rien-en-dire (accessed May 9, 2019).

Lester, Neal A. (2019), "African-American Adaptations of Fairy Tales," in Andrew Teverson (ed.), *The Fairy Tale World*, 232–47, London: Routledge.

Lesuma, Caryn Kunz (2018), "Contemporary Young Adult Literature in Hawai'i and the Pacific: Genre, Diaspora, and Oceanic Futures," PhD diss., University of Hawai'i at Manoa, Honolulu.

Lewis, C. S. (1950), *The Lion, the Witch and the Wardrobe*, London: Geoffrey Bles.

Lewis, C. S. (1951), *Prince Caspian*, London: Geoffrey Bles.

Lewis, C. S. (1954), *The Horse and His Boy*, London: Geoffrey Bles.

Lewis, C. S. (1956), *The Last Battle*, London: Bodley Head.

Lezubski, Kirstian (2014), "The Power to Revolutionize the World, or Absolute Gender Apocalypse?: Queering the New Fairy-Tale Feminine in *Revolutionary Girl Utena*," in Pauline Greenhill and Jill Terry Rudy (eds.), *Channeling Wonder: Fairy Tales on Television*, 163–86, Detroit, MI: Wayne State University Press.

Lieberman, Marcia R. (1972), "'Some Day My Prince Will Come': Female Acculturation through the Fairy Tale," *College English*, 34 (3): 383–95.

Lindsay, Julianna (2016), "The Magic and Science of Grimm: A Fairy Tale for Modern Americans," *Humanities*, 5 (35): 34. https://doi.org/10.3390/h5020034.

Linkin, Harriet Kramer (1994), "Isn't It Romantic?: Angela Carter's Bloody Revision of the Romantic Aesthetic in 'The Erl King'," *Contemporary Literature*, 35 (2): 305–23.

The Little Mermaid (1989), [Film] Dir. Ron Clements and John Musker, Burbank: Buena Vista Pictures.

The Little Mermaid (2008), [Musical] music by Alan Menken, lyrics by Howard Ashman and Glenn Slater, and book by Doug Wright, Broadway. USA.

Little Otk (2000), [Film] Dir. Jan Švankmajer, Czech Republic: Zeitgeist Films.

Little Red Riding Hood (1997), [Film] Dir. David Kaplan, New York: Caruso/Mendelsohn Productions.

"Little Red Riding Hood" (2011), [Television Episode/Cartoon] written by E. Boucher, *Fairy Tales for Kids*, UK: Cartoonito.

Lo, Malinda (2009), *Ash*, New York: Little, Brown, and Company.

Locke, John ([1689] 1988), *Two Treatises on Government*, ed. Peter Laslet, Cambridge: Cambridge University Press.

Lorde, Audre ([1984] 2010), "The Master's Tools Will Never Dismantle the Master's House," in *Sister Outsider*, 110–14, London: Crossing Press.

Lost Girl (2010–16), [Television Series] created by Michelle Lovretta, USA: Showcase.

Love Island (2015–), [TV Program] ITV, June 7, 2015.

Lukasiewicz, Tracie D. (2010), "The Parellelism of the Fantastica and the Real: Guillermo Del Toro's *Pan's Labyrinth/El Laberinto Del Fauno* and Neomagical Realism," in Pauline Greenhill and Sidney Eve Matrix (eds.), *Fairy Tale Films: Visions of Ambiguity*, 60–78, Logan: Utah State University Press.

Lundell, Torborg (1986), "Gender-Related Biases in the Type and Motif Indexes of Aarne and Thompson," in Ruth B. Bottigheimer (ed.), *Fairy Tales and Society: Illusion, Allusion, and Paradigm*, 149–63, Philadelphia: University of Pennsylvania Press.

Lurie, Alison (1970), "Fairy Tale Liberation," *New York Review of Books*, December 17: 42–4. Available online: https://www.nybooks.com/articles/1970/12/17/fairy-tale-liberation/ (accessed December 10, 2020).

Lüthi, Max ([1947] 1982), *The European Folktale: Form and Nature*, trans. John D. Niles, Philadelphia: Institute for the Study of Human Issues.
Maas, Sarah J. (2015), *A Court of Thorns and Roses*, London: Bloomsbury.
Maas, Sarah J. (2016), *A Court of Mist and Fury*, London: Bloomsbury.
Macleod, Mark (2016), "Home by Midnight: The Male Cinderella in LGBTI Fiction for Young Adults," in Martine Hennard Dutheil de la Rochère, Gillian Lathey, and Monika Woźniak (eds.), *Cinderella Across Cultures: New Directions and Interdisciplinary Perspectives*, 197–214, Detroit, MI: Wayne State University Press.
Maguire, Gregory (1995), *Wicked: The Life and Times of the Wicked Witch of the West*, New York City: HarperCollins Publishers.
Maguire, Gregory (1999), *Confessions of an Ugly Stepsister*, New York: HarperCollins Publishers.
Maitland, Sara (2012), *Gossip from the Forest*, London: Granta.
Makinen, Merja (1992), "Angela Carter's *The Bloody Chamber* and the Decolonization of Feminine Sexuality," *Feminist Review*, 42 (1): 2–15.
Maleficent (2014), [Film] Dir. Robert Stromberg, Burbank: Buena Vista Pictures.
Maleficent: Mistress of Evil (2019), [Film] Dir. Joachim Rønning, US: Walt Disney Pictures/Roth Films.
Maliani, Michael, dir. (1987), [Television Episode] *Hello Kitty Furry Tale Theater*, season 1, episode 7, "Little Red Bunny Hood," aired October 31, 1987, English dubbing, Canada/US/Japan: DIC Animation City/MGM/UA Television.
Martin, Ann (2006), *Red Riding Hood and the Wolf in Bed: Modernism's Fairy Tales*, Toronto: University of Toronto Press.
Marx, Karl ([1867] 1977), *Capital*, vol. 1, trans. Ben Fowkes, London: Vintage Books.
McAra, Catriona (2017), "Dollhouse Architecture: Leonora Carrington and Children's Literature," *Gramarye: Journal of the Sussex Centre for Folklore, Fairy Tales and Fantasy*, 12 (Winter): 35–45.
McCann, Sharon (2010), "'With Redundance of Blood': Reading Ireland in Neil Jordan's *The Company of Wolves*," *Marvels & Tales*, 24 (1): 68–85.
McCoola, Marika and Emily Carroll (2015), *Baba Yaga's Assistant*, Somerville, MA: Candlewick Press.
McDougall, Brandy Nalani (2016), *Finding Meaning: Kaona and Contemporary Hawaiian Literature*, Tucson: University of Arizona.
McGuire, Seanan (2011a), "Jack's Place," track 5 on *Wicked Girls*, Independently produced, MP3.
McGuire, Seanan (2011b), "Wicked Girls," track 15 on *Wicked Girls*, Independently produced, MP3.
McGuire, Seanan (2016), *Every Heart a Doorway*, New York City: Tor.
McHale, Brian ([1987] 2001), *Postmodern Fiction*, London: Routledge.
McKillip, Patricia A. (2002), *Ombria in Shadow*, New York City: Ace.
McKinley, Robin (1978), *Beauty: A Retelling of the Story of Beauty and the Beast*, New York: Harper and Row.
Mendlesohn, Farah (2013), *Rhetorics of Fantasy*, Middletown, CT: Wesleyan University Press.
Messerli, Alfred (2005), "Spatial Representation in Popular European Fairy Tales," *Marvels & Tales*, 19 (2): 274–84.
Mikulak, Michael (2008), "The Rhizomatics of Domination: From Darwin to Biotechnology," in Bernd Herzogenrath (ed.), *An [Un]likely Alliance: Thinking Environment[s] with Deleuze and Guattari*, 66–83, Newcastle: Cambridge Scholars Publishing.

Miller, D. Scott (2016) "Afrosurreal: The Marvelous and the Invisible," *Open Space*, October 4. Available online: https://openspace.sfmoma.org/2016/10/afrosurreal-the-marvelous-and-the-invisible/ (accessed May 1, 2020).

Miller, Vincent (2011), *Understanding Digital Culture*, London: Sage Publications.

Mirror, Mirror (2012), [Film] Dir. Tarsem Singh, Beverly Hills: Relativity Media.

Moana (2016), [Film] Dir. Ron Clements and John Musker, USA: Walt Disney Pictures/Animation Studios.

Mollet, Tracey (2019), "The American Dream: Walt Disney's Fairy Tales," in Andrew Teverson (ed.), *The Fairy Tale World*, 221–31, London: Routledge.

Monster, Sfé R. (2014), *Eth's Skin*. Available online: http://www.eths-skin.com/ (accessed July 20, 2019).

A Monster Calls (2016), [Film] Dir. J. A. Bayona, Spain/UK/USA: Apaches Entertainment/Participant Media.

Monsters, Inc. (2001), [Film] Dir. Pete Docter, USA: Walt Disney Pictures/Pixar Animation Studios.

Moon, Sarah ([1983] 2002), *Little Red Riding Hood*, Mankato, MN: Creative Editions.

Moore, Bryan L. (2008), *Ecology and Literature: Ecocentric Personification from Antiquity to the Twenty-First Century*, New York: Palgrave MacMillan.

Moore, Leah and John Reppion (2017), *Damsels*, vol. 1, Runnemede: Dynamite Entertainment.

Morrison, Toni ([1987] 2007), *Beloved*, London: Vintage.

Morrison, Toni (1998), "Home," in Wahneema Lubiano (ed.), *The House That Race Built*, 3–12, London: Vintage.

Mueller, Andreas and Michael Schade (2012), "Symbols and Place Identity: A Semiotic Approach to Internal Place Branding—Case Study Bremen (Germany)," *Journal of Place Management and Development*, 5 (1): 81–92.

Muhawi, Ibrahim and Sharif Kanaana (1989), *Speak, Bird, Speak Again: Palestinian Arab Folktales*, Berkeley: University of California Press.

Müller-Wood, Anja (2012), "Angela Carter, Naturalist," in Sonya Andermahr and Lawrence Phillips (eds.), *Angela Carter: New Critical Readings*, 105–16, London: Continuum.

The Muppet Musicians of Bremen (1972), [Television Film] Dir. Jim Henson, written by J. Juhl, USA: Jim Henson Productions.

Murai, Mayako (2012), "Voicing Authenticities through Translation: Framing Strategies in the Multicultural Fairy Tale Collections of Andrew Lang and Angela Carter," *Synthesis*, 4. https://doi.org/10.12681/syn.17285.

Murai, Mayako (2013), "The Princess, the Witch and the Fireside: Yanagi Miwa's Uncanny Restaging of Fairy Tales," *Marvels & Tales*, 27 (2): 234–53.

Murai, Mayako (2015), *From Dog Bridegroom to Wolf Girl: Contemporary Japanese Fairy-Tale Adaptations in Conversations with the West*, Detroit, MI: Wayne State University Press.

Murai, Mayako (2018), "Photographic," in Pauline Greenhill, Jill Terry Rudy, Naomi Hamer, and Lauren Bosc (eds.), *The Routledge Companion to Media and Fairy-Tale Cultures*, 348–56, New York: Routledge.

Murai, Mayako (2019a), "The Fairy Tale in Contemporary Japanese Literature and Art," in Andrew Teverson (ed.), *The Fairy Tale World*, 347–55, London: Routledge.

Murai, Mayako (2019b), "'The Tongue-Cut Sparrow' and the Art of Translating Animals in Fairy Tales," *Voské Divan: Journal of Fairy-Tale Studies*, 6: 41–50.

Murai, Mayako and Luciana Cardi, eds. (2020), *Re-Orienting the Fairy Tale: Contemporary Adaptations across Cultures*, Detroit, MI: Wayne State University Press.

Murray, Simone (2012), *The Adaptation Industry: The Cultural Economy of Literary Adaptation*, New York: Routledge.

Myers, Benjamin (2018), "Folk by Zoe Gilbert Review—A Dreamlike Tapestry of Island Fables," *The Guardian*, March 8. Available online: https://www.theguardian.com/books/2018/mar/08/folk-zoe-gilbert-review-island-fables (accessed December 15, 2020).

Napoli, Donna Jo (2000), *Beast*, New York City: S. and Schuster Books for Young Readers.

Nicolaisen, W. F. H. (1976), "Place Name Legends: An Onomastic Mythology," *Folklore*, 87 (2): 146–59.

Nicolaisen, W. F. H. (1980), "Space in Folk Narrative," in Nikolai Burlakoff, Carl Lindahl, and W. F. H. Nicolaisen (eds.), *Essays in Honour of L. Dégh*, 14–18, Bloomington: Trickster.

Nicolaisen, W. F. H. (1991), "The Past as Place: Names, Stories and the Remembered Self," *Folklore*, 102 (1): 3–15.

Nicolaisen, W. F. H. (2002), "Narrating Names," *Folklore*, 113 (1): 1–9.

Nightwish (1997), "Beauty and the Beast," track 2 on *Angels Fall First*, Spinefarm, MP3.

Nikolajeva, Maria (2014), *Reading for Learning: Cognitive Approaches to Children's Literature*, Amsterdam: J. Benjamins.

Niles, John D. (1982), "Translator's Preface," in Max Lüthi (ed.), *The European Folktale: Form and Nature*, xvii–xxv, Philadelphia: Institute for the Study of Human Issues.

Novik, Naomi (2015), *Uprooted*, New York City: Del Rey.

Nugent, Cynthia (2018), "Mobile Apps," in Pauline Greenhill, Jill Terry Rudy, Naomi Hamer, and Lauren Bosc (eds.), *The Routledge Companion to Media and Fairy-Tale Cultures*, 539–47, New York: Routledge.

The Numbers (1997–2020), "Box Office History for Barbie Movies." Available online: https://www.the-numbers.com/movies/franchise/Barbie#tab=video (accessed December 12, 2020).

Oh, Ellen and Elsie Chapman, eds. (2018), *A Thousand Beginning and Endings*, New York: HarperCollins Publishers.

Okja (2017), [Film] Dir. Bong Joon-ho, South Korea/USA: Plan B Entertainment/Lewis Pictures/Kate Street Picture Company.

Once Upon a Mattress (1959), [Stage Musical] Music by Mary Rodgers, lyrics by Marshall Barer, book by Jay Thompson, Marshall Barer, and Dean Fuller. USA: Broadway.

Once Upon a Time (1994), [Card Game] Created by James Wallis and Andrew Rilstone, Paul, MN: Atlas Games.

Once Upon a Time (2011–18), [Television Series] Created by Edward Kitsis and Adam Horowitz, USA: ABC.

O'Neill, Katie (2017), *The Tea Dragon Society*, Portland: Oni Press.

Orenstein, Peggy (2011), *Cinderella Ate My Daughter: Dispatches from the Front Lines of the New Girlie-Girl Culture*, New York: Harper.

Orme, Jennifer (2015), "A Wolf's Queer Invitation: D. Kaplan's *Little Red Riding Hood* and Queer Possibility," *Marvels & Tales*, 29 (1): 87–109.

Orr, Lisa (2009), "'Difference That Is Actually Sameness Mass-Reproduced': Barbie Joins the Princess Convergence," *Jeunesse*, 1 (1): 9–30.
O'Toole, Allison (2018), *Wayward Sisters: An Anthology of Monstrous Women*, Toronto: TO Comix Press.
Oxford English Dictionary (n.d.-a), s.v. "beast." Available online: https://en.oxforddictionaries.com/definition/beast (accessed March 27, 2019).
Oxford English Dictionary (n.d.-b), s.v. "monster." Available online: http://www.oed.com/viewdictionaryentry/Entry/121738 (accessed March 23, 2019).
Oyeyemi, Helen (2005), *The Icarus Girl*, London: Bloomsbury.
Oyeyemi, Helen (2007), *The Opposite House*, New York: Penguin.
Oyeyemi, Helen (2009), *White Is for Witching*, New York: Riverhead Books.
Oyeyemi, Helen (2011), *Mr. Fox*, London: Picador.
Oyeyemi, Helen (2014), *Boy, Snow, Bird*, London: Picador.
Oyeyemi, Helen (2019), *Gingerbread*, London: Picador.
Oziewicz, Marek C. (2015), *Justice in Young Adult Speculative Fiction: A Cognitive Reading*, New York: Routledge.
Paes-Kada, Anne-Paule (2014), "Les Contes en perspective," in Marcel Aymé (ed.), *Les Contes du chat perché: 6 contes choisis*, choice of texts, dossier and notes by Anne-Paule Paes-Kada, 131–92, Paris: Gallimard.
Pan's Labyrinth (*El laberinto del fauno*) (2006), [Film] Dir. Guillermo del Toro, Spain/Mexico/USA: Estudios Picasso/Tequila Gang.
Parisien, Dominik and Navah Wolfe, eds. (2016), *The Starlit Wood: New Fairy Tales*, New York: Saga Press.
Parry, Catherine (2017), *Other Animals in Twenty-First Century Fiction*, London: Palgrave Macmillan.
The Path (2009), [Video Game] USA: Tale of Tales.
Paucard, Alain (1985), *Gripari mode d'emploi*, Lausanne: Éditions L'Âge d'homme.
Pearce, Joseph (1998), *Tolkien: Man and Myth. A Literary Life*, London: HarperCollins.
Penelope (2006), [Film] Dir. Mark Palansky, Santa Monica: Summit Entertainment.
Peter Pan (1955), [TV Film] Dir. Clarke Jones, written by J. M. Barrie and Jerome Robbins, USA: NBC.
Peter Pan (1960), [TV Film] Dir. Vincent J. Donehue, written by J. M. Barrie and Jerome Robbins, USA: NBC.
Peter Pan Live! (2014), [TV Film] Dir. Rob Ashford and Glenn Weiss, written by Irene Mecchi, USA: NBC.
Peterson, Andrea L. (2003), *No Rest for the Wicked*. Available Online: http://www.forthewicked.net/archive/ (accessed July 20, 2019).
Pete's Dragon (1977), [Film] Dir. Don Chaffey, USA: Walt Disney Productions.
Pete's Dragon (2016), [Film] Dir. D. Lowery, USA: Walt Disney Pictures/Whitaker Entertainment.
Peyroutet, Jean-Luc and Pierre Gripari (1964), *Pierre Gripari et ses contes pour enfants: entretiens avec Jean-Luc Peyroutet*, Mérignac: Girandoles.
Pharo, Patrick (2009), "La monstruosité morale," in Didier Manuel (ed.), *La Figure du monstre: Phénoménologie de la monstruosité dans l'imaginaire contemporain*, 157–69, Nancy: Presses universitaires de Nancy.
The Piano (1993), [Film] Dir. Jane Campion, USA: Miramax.
Ponyo (2008), [Film] Dir. Hayao Miyazaki, Japan: Studio Ghibli.

Popkin, Michael (1982), "Cocteau's *Beauty and the Beast*: The Poet as Monster," *Literature and Film Quarterly*, 10 (2): 100–9. Available online: http://film110.pbworks.com/f/Beauty+and+the+Beast.pdf (accessed June 15, 2019).

Porter, Jessica (2013), "[Im]Migrating Witchcraft: Transatlantic Gothic Hybridity in *White Is for Witching*," *Monsters and the Monstrous*, 3 (1): 23–38.

Poston, Ashley (2017), *Geekerella: A Fangirl Fairy Tale*, Philadelphia: Quirk Books.

The Princess and the Frog (2009), [Film] Dir. Ron Clements and John Musker, USA: Disney Pictures.

Princess Tutu (2002–3), [Film] Dir. Junichi Sato and Shogo Koumoto, written by Michiko Yokote, Japan: NHK.

Propp, Vladímir ([1928] 1968), *The Morphology of the Folktale*, trans. Laurence Scott, Bloomington: Indiana University Press.

Puella Magi Madoka Magica (2011), [Film] Dir. Yukihiro Miyamoto and Akiyuki Shinbo, written by Gen Urobuchi, Japan: MBS.

Pullman, Philip ([1995–2000] 2011) *His Dark Materials: Northern Lights, The Subtle Knife, The Amber Spyglass*, London: Everyman's Library.

Ragan, Kathleen (2009), "What Happened to the Heroines in Folktales? An Analysis by Gender of a Multicultural Sample of Published Folktales Collected from Storytellers," *Marvels & Tales*, 23 (2): 227–47.

Rankin, Walter (2007), *Grimm Pictures: Fairy Tale Archetypes in Eight Horror and Suspense Films*, Jefferson, NC: McFarland.

Rao, Sirish (text) and Durga Bai (art) (2008), *The Old Animals' Forest Band*, Chennai: Tara Books.

The Red Shoes (2016), [Ballet] Dir. Matthew Bourne, music by Bernard Herrmann, Plymouth: Theatre Royal.

Rehm, Rush (2002), *The Play of Space: Spatial Transformation in Greek Tragedy*, Princeton, NJ: Princeton University Press.

Reubins, Beatriz Markman (2014), *Pioneers of Child Psychoanalysis: Influential Theories and Practices in Healthy Child Development*, ed. Marc Stephen Reubins, London: Karnac.

Revolutionary Girl Utena (1997), [Television Series] Dir. Kunihiko Ikuhara, written by Yōji Enokido, Japan: TV Tokyo.

Revolve8 (2019), [Mobile Game] Dir. Masaru Kurusawa, Japan: Sega Corporation.

Ritchie, Anne Thackeray ([1868–74] 2010), *The Fairy Tale Fiction of A. Thackery Ritchie: Selections from "Five Old Friends" and 'Bluebeard's Keys'*, ed. Heidi Anne Heiner, Scotts Valley, CA: CreateSpace.

Rogoff, Barbara (1990), *Apprenticeship in Thinking: Cognitive Development in Social Context*, Oxford: Oxford University Press.

Rosemont, Penelope, ed. (1998), *Surrealist Women: An International Anthology*, Austin: University of Texas Press.

Rossetti, Christina (1862), *Goblin Market and Other Poems*, London: Macmillan.

Roughgarden, Joan ([2004] 2013), *Evolution's Rainbow: Diversity, Gender, and Sexuality in Nature and People. Tenth Anniversary Edition with a New Preface by the Author*, Berkeley: University of California Press.

Rowe, Karen E. (1989), "To Spin A Yarn: The Female Voice in Folklore and Fairy Tale," in Ruth B. Bottigheimer (ed.), *Fairy Tales and Society: Illusion, Allusion, and Paradigm*, 53–74, Philadelphia: University of Pennsylvania Press.

Roy, Malini (2014), "The Grimm Brothers' *Kahaniyan*: Hindi Resurrections of the Tales in Modern India by Harikrishna Devsare," in Vanessa Joosen and

Gillian Lathey (eds.), *Grimms' Tales Around the Globe: The Dynamics of Their International Reception*, 135–52, Detroit, MI: Wayne State University Press.

Rudy, Jill Terry (2018a), "Formalism," in Pauline Greenhill, Jill Terry Rudy, Naomi Hamer, and Lauren Bosc (eds.), *The Routledge Companion to Media and Fairy-Tale Cultures*, 31–9, New York: Routledge.

Rudy, Jill Terry (2018b), "Overview of Basic Concepts: Folklore, Fairy Tale, Culture, Media," in Pauline Greenhill, Jill Terry Rudy, Naomi Hamer, and Lauren Bosc (eds.), *The Routledge Companion to Media and Fairy-Tale Cultures*, 21–31, New York: Routledge.

Rudy, Jill Terry and Pauline Greenhill (2020), *Fairy-Tale TV*, New York: Routledge.

Rushdie, Salman (1990) *Haroun and the Sea of Stories*, New York: Penguin.

Rushdie, Salman (1998), Interview with David Tushingham, Theatre Program for *Haroun and the Sea of Stories*, adapted by Tim Supple, n.p., London: National Theatre.

Russell, Karen (2013), *Vampires in the Lemon Grove*, London: Chatto and Windus.

Said, Edward W. (1993), *Culture and Imperialism*, London: Chatto and Windus.

Said, Edward W. (2000), "Invention, Memory, and Place (Geography, Palestine)," *Critical Inquiry*, 26 (2): 175–92.

Sam the Sham and the Pharaohs (1966), "Li'l Red Riding Hood," written by Ron Blackwell, track 1 on *Li'l Red Riding Hood*, MGM, MP3.

Sasami: Magical Girls Club (2006–7), [Television Series] Dir. Yoshihiro Takamoto, written by Mari Okada, Japan: WOWOW.

Sawin, Patricia (2014), "Things Walt Disney Didn't Tell Us (But at Which Rodgers and Hammerstein at Least Hinted): The 1965 Made-for-TV Musical of Cinderella," in Pauline Greenhill and Jill Terry Rudy (eds.), *Channeling Wonder: Fairy Tales on Television*, 103–24, Detroit, MI: Wayne State University Press.

Schacker, Jennifer (2003), *National Dreams: The Remaking of Fairy Tales in Nineteenth-Century England*, Philadelphia: University of Pennsylvania.

Schacker, Jennifer (2018), "Theater," in Pauline Greenhill, Jill Terry Rudy, Naomi Hamer, and Lauren Bosc (eds.), *The Routledge Companion to Media and Fairy-Tale Cultures*, 337–47, New York: Routledge.

Schickel, Richard (1997), *The Disney Version*, 3rd edn., Chicago: Ivan R. Dee.

Schlegel, Friedrich von (1799), "Die Gebüsche," *Abendröte*. Available online: http://www.zeno.org/Literatur/M/Schlegel,+Friedrich/Gedichte/Abendr%C3%B6te/Zweiter+Teil/Die+Geb%C3%BCsche (accessed May 8, 2020).

Schmiesing, Ann (2014), *Disability, Deformity, and Disease in the Grimms' Fairy Tales*, Detroit, MI: Wayne State University Press.

Schwabe, Claudia (2014), "Getting Real with Fairy Tales: Magic Realism in *Grimm* and *Once Upon a Time*," in Pauline Greenhill and Jill Terry Rudy (eds.), *Channeling Wonder: Fairy Tales on Television*, 294–315, Detroit, MI: Wayne State University Press.

Seaton, Cat and Kit Seaton (2018), *Norroway Book 1: The Black Bull of Norroway*, Portland, OR: Image Comics.

Seifert, Lewis C. (1996), *Fairy Tales, Sexuality, and Gender in France, 1690–1715*, Cambridge: Cambridge University Press.

Sells, Laura (1995), "'Where Do the Mermaids Stand?' Voice and Body in *The Little Mermaid*," in Elizabeth Bell, Lynda Haas, and Laura Sells (eds.), *From Mouse to Mermaid: The Politics of Film, Gender, and Culture*, 175–92, Bloomington: Indiana University Press.

Sexton, Anne ([1971] 2016), *Transformations*, New York: Open Road Media.
The Shape of Water (2017), [Film] Dir. Guillermo del Toro, USA: Fox Searchlight Pictures/Double Dare You/Bull Productions.
Sheets, Robin Ann (1991), "Pornography, Fairy Tales, and Feminism: Angela Carter's *The Bloody Chamber*," *Journal of the History of Sexuality*, 1 (4): 633–57.
Shelley, Mary (1818), *Frankenstein; or, The Modern Prometheus*, London: Lackington, Hughes, Harding, Mavor & Jones.
Shen, Qinna (2015), *The Politics of Magic: DEFA Fairy-Tale Films*, Detroit, MI: Wayne State University Press.
Sherman, Cindy (1992), *Fitcher's Bird*, New York: Rizzoli.
Short, Sue (2018), "Horror," in Pauline Greenhill, Jill Terry Rudy, Naomi Hamer, and Lauren Bosc (eds.), *The Routledge Companion to Media and Fairy-Tale Cultures*, 532–8, New York: Routledge.
Shrek (2001), [Film] Dir. Andrew Adamson and Vicky Jenson, USA: DreamWorks Animation.
Shrek 2 (2004), [Film] Dir. Andrew Adamson, Kelly Asbury, and Conrad Vernon, USA: DreamWorks SKG.
Shrek Forever After (2010), [Film] Dir. Mike Mitchell, USA: Pacific Data Images.
Shrek the Musical (2008), [Stage Musical] Music by Jeanine Tesori, lyrics and book by David Lindsay-Abaire, Broadway: USA.
Shrek the Third (2007), [Film] Dir. Chris Miller and Raman Hui, USA: DreamWorks Animation.
Simpson, Helen (2006), "Introduction," in Angela Carter, *The Bloody Chamber*, vii–xix, London: Vintage.
The Simpsons (1989–), [Television Series] Created by Matt Groening, USA: Fox.
Slack-Smith, Amanda (2018), "Contemporary Art," in Pauline Greenhill, Jill Terry Rudy, Naomi Hamer, and Lauren Bosc (eds.), *The Routledge Companion to Media and Fairy-Tale Cultures*, 492–500, New York: Routledge.
Sleeping Beauty (1922), [Film] Dir. Lotte Reiniger, Germany: Sochatschewer.
Sleeping Beauty (1959), [Film] Dir. Clyde Geronimi, Eric Larson, Wolfgang Reitherman, and Les Clarke, New York: RKO Radio Pictures.
Sleeping Beauty: A Gothic Romance (2012), [Ballet] Dir. Matthew Bourne, music by Pyotr Ilyich Tchaikovsky, Plymouth: Theatre Royal.
Smart Kids TV (2014–), [YouTube Channel]. Available online: https://www.youtube.com/channel/UC5cF0JfounoraesRd3zBlxQ (accessed July 20, 2019).
Smith, Kiki (2001), *Rapture* [Bronze Sculpture], Pace Gallery, New York.
Smith, Kiki (2002a), *Born* [Bronze Sculpture], Albright-Knox Gallery, New York.
Smith, Kiki (2002b), *Born* [Lithograph], Universal Limited Art Editions, New York.
Snow White and the Huntsman (2012), [Film] Dir. Rupert Sanders, Universal City: Universal Pictures.
Snow White and the Seven Dwarfs (1937), Dir. David Hand, USA: Walt Disney Productions.
Snow White: A Tale of Terror (1997), [Film] Dir. Michael Cohn, written by Tom Szollosi and Deborah Serra, USA: Showtime.
Snow White with the Red Hair (2015–16), [Television Series] Dir. Masahiro Andō, written by Deko Akao, Japan: Tokyo MX.
Snyder, Louis L. (1951), "Nationalistic Aspects of the Grimm Brothers' Fairy Tales," *Journal of Social Psychology*, 33 (2): 209–23.
Soja, Edward (1996), *Thirdspace: Journeys to Los Angeles and Other Real-and-Imagined Places*, Oxford: Blackwell.

Somtow, S. P. (2003), *Bluebeard's Castle*, Indiana: iUniverse.
Spivak, Gayatri Chakravorty ([1988] 2000), "Can the Subaltern Speak?," in Diana Brydon (ed.), *Postcolonialism: Critical Concepts in Literary and Cultural Studies*, 1427–77, London: Routledge.
Stephanou, Aspasia (2014), "Helen Oyeyemi's *White Is for Witching* and the Discourse of Consumption," *Callaloo*, 37 (5): 1245–59.
Stern, Scott W. (2018), *The Trials of Nina McCall: Sex, Surveillance, and the Decades-Long Plan to Imprison "Promiscuous" Women*, Boston: Beacon Press.
Stewart, Susan (1991), *Crimes of Writing: Problems in the Containment of Representation*, Oxford: Oxford University Press.
Stockinger, Günther von (2004), "The Wolf People: The Curse of the Hair," *Spiegel Online*, December 31. Available online: https://www.spiegel.de/international/spiegel/the-wolf-people-the-curse-of-the-hair-a-335660.html (accessed August 23, 2019).
Stone, Kay (1985), "The Misuses of Enchantment: Controversies on the Significance of Fairy Tales," in Rosan A. Jordan and Susan J. Kalčik (eds.), *Women's Folklore, Women's Culture*, 125–45, Philadelphia: University of Pennsylvania Press.
Stone, Kay (2008), *Some Day Your Witch Will Come*, Detroit, MI: Wayne State University Press.
The Storyteller (1987), [Television Series] created by Jim Henson, USA: TVS Television.
Suddath, Claire (2015), "The $500 Million Battle over Disney's Princesses," *Bloomberg*, December 17. Available online: https://www.bloomberg.com/features/2015-disney-princess-hasbro/ (accessed August 13, 2019).
Super Mario Bros. (1985), [Video Game] Dir. Shigeru Miyamoto, Japan: Nintendo.
Szugajew, Aleksandra (2020), "Adults Reclaiming Fairy Tales through Cinema: Popular Fairy-Tale Movie Adaptations from the Past Decade," in Mayako Murai and Luciana Cardi (eds.), *Re-Orienting the Fairy Tale: Contemporary Adaptations across Cultures*, 207–45, Detroit, MI: Wayne State University Press.
Taggart, James (1990), *Enchanted Maidens: Gender Relations in Spanish Folktales of Courtship and Marriage*, Princeton, NJ: Princeton University Press.
The Tale of Princess Kaguya (2013), [Film] Dir. Isao Takahata, Japan: Studio Ghibli.
Tale of Tales (2015), [Film] Dir. Matteo Garrone, Rome: 01 Distribution.
Tangled (2010), Dir. Nathan Greno and Byron Howard, USA: Walt Disney Animation Studios.
Tasty Tales (2014), [Mobile Game], USA: Sweet Nitro.
Tatar, Maria (1987), *The Hard Facts of the Grimms' Fairy Tales*, Princeton, NJ: Princeton University Press.
Tatar, Maria (1992), *Off with Their Heads!: Fairy Tales and the Culture of Childhood*, Princeton, NJ: Princeton University Press.
Tatar, Maria (2009), *Enchanted Hunters: The Power of Stories in Childhood*, New York: Norton.
Tatar, Maria, ed. (2014), *The Annotated Brothers Grimm: The Bicentennial Edition*, New York: Norton.
Tchombe, Theresa Mungah Shalo and Tani Emmanuel Lukong (2016), "Dynamics of Indigenous Socialization Strategies and Emotion Regulation Adjustment among Nso Early Adolescents, North West Region of Cameroon," *International Journal of Humanities, Social Sciences and Education*, 3 (8): 86–124.
Tell Me a Story (2018–), [Television Series] Created by Kevin Williamson, USA: CBS.

Telotte, J. P. (2004), *Disney TV*, Detroit, MI: Wayne State University Press.
Teverson, Andrew (2001), "Fairy Tale Politics: Issues of Free Speech and Multiculturalism in Salman Rushdie's *Haroun and the Sea of Stories*," *Twentieth Century Literature*, 47 (4): 444–66.
Teverson, Andrew (2008), "Migrant Fictions: Salman Rushdie and Fairy Tale," in Stephen Benson (ed.), *Contemporary Fiction and the Fairy Tale*, 47–73, Detroit, MI: Wayne State University Press.
Teverson, Andrew (2013), *Fairy Tale*, New York: Routledge.
Teverson, Andrew, ed. (2019), *The Fairy Tale World*, London: Routledge.
Teverson, Andrew and Sara Upstone, eds. (2011), *Postcolonial Spaces: The Politics of Place in Contemporary Culture*, London: Palgrave.
Then She Fell (2012), [Play] Created by Zach Morris, Tom Pearson, and Jennine Willett, USA: Third Rail Projects.
Thompson, Stith (1928), *The Types of the Folk-Tale: A Classification and Bibliography*, Folklore Fellows Communications, vol. 74, Helsinki: Suomalainen Tiedeakatemia.
Thompson, Stith (1961), *The Types of the Folk-Tale: A Classification and Bibliography*, 2nd edn., Folklore Fellows Communications 184, Helsinki: Academia Scientiarum Fennica.
Thornton, Gypsy (2009–), *Once Upon a Blog*. Available online: http://fairytalenewsblog.blogspot.com/ (accessed July 20, 2019).
Tolkien, J. R. R. (1937), *The Hobbit*, London: George Allen and Unwin.
Tolkien, J. R. R. (1947), "On Fairy Stories." Available online: http://brainstorm-services.com/wcu-2005/fairystories-tolkien.html (accessed May 9, 2020).
Tolkien, J. R. R. (1955), *The Lord of the Rings*, London: George Allen and Unwin.
Tolkien, J. R. R. (1977), *The Silmarillion*, London: George Allen and Unwin.
Traister, Rebecca (2016), *All the Single Ladies: Unmarried Women and the Rise of an Independent Nation*, New York: S. & Schuster.
Trolls (2016), [Film] Dir. Mike Mitchell, Walt Dohrn, USA: DreamWorks Animation.
Turner, Kay and Pauline Greenhill, eds. (2012), *Transgressive Tales: Queering the Grimms*, Detroit, MI: Wayne State University Press.
Turnquist, Kristi (2017), "*Grimm* May be Ending, but its Impact on Portland Remains," *The Oregonian*, March 29. Available online: https://www.oregonlive.com/tv/2017/03/grimm_may_be_ending_but_its_im.html (accessed May 9, 2020).
Ungerer, Tomi (1967), *Zeralda's Ogre*, New York: Harper & Row.
Upstone, Sara (2005), "'LA's Got it All': Hybridity and Otherness in *Angel*'s Postmodern City," in Stacey Abbott (ed.), *Reading Angel*, 101–16, London: I.B. Tauris.
Upstone, Sara (2009), *Spatial Politics in the Postcolonial Novel*, Aldershot: Ashgate.
Uther, Hans-Jörg (2004), *The Types of International Folktales: A Classification and Bibliography*, Folklore Fellows Communications, 284–6, Helsinki: Academia Scientiarum Fennica.
Valente, Catherynne M. (2011), *Deathless*, New York: Tom Doherty Associates, LLC.
Valente, Catherynne M. (2015), *Six-Gun Snow White*, repr. edn., New York City: Saga Press.
von Franz, Marie-Louise (1997), *Archetypal Patterns in Fairy Tales*, Toronto: Inner City Books.
Warner, Marina (1994a), *From the Beast to the Blonde: On Fairy Tales and their Tellers*, London: Chatto and Windus.
Warner, Marina (1994b), *Managing Monsters: Six Myths of Our Time*, London: Vintage.

Warner, Marina (2014), *Once Upon a Time: A Short History of Fairy Tale*, Oxford: Oxford University Press.
Warner, Marina (2015), *Fly Away Home: Stories*, Cromer: Salt.
Wasko, Janet (2001), *Understanding Disney: The Manufacture of Fantasy*, Cambridge: Blackwell.
Weaver, Jace (1997), *That the People Might Live: Native American Literatures and Native American Community*, Oxford: Oxford University Press.
Weber, Max ([1922] 1978), *Economy and Society: An Outline of Interpretive Sociology*, Berkeley: University of California Press.
Wells, H. G. (1895), *The Time Machine*, London: William Heinemann.
Whatman, Emma and Victoria Tedeschi (2018), "Video Games," in Pauline Greenhill, Jill Terry Rudy, Naomi Hamer, and Lauren Bosc (eds.), *The Routledge Companion to Media and Fairy-Tale Cultures*, 634–41, New York: Routledge.
Whitley, David ([2008] 2016), *The Idea of Nature in Disney Animation: From Snow White to WALL-E*, London: Routledge.
Wicked (2003), [Stage Musical] Music and lyrics by Stephen Schwartz, book by Winnie Holzman, Broadway, USA.
Willingham, Bill (2002–15), *Fables*, New York: DC Vertigo.
Willingham, Bill (2006), *1001 Nights of Snowfall*, New York: DC Vertigo.
Willocq, Philippe (2008), "Analyse de *Truismes* (1996) de Marie Darrieussecq sous l'angle critique de *La Morphologie du conte de Propp*," *Initiales*: 242–59.
Wilson, Rawdon (1995), "The Metamorphoses of Fictional Space," in Lois Parkinson Zamora and Wendy B. Faris (eds.), *Magical Realism: Theory, History Community*, 209–34, Durham: Duke University Press.
Windling, Terri (2008–), *Myth and Moor*. Available online: https://www.terriwindling.com/blog/ (accessed July 20, 2019).
The Wolf Among Us (2013), [Video Game] Dir. Nick Herman, Jason Latino, Dennis Lenart, USA: Telltale Games.
Wood, Lucy (2012), *Diving Belles*, London: Bloomsbury.
The Woodsman (2012), [Play] Written by James Ortiz, USA: Off Broadway.
Woolf, Virginia ([1925] 2019), *Mrs Dalloway*, London: Penguin.
Xandria (2003–4), "Snow-White," track on *Ravenheart*, Drakkar Entertainment, MP3.
Yasunari, Kawabata ([1961] 1997), *House of the Sleeping Beauties*, New York: Kodansha America.
Yolen, Jane (1992), *Briar Rose*, New York: Tor Books.
Yoshinaga, Ida (2018), "Convergence Culture," in Pauline Greenhill, Jill Terry Rudy, Naomi Hamer, and Lauren Bosc (eds.), *The Routledge Companion to Media and Fairy-Tale Cultures*, 233–45, New York: Routledge.
Zamora, Lois Parkinson and Wendy B. Faris (1995), "Introduction: Daiquiri Birds and Flaubertian Parrot(ie)s," in Lois Parkinson Zamora and Wendy B. Faris (eds.), *Magical Realism: Theory, History Community*, 1–14, Durham, NC: Duke University Press.
Ziolkowski, Jan M. (2009), *Fairy Tales from Before Fairy Tales: The Medieval Latin Past of Wonderful Lies*, Ann Arbor: University of Michigan Press.
Zipes, Jack ([1979] 2002), *Breaking the Magic Spell: Radical Theories of Folk and Fairy Tales*, rev. and exp. edn., Lexington: University Press of Kentucky.
Zipes, Jack (1983), *The Trials and Tribulations of Little Red Riding Hood: Versions of the Tale in Sociocultural Context*, South Hadley, MA: Bergin & Garvey Publishers.

Zipes, Jack ([1987] 1989), *Don't Bet on the Prince: Contemporary Feminist Fairytales in North America and England*, New York: Routledge.

Zipes, Jack (1995), *Creative Storytelling: Building Community, Changing Lives*, New York: Routledge.

Zipes, Jack (1997), *Happily Ever After: Fairy Tales, Children, and the Culture Industry*, New York: Routledge.

Zipes, Jack (1999), "Breaking the Disney Spell," in Maria Tatar (ed.), *The Classic Fairy Tales*, 332–52, New York: Norton.

Zipes, Jack (2000), *The Oxford Companion to Fairy Tales*, Oxford: Oxford University Press.

Zipes, Jack (2002), *The Brothers Grimm: From Enchanted Forests to the Modern World*, Basingstoke: Palgrave Macmillan.

Zipes, Jack (2008), "Review of *Pan's Labyrinth*," *Journal of American Folklore*, 121 (480): 236–40.

Zipes, Jack (2011), *The Enchanted Screen: The Unknown History of Fairy-Tale Films*, New York: Routledge.

Zipes, Jack (2012a), *Fairy Tales and the Art of Subversion*, Routledge Classics edn., London: Routledge.

Zipes, Jack (2012b), *The Irresistible Fairy Tale: The Cultural and Social History of a Genre*, Princeton, NJ: Princeton University Press

Zipes, Jack (2017) "Breaking the Disney Spell," in Maria Tatar (ed.), *The Classic Fairy Tales*, 2nd Norton Critical edn., 414–35, New York: W. W. Norton and Company.

CONTRIBUTORS

Sara Cleto and **Brittany Warman** received their PhDs in English and Folklore from the Ohio State University in 2018 and currently co-run and teach at the Carterhaugh School of Folklore and the Fantastic, an online hub for creative souls who want to re-enchant their lives through folklore and fairy tales. In 2019, Carterhaugh won the Dorothy Howard Award from the American Folklore Society. Their research centers on folk- and fairy-tale studies, gender and sexuality studies, disability studies, and nineteenth-century literature. Their coauthored academic writing has appeared in various books and journals including *Marvels & Tales* and *Gramarye*.

Amy Greenhough is a lecturer in English and Creative Writing at Falmouth University. Her research is in the use of fairy tales in contemporary literature, with a focus on nature and materiality. Her most recent work includes a publication in *The Fairy Tale World* (2019), a short film entitled "The Vanishing Princess" (based on the short story by Jenny Diski and accepted into New York Shorts Film Festival 2019) and a recently submitted PhD manuscript. She is currently writing a feature-length screenplay about a metamorphosis.

Christa Jones is Professor of French at Utah State University. Her research centers on postcolonial North African Francophone literature and culture; folk- and fairy-tale studies; gender and sexuality studies; and ecocriticism. She is the author of *Cave Culture in Maghrebi Literature* (2012) and coeditor of *Women from the Maghreb* (2014), *New Approaches to Teaching Folk and Fairy Tales* (2016), and *Algerian Filmmaker Merzak Allouache* (2017). She is currently working on a study of the Maghrebian trickster Si Djeh'a.

Jeana Jorgensen earned her PhD in folklore from Indiana University and has gone on to teach in folklore and anthropology programs at Indiana University,

Butler University, and the University of California, Berkeley. Her articles have appeared in journals such as *Marvels & Tales*, *The Journal of American Folklore*, and *Cultural Analysis* and in books such as *Transgressive Tales: Queering the Grimms*, *Channeling Wonder: Fairy Tales on Television*, and *The Fairy Tale World*. She also writes poetry, directs a dance troupe, and nurtures a sourdough culture.

Kimberly J. Lau is Professor of Literature at the University of California, Santa Cruz. She is the author of numerous articles, most recently addressing race and the fairy tale in both historical and contemporary contexts, as well as the books *New Age Capitalism: Making Money East of Eden* (2000), *Body Language: Sisters in Shape, Black Women's Fitness, and Feminist Identity Politics* (2011), and *Erotic Infidelities: Love and Enchantment in Angela Carter's* The Bloody Chamber (2015).

Mayako Murai is Professor at Kanagawa University, Japan. She is author of *From Dog Bridegroom to Wolf Girl: Contemporary Japanese Fairy-Tale Adaptations in Conversation with the West* (2015) and coeditor of *Re-Orienting the Fairy Tale: Contemporary Adaptations across Cultures* (2020). She curated the exhibition *Tomoko Konoike: Fur Story* at the Blenheim Walk Gallery, Leeds Arts University in 2018. She is currently writing a book tentatively titled *Re-Storying the World for Multispecies Survival: Fairy-Tale Animals in Contemporary Art and Picturebook Illustrations*.

Jill Terry Rudy is Associate Professor of English at Brigham Young University, Provo, Utah. She edited *The Marrow of Human Experience: Essays on Folklore* by William A. Wilson (2006) and coedited, with Pauline Greenhill, *Channeling Wonder: Fairy Tales on Television* (2014) and, with Greenhill, Naomi Hamer, and Lauren Bosc, *The Routledge Companion to Media and Fairy-Tale Cultures* (2018). Most recently, she coauthored, with Greenhill, *Fairy-Tale TV* (2020). She codirects a digital humanities project, "Visualizing Wonder," at fttv.byu.edu.

Claudia Schwabe is Associate Professor of German at Utah State University. She is author of *Craving Supernatural Creatures: German Fairy-Tale Figures in American Pop Culture* (2019), editor of *The Fairy Tale and Its Uses in Contemporary New Media and Popular Culture* (2016), and coeditor, with Christa C. Jones, of *New Approaches to Teaching Folk and Fairy Tales* (2016). Most recent works have appeared in *Contemporary Fairy-Tale Magic: Subverting Gender and Genre* (2020), *Marvels & Tales: Journal of Fairy-Tale Research* (2020, 2017, 2015), *The Routledge Companion to Fairy-Tale Cultures and Media* (2018), and *Contemporary Legend* (2016).

Andrew Teverson is Dean of Academic Strategy and Professor of Cultural History and Critical Thinking at the London College of Fashion, University of the Arts, London. His recent publications include the edited collection *The Fairy Tale World* (2019), and a two-volume critical edition of the scholarly writings of Andrew Lang (2015, with Alexandra Warwick and Leigh Wilson). Currently he is completing a critical edition of the children's fictions of Andrew Lang, due for publication in 2021. Previous publications include *Fairy Tale* (2013) and, edited with Sara Upstone, *Postcolonial Spaces: The Politics of Place in Contemporary Culture* (2011).

Sara Upstone is Professor of Contemporary Literature and Head of School of Arts, Culture and Communication at Kingston University, London. She is currently editing a collection on the contemporary novelist Hari Kunzru (2021, with Kristian Shaw). Previous publications include *Spatial Politics in the Postcolonial Novel* (2010), *Rethinking Race and Identity in the Contemporary British Novel* (2016), and, edited with Andrew Teverson, *Postcolonial Spaces: The Politics of Place in Contemporary Culture* (2011). Her most recent publications are *Literary Theory: A Complete Introduction* (2017) and *Against* (2020), a collection of creative fiction and nonfiction.

INDEX

Notes: Fairy tales to receive multiple references or general treatment are indexed by title as well as at the authors' names.
Page numbers in *italic* refer to illustrations.
n = endnote.

The 10th Kingdom (TV, 2000) 35

Aarne, Antti 185–6
Aarne-Thompson-Uther (ATU) Tale Type Index 55, 72, 79, 105, 162, 185–7, 199*n*10
    Eurocentrism 186–7
Aboulela, Leila, *Bird Summons* 155–6
Abram, David 102
Aceval, Nora 114
adaptation(s) 43–54, 66–7
    interdisciplinary 51–4
    intergeneric 50–1
    intermedia 44–50 *see also* "The Bremen Town Musicians"
The Adventures of Prince Achmed (1926) 1
The Adventures of Rocky and Bullwinkle and Friends (TV, 1959-64) 35, 77
Aeschylus, *Agamemnon* 188
Afanasyev, Alexander 130
Africa, indigenous cultures/tales 114, 155, 178
Aladdin (1992) 34, 76
Aladdin (2019) 34
Aldred, B. Grantham 62
Ali, Agha Shahid, "The Wolf's Postscript to 'Little Red Riding Hood'" 103

Alice (1988) 7
alien productions (artist group) 66
American McGee's Alice (computer game) 41
Andersen, Hans Christian 4, 7, 35, 77, 161–2, 197*n*6
    "The Princess and the Pea" 37
    "The Snow Queen" 125 *see also* "The Little Mermaid"
Anderson-Grégoire, Emilie 79
Andrews, Julie 35
Angel (TV, 1999–2004) 153
animals 91–111
    artistic/sculptural representations 55–61, *56, 57, 59, 60*
    focus on, in retellings 54
    hybrid/metamorphosed 107–10, 128–30
    links with music 61–6
anime 36
Ankoku Gurimu Dōwashu (*Dark Grimm's Tales*, anthology) 84
anthologies 32, 69–70
Anthropocene Age 106, 109
anthropocentrism 95–8
    moves away from 54, 106–10
anthropomorphism 22–3, 54, 66, 94–8
Anwar, Gabrielle *163*

Arendt, Hannah 6
Ashliman, D. L. 41, 162
Ashwin, Kate, and Kel McDonald (eds), *Cautionary Fables and Fairytales* 33
Attar, Farid ud-Din, *The Conference of the Birds* 156
Atwood, Margaret 51, 53, 98, 189
  Bluebeard's Egg and Other Stories 115, 139
  "I Dream of Zenia with the Bright Red Teeth" 144
  The Robber Bride 144
Auden, W. H. 4, 25
Aulnoy, Marie-Catherine d' 52, 184–5, 198–9n6
  Contes de fées (Fairy Tales) 50
Australia, colonial *vs.* indigenous tales/culture 187
Avery, Tex 77
Aymé, Marcel
  Les contes du chat perché (The Wonderful Farm) 132
  "Le Loup" 132
Azzolina, David 199n10

Bacchilega, Cristina 17, 29, 43–4, 45, 46, 49, 54, 72, 78, 95, 169, 173
  Postmodern Fairy Tales: Gender and Narrative Strategies 51, 53
Bae, Chan-Hyo 47, 54
Bai, Durga 63–5, *64, 65,* 198n9
Bakhtin, Mikhail 16
Bandura, Albert 174
Baquero, Ivana 120, *121*
Barad, Karen 108
Barbe bleue (2009) 34, 46, 77, 115, *116,* 117
Barbie in the 12 Dancing Princesses (2006) 170–1, 172–3
Bareilles, Sara 38
Barnes, Djuna 1–3, 50
  Nightwood 2–3
Barron, Steve 35
Barthelme, Donald 51
Barthes, Roland 17–20, 25
  Mythologies 17–18, 19, 20
Basile, Giambattista, *Lo cunto de li cunti (Tale of Tales)* 50, 78, 183, 198n2, 198n4

Baum, L. Frank, *The Wonderful Wizard of Oz* 3, 30–1, *31,* 37
Bayona, J. A. 122–3
"Beauty and the Beast" (tale/theme)
  film versions 34, 114
  literary reworkings 7, 11, 18, 29, 30, 32, 82, 83
  non-anthropocentric adaptations 54
  parodies 46
Beauty and the Beast (1991 film) 34, 114
Beauty and the Beast (2017 film) 34, 76–7, 114
Beauty and the Beast (stage musical) 37
Beauty and the Beast (TV, 1987–90/2012–16) 35, 140
Beauvoir, Simone de 13, 25
  Le deuxième sexe 16–17, 52
Beckett, Sandra 172
Bell, Kristen 125
La Belle et la Bête (1946) 11, 34, 46, 96, 97–8, 114
La Belle et la Bête (2014) 114
Benjamin, Walter 6, 16, 25, 170
  "The Storyteller: Reflections on the Work of Nikolai Leskov" 4
Bennett, Jane 94, 109
Benson, Stephen 80
Bernheimer, Kate 16
  The Complete Tales of Ketzia Gold 7
  "Fairy Tale Is Form, Form Is Fairy Tale" 29
  Horse, Flower, Bird 7–9
  "Whitework" 7–9
Bettelheim, Bruno 3
  The Uses of Enchantment: The Meaning and Importance of Fairy Tales 52, 98, 165–6
Bhabha, Homi K. 150, 151, 152, 154–5, 156
Blackwell, Jeannine, and Shawn C. Jarvis, *The Queen's Mirror: Fairy Tales by German Women, 1780–1900* 53
Blank, Hanne 70–1
Bloch, Ernst 6, 25
  "Better Castles in the Sky at the Country Fair and Circus, in Fairy Tales and Colportage" 4
  "The Fairy Tale Moves on Its Own Time" 4
Block, Francesca Lia 189
  The Rose and the Beast 32, 80, 84

"Bluebeard" (tale/theme)
    films based on 34, 46, 77, 115
    literary reworkings 18, 51, 84, 115–18, 139, 189
Bluebeard's Bride (board game) 39
board games 39
Boccaccio, Giovanni, *Decameron* 183
Bong Joon-ho 126–7
Bonner, Sarah 79–80
Borges, Jorge Luis, "The House of Asterion" 133–4
Borja-Villel, Manuel 9
Bosc, Lauren 44
Bottigheimer, Ruth B. 3, 162
    Grimm's Bad Girls and Bold Boys 53, 167
Bourne, Matthew 37
Braidotti, Rosi 98, 105, 107, 109, 111
Brave (2012) 76
Breillat, Catherine 34, 46, 77, 115, 117
Breindl, Martin 66
Bremen (city), history/public attractions 57, 57–8
"The Bremen Town Musicians" 22, 54, 55–66
    film/TV adaptations 45, 61
    interdisciplinary possibilities 65–6
    pictorial representations 55–7, 56
    plot 55
    reasons for popularity 55, 61
    retellings in other cultures 62–5
    sculptures 57, 57–61, 59, 60
Breton, André 13
    Manifesto of Surrealism 6–7
Brooke, Leslie 56
Broumas, Olga 189
    Beginning with O 32, 50–1
Brown, Bill, "Thing Theory" 106
Buchan, David 162
Buchanan, Rowan Hisayo 143
Buffy the Vampire Slayer (TV, 1997–2003) 153
Burnett, Carol 37
Byatt, A. S. 80, 91, 98
    "Cold" 104
    The Djinn in the Nightingale's Eye 104
    Elementals 104
    "The Glass Coffin" 104
    The Little Black Book of Stories 104
    "The Stone Woman" 104

Calvino, Italo 133
Cameroon, folk tales/traditional culture 178
Campagnaro, Marnie 138–9
Campbell, Joseph 3
    The Hero with a Thousand Faces 52
Campion, Jane 139
Canada, indigenous cultures/tales 178–9, 179
capitalism, cinematic critiques 109–10, 125–7
Carastathis, Anna 74
card games 39
Cardcaptor Sakura (TV, 1998–2000) 36
Carrington, Leonora 7, 46, 50
    "La Débutante" 7
    Self-Portrait (Inn of the Dawn Horse) 9, 9–10
Carroll, Emily
    Through the Woods 33
    (with Marika McCoola) *Baga Yaga's Assistant* 33
Carroll, Lewis 37
    Alice's Adventures in Wonderland 38–9, 41, 150
Carter, Angela 16, 25, 48–9, 53, 80–1, 98, 99–102
    "The Alchemy of the Word" 10–11
    The Bloody Chamber (and Other Stories) 18–19, 32, 48–9, 51, 52, 94, 99–102, 115, 139, 140–1, 149, 152, 188–9
    Come Unto These Yellow Sands: Four Radio Plays 48–9
    "The Company of Wolves" 34, 48–9, 81, 101, 149
    "The Courtship of Mr Lyon" 11, 94, 139
    "The Erl-King" 100–1, 145
    Nights at the Circus 32
    "Notes from the Front Line" 18–19
    The Passion of New Eve 19
    The Second Virago Book of Fairy Tales (ed.) 49–50
    "The Tiger's Bride" 18, 100, 102, 141
    The Virago Book of Fairy Tales (ed.) 49–50, 138
    "The Werewolf" 101
    "Wolf-Alice" 101

comments on own work/fairy-tale genre 52, 139, 140–1, 148
legacy 81, 102–3, 139
as translator 48, 49
treatment of animal-human relations 95, 99–102
treatment of place 140–1, 145, 152
Cartoonito UK (TV channel) 175, *176*, 177
Cattelan, Maurizio 58–61
   Love Lasts Forever 59–61, *60*
   Love Saves Life 58, *59*
   La Nona Ora 61
Ceccoli, Nicoletta 39
Césaire, Aimé 13–14, 15, 16
   Cahier d'un retour au pays natal 13
Césaire, Suzanne 14–15, 16
Chamoiseau, Patrick 16
   "Une affaire de mariage" 115
   Au temps de l'antan: Contes du pays Martinique (Strange Words) 15, 53
   "Glan-Glan the Spat-Out Bird" 15
Chapman, Elsie *see* Oh, Ellen
Churchill, Frank 45
"Cinderella" (tale/theme)
   film/stage versions 34, 35, 37, 45, 54, 82
   queered retellings 82–3, 88
   verse retellings 50–1
   visual adaptations 44–5, 47–8
Cinderella (1922 film) 1
Cinderella (1950 film) 34, 75–6, 96–7
Cinderella (2015 film) 34
Cinderella (ballet) 37
Cinderella (TV Film, 1957/1965/1997) 35
Cinders (computer game) 41
Clark, Timothy 93
classification (of tale types) 185–6 *see also* Aarne-Thompson-Uther (ATU) Tale Type Index
clothing, fairy-tale themed 39–41
Cocteau, Jean 11, 34, 46, 96, 97–8, 114
Cole, Babette, *Princess Smartypants* 80
colonialism, impact on indigenous cultures 187–8
The Company of Wolves (1984) 34, 49, 149
conteuses 183–4, 198–9nn6–7
   contemporary critiques 184–5
Coole, Diana 105, 107

Coover, Robert 51, 80, 98
Craft, Kuniko 39
Crane, Walter 39
Crenshaw, Kimberlé Williams 74
Créton, Lola 115, *116*
Crofts, Charlotte 49
Crystal, Billy 125
cultural appropriation 178

Dahan, Olivier 115
Dahl, Roald, *Revolting Rhymes* 32–3
Dam, Thomas 125
D'Amore, Laura 83–4
dance productions 37
Dancehall Queen (1997) 54
Darrieussecq, Marie, *Truismes* (Pig Tales) 128–30, 134
databases 41–2
Datlow, Ellen, and Terri Windling, *Snow White, Blood Red* 32
del Toro, Guillermo 7, 34, 77, 119–22, 123
Deleuze, Gilles 100, 101, 104, 107
Demy, Jacques 34, 46
Desblache, Lucille 102
Descartes, René 95, 105, 108
Devsare, Harikrishna 88
Diaz, Cameron 124
digital media 41–2
Dimaline, Cherie, *The Marrow Thieves* 168–9
Dinsdale, Reece *163*
Disenchantment (TV, 2018–) 36
Disney, Walt/Disney Studios 1, 21, 22–3, 29, 33–4, 45, 61
   characterisation of heroines/villains 75, 76–7, 172–3
   critiqued 52–3
   digital media 41, 42, 45–6, 170
   and gender/sexuality 69–70, 75–7
   impact on modern perceptions 52, 69–70, 96–7, 169–73
   merchandising 45–6, 76, 169–70, 198n5
   theme park rides 45, 198n3
   treatment of animal characters 96–7
Divine 76
Do Rozario, Rebecca-Anne 187
Dolce and Gabbana 40

Dollerup, Cay 199*n*8
Donkeyskin (1970) 34, 46
Donoghue, Emma 189
  Kissing the Witch: Old Tales in New Skins 29, 32, 53, 82, 84, 138, 158
Doré, Gustave 11–13
  Les Océanides (Naiades de la Mer) 12, 12–13
Dorson, Richard 78
DragonHeart (1996) 118
dragons, comic/sympathetic representations 118–19
"Dread and Delight: Fairy Tales in an Anxious World" (exhibition, 2018) 39
Duggan, Anne E. 198–9*n*6
Dukas, Paul, *The Sorcerer's Apprentice* 174
Dulac, Edmund 39
Dundes, Alan 28, 166
Duvall, Shelley 35
Dworkin, Andrea 17

ecocriticism 54, 102–5, 157
The Elephant Man (1980) 114
Elias, Norbert 167
Eliot, T. S. 1
Emilie Autumn 38
Enchanted (2007) 34, 147
Ende, Michael, *The NeverEnding Story* 118
Eragon (2006) 119
Erb, Cynthia 97
Estés, Clarissa Pinkola, *Women Who Run with the Wolves* 52
Eurocentrism, of studies/classification systems 186–8
Ever After (1998) 34
Evernden, Neil 111
Ex Machina (2014) 117–18

Faerie Tale Theatre (TV, 1982–87) 35
"Fairy Tale Fashion" (exhibition, 2016) 40
"fairy-tale generation" 98–9
Fairy Tales for Kids (TV, 2011) 175, 176, 177
Fairytale Gloom (card game) 39
fan culture 42
Fanon, Frantz 16
Fantasia (1940) *see* "The Sorcerer's Apprentice"

"Fantasies and Fairy Tales" (exhibition, 2018–19) 39
Faris, Wendy B. 152
fashion 40–1, 48, 126
feminism 16–20, 52–3, 116–17
  and representations of power 188–96
  and gender/sexuality 70–1, 73–5, 79–88, 170–1
  history 73
  second-wave 73, 81–2
  and treatments of socialization 166–9
Figes, Eva, *Tales of Innocence and Experience* 159–60, 161, 168–9
film 33–4
fine arts, representations of fairy tales 39
Florence + the Machine 38–9
folk tale(s) 77–9
  defined/distinguished from fairy tale(s) 72–3, 140
Folktexts (online database) 41
form, and the modern fairy tale 27–9
  see also digital media; film; literature; music; musicals; television; theatre; visual arts
Foucault, Michel 24, 181–3, 198*n*3
The Four Musicians of Bremen (1922) 61
France, development of fairy tale in 183–4
Frank, Arthur 173–4
Franz, Marie-Louise von 3, 171
  Shadow and Evil in Fairy Tales 52
Freeman, Martin 124
Freud, Sigmund 3, 51, 60–1, 164–5
Frost, Samantha 107
Frozen (2013) 34, 76, 125

Gaiman, Neil
  American Gods 147
  Anansi Boys 147
  Coraline 32
  Stardust 32
Gans, Christophe 114
Garland, Alex 117–18
Garner, Alan, *The Weirdstone of Brisingamen* 31–2
Garrone, Matteo 34
gay characters, in retellings of fairy tales 76–7, 82–3
Geetha, V. 63
gender/sexuality 22, 69–89, 157–8

definitions 70–1
and fairy-tale plots 71–2
feminism and 73–5, 79–88
historical contexts 73–5
modern terminology 71–2
in monster narratives 114, 117–18, 119, 128–30
national contexts 77–9
stereotypical representations 75–7, 98–9, 114
Georges, Robert 185–6
"German Fairy Tale Route" 58
Gil, Ariadna 120
Gilbert, Sandra M. and Susan Gubar, *The Madwoman in the Attic* 17, 53
Gilbert, Zoe
  Folk 142–3, 146, 148, *149*, 156
  "Tether" 146, 148
Giroux, Henry 97
Giuntoli, David 135
Gleeson, Domhnall 117
Goldman, William, *The Princess Bride* 31–2
Goldstein, Dina 16, 39
  Fallen Princesses series 7, 48
  Princess Pea 7, 8
  Snowy 7, 8
González, Pedro 114
Goodman, John 125
Gramsci, Antonio 16
graphic novels 33
Greenhill, Pauline 44, 79, 82, 162
Greenwalt, David 140, 153
Grimm, Jacob/Wilhelm 3–4, 35, 77, 147
  Children's and Household Tales 50, 62, 168, 184–5
  "The Donkey" 62
  "Hans My Hedgehog" 62
  "Little Snow White" 96
  "The Robber Bridegroom" 144
  "The Story of a Boy Who Went Forth to Learn Fear" 162
  "The Wolf and the Seven Young Goats" 132
  adoption by Nazi regime 5–6
  comments on predecessors 184–5
  illustrated editions *40*
  legacy 88, 130, 185
  modern commentaries 52, 78, 161–2, 165–6, 167, 168, 184–5
  modern reworkings of tales 32–3, 48, 88
  numbering of stories 185, 186
  tourist trail 58, 197*n*6
  translations of tales 3–4, 88, 185, 199*n*8 *see also titles of tales*
Grimm (TV, 2011–17) 35–6, 135, 145
  use of urban setting 139, 140, 153
Grint, Rupert 124
Gripari, Pierre 114, 130–2
  "Le Gentil petit diable" 130–1
Groening, Matt 36
Groff, Jonathan 125
Grosz, Elizabeth 107
Guattari, Félix 100, 107
Gubar, Susan *see* Gilbert, Sandra M.
Gunawan, Michelle 109
Gupfinger, Reinhard, and Martin Kaltenbrunner, "Animals Make Music: A Look at Non-Human Musical Expression" 66
Guran, Paula (ed.), *Beyond the Woods: Fairy Tales Retold* (2016) 32
Gurimu meisaku gekijou (*Grimm's Fairy Tale Classics*, TV 1987–9) 36

Haas, Lynda 169–70
Haase, Donald 55, 57, 162, 168, 172
Hadestown (stage musical) 37
Hall, Sarah, "Mrs. Fox" 110
Hallett, Martin 39
Halsey, Mark 101
Hamer, Naomi 44
Hammerstein, Oscar 35
Hansel and Gretel: Witch Hunters (2013) 34, 83–4
"Hansel and Gretel" (tale/theme), modern reworkings 8–9, 30, 140, 189, 196
Haraway, Donna 100, 110
  "Cyborg Manifesto" 104, 107
Harries, Elizabeth Wanning 161, 183, 184–5, 199*n*7
Harris Satkunananthan, Anita 199*n*14
Harry Potter and the Philosopher's Stone (2001) 124
Hassenpflug, Marie/Amalie/Jeannette 52
Hawaii, folk tales/traditional culture 160–1, 178
Hawkins, Sally 119, *120*

Haxthausen, Ludowine von 52
Hearne, Joanna 178–9
Heiner, Heidi Anne 41
Heise, Ursula K. 102–3, 104
Hello Kitty's Furry Tale Theatre (1987) 175
Hennard Dutheil de la Rochère, Martine 48
Henson, Jim 35, 61, 162
Hirst, Damien 58
Hitler, Adolf 5, 153
The Hobbit: An Unexpected Journey (2012) 124–5
Hockney, David 39
Hoffmann, E. T. A., "The Sandman" 51
Hoggard, Liz 190
Holbek, Bengt 72
hoʻomanawanui, kuʻualoha 160–1, 178
Hopkinson, Nalo
    "Precious" 105–6
    Skin Folk 94, 105–6
horror, relationship with fairy tale 34
Hot Topic (retail chain) 40
How to Train Your Dragon (2010) 119
Humperdinck, Engelbert, *Hansel and Gretel* 151
Hunt, Margaret 3–4
Hurt, John 35
Hutcheon, Linda 44

illustrations, book 39, *40*
inanimate objects, interaction with 104–6
indigenous cultures 160–1, 177–80
    colonial suppression 187–8
    cultural appropriation 178
    oral-to-electronic transmission 179
    relationship with fairy-tale socialization 179–80
installations 47, 61, 65–6, 91–3
Into the Woods (2014 film) 37
Into the Woods (stage musical) 37
Isaac, Oscar 117

Jagger, Mick 35
James, Marlon, *Black Leopard, Red Wolf* 110
Japan/Japanese culture
    animated film genres 36
    contemporary fairy tales 93
    'Grimm boom' (1980s) 84
    photography 152

Jarvis, Shawn C. *see* Blackwell, Jeannine
John Paul II, Pope 61
Johnson, Virginia 74
Jones, Christine 42
Jones, Doug 119–21, *120*
Jones, Ernst 51
Jones, Felicity 122
Joosen, Vanessa 72, 80, 82, 85
    Critical and Creative Perspectives on Fairy Tales 53
Jordan, Neil 34, 49, 149
Joyce, James
    Finnegans Wake 1
    Ulysses 1
Jung, Carl Gustav 3, 51–2, 164, 165
The Juniper Tree (1990) 34

Kakelaka, Sarah Poniʻala 160–1
Kaltenbrunner, Martin *see* Gupfinger, Reinhard
Kamenetzky, Christa 5
Kanaana, Sharif *see* Muhawi, Ibrahim
Kaplan, David 34, 77
Karasek, Barbara 39
Kawai, Hayao, *The Japanese Psyche: Major Motifs in the Fairy Tales of Japan* 52
Kendrick, Anna 125
Kingdom Hearts (computer game series) 41
Kinsey, Alfred 74
Kipling, Rudyard
    Puck of Pook's Hill 3
    Rewards and Fairies 3
Kolbenschlag, Madonna, *Kiss Sleeping Beauty Goodbye* 53
Kōnoike, Tomoko 47, 54, 91–3, 94, 95, 104
    Donning Animal Skins and Braided Grass 91, 92
    The Planet is Covered by Silvery Sleep 91, 92
Krohn, Karle 185
Kustriz, Anne 171–2

la Fontaine, Jean de 132–3
Lang, Andrew 49, 52–3, 167
    Brown Fairy Book 187
    "The Bunyip" 187
    Colored Fairy Books 3

The Gold of Fairnilee 3
Prince Prigio 3
Lapine, James 37
Lau, Kimberly 81, 85–6
Le Guin, Ursula K. 142
Lebeau, Suzanne, *L'Ogrelet* 114–15
Lee, Sung-Ae 85
Lee, Tanith 51, 189
The Legend of Zelda (computer game) 41
Leprince de Beaumont, Jeanne-Marie, "Beauty and the Beast" 18, 30, 114
Lester, Neal A. 86
Lesuma, Caryn 180
Lewis, C. S. 150–1
   The Horse and His Boy 151
   The Last Battle 151
   The Lion, the Witch and the Wardrobe 30–1, 150–1
   Prince Caspian 151
Lieberman, Marcia, "Some Day My Prince Will Come: Female Acculturation through the Fairy Tale" 52–3, 166–7
Lieberman, Marcia K. 166–7
Linkin, Harriet Kramer 145
The Lion King (1994) 76
literature 29–33
"The Little Mermaid" (Andersen) 13
   modernized retellings 46, 54, 84–5
The Little Mermaid (1989) 34, 76
The Little Mermaid (2021/22, projected) 149
The Little Mermaid (stage musical) 37
Little Otik (2000) 7
"Little Red Riding Hood" (tale/theme)
   cognitive-affective approaches 175
   film/stage versions 34, 37, 45, 77, 175
   literary reworkings 32–3, 49–50, 81, 132–3
   non-anthropocentric adaptations 54
   queered retellings 77
   retellings in song 38
   socializing role 164
   studies 172, 175
   versions aimed at young children 175, 176
   visual adaptations 44–5, 47, 48
Little Red Riding Hood (1922 film) 77
Little Red Riding Hood (1997 film) 34
Lo, Malinda, *Ash* 83

Loaiza Ontiveros, José Rodolfo 39
López, Sergi 120
Lorde, Audre 195–6
Lost Girl (TV, 2010–16) 87, 89
Love Island (TV, 2015–) 137–8
Lukasiewicz, Tracie 147
Lukong, Tani Emmanuel 178, 180
Lurie, Alison 166–7
Lüthi, Max 28–9, 139
Lynch, David 114

Maas, Sarah J.
   A Court of Mist and Fury 83
   A Court of Thorns and Roses 83
MacDonald, George 3
MacDougall, Lewis 122
Macleod, Mark 83
magical realism 109, 140, 143–7, 152
   socio-political elements 147–50
Magritte, René, *The Collective Invention* 46
Maguire, Gregory
   Confessions of an Ugly Stepsister 30
   Mirror, Mirror 154
   Wicked: The Life and Times of the Wicked Witch of the West 30, 154
Maitland, Sara, *Gossip from the Forest* 138, 145, 156–7
Maleficent: Mistress of Evil (2019) 172
Maleficent (2014) 29, 46, 53, 172
Marchesa 41
Marcks, Gerhard 57
Martin, Ann 1–3, 7
Martin, George R. R. 142
Massenet, Jules, *Cendrillon* 151
Masters, William 74
material culture 39–41
Math, Norbert 66
Matrix, Sidney Eve 162
Mattel (toy company) 125, 170–1, 198*n*5
Mayer, Mercer 39
McCoola, Marika *see* Carroll, Emily
McDonald, Kel *see* Ashwin, Kate
McGuire, Seanan 38
McHale, Brian 99
McKillip, Patricia, *Ombria in Shadow* 32
McKinley, Robin, *Beauty: A Retelling of the Story of Beauty and the Beast* 30
McQueen, Alexander 40

Méliès, Georges 1
Mendlesohn, Farah 31
Ménil, René 13–14
Merrick, Joseph 114
Messerli, Alfred 140
metamusic (interdisciplinary art project) 66
Mikulak, Michael, *An [Un]likely Alliance* 111
Miller, D. Scott 15
Minnelli, Liza 35
Mirror Mirror (2012) 34
Misao, Kiryū, *Hontō wa osoroshii Gurimu dōwa (Grimms' Tales really Are Horrific)* 84
Mitchell, Silas Weir 135
Miwa, Yanagi, *Fairy Tale: Strange Stories of Women Young and Old* 152
Mizuno, Sonoya 117
Moana (2016) 76, 178
modernity, of fairy tales 20–2
    destabilization of canon 21–2
    engagement with gender/sexuality 79–88
    and technological developments 20–1
Mohamed, Salima Aït 114
Mollet, Tracey 75, 76
A Monster Calls (2016) 122–3, *123*
Monster High (toy franchise) 125–6
Monsters, Inc. (2001) 125–6
monsters/monstrosity 23, 113–36
    comedic treatments 123–6
    dictionary definitions 113, 136
    French/Argentinian treatments 115–18, 128–35
    merchandising 125–6
    reimagining of traditional figures 114–18
    sympathetic/ambiguous treatments 118–23, 126–8, 135–6
    traditional depictions 114, 133–4
Moon, Sarah 48
Moore, Bryan L. 98
Moore, Leah, and John Reppion, *Damsels* 33
Morey, Larry 45
Morris, Zach 37
Morrison, Toni 195–6
    Beloved 151
Mueller, Andreas 58

Muhawi, Ibrahim, and Sharif Kanaana (eds), *Speak, Bird, Speak Again* 78
Müller-Wood, Anja 100
The Muppet Musicians of Bremen (TV, 1972) 61
Murai, Mayako 84, 91–3, 152
Murait, Henriette-Julie de 184–5
Murphy, Eddie 124
music, interpretations of fairy tales 38–9
musicals (stage) 37
Myers, Mike 124

Napoli, Donna Jo, *Beast* 30
Natalia Kills 38
Nazi regime, role of fairy tale in 5–6
Neeson, Liam 122
Nesbit, E. 3
Ness, Patrick, *A Monster Calls* 122
The NeverEnding Story (1984) 118
'Neverness' (fictional location) 142–3, *149*
Nicolaisen, W. F. H. 137, 139, 140, 141, 143, 148, 151
Nielsen, Kay 39
Nightwish 38
Nikolajeva, Maria 174–5
Norwood, Brandy 35
Nothomb, Amélie, *Barbe bleue* 115–17
Novik, Naomi, *Uprooted* 32
Nugent, Cynthia, *The King's Ears* 41

Oceania, young adult literatures (YALO) 180
ogres
    comic depictions 124
    sympathetic depictions 114–15
    in traditional folk tales 114
Oh, Ellen, and Elsie Chapman (eds), *A Thousand Beginnings and Endings* 32
Okja (2017) 109–10, 126–7, *127*
Once Upon a Mattress (stage musical) 37
Once Upon a Time (card game) 39
Once Upon a Time (TV, 2011–18) 35, 153–4
O'Neill, Katie, *The Tea Dragon Society* 33
Orenstein, Peggy, *Cinderella Ate My Daughter: Dispatches from the Front Lines of the New Girlie-Girl Culture* 170–1
Orr, Lisa 171, 172–3

Ortiz, James, *The Woodsman* 37
O'Toole, Allison, *Wayward Sisters: An Anthology of Monstrous Women* 33
Oyeyemi, Helen 24, 189–96
   Boy, Snow, Bird 30, 53–4, 85–7, 139, 140, 149–50, 151, 189
   Gingerbread 30, 147, 149, 154, 189, 196
   The Icarus Girl 155, 189
   Mr. Fox 139, 140, 151, 155, 189, 194
   The Opposite House 193
   White Is for Witching 189, 190–6
   commentaries on 189–90, 199nn13–15
   manipulation of fairy-tale tropes 180, 193–5
Oziewicz, Marek C. 172, 174, 176–7

Palansky, Mark 34
Pan's Labyrinth (2006) 7, 34, 77, 119–22, *121*, 147–8
Paolini, Christopher, *Eragon* 119
Parisien, Dominik, and Navah Wolfe (eds), *The Starlit Wood: New Fairy Tales* 32
parrots, musical experiments involving 66
Parry, Catherine 94, *95*
The Path (computer game) 41
Pearce, Jackson, *Sisters Red* 84
Pearson, Tom 37
Penelope (2006) 34
Perrault, Charles 18, 51, 52, 130, 198n2
   "Little Red Riding Hood" 38, 48, 49, 132, 168
   "Sleeping Beauty" 157–8
   contemporary/later repute 184–5
   modern commentaries 78, 81, 161–2, 168 *see also* "Bluebeard"
Peter Pan (TV, 1955/1960/2014) 35
Peterson, Andrea L. 42
Pete's Dragon (1977) 118
Pete's Dragon (2016) 118
Le Petit Poucet (2001) 115
photography 47–8, 152
The Piano (1993) 139
Plato 98
Ponyo (2008) 46
Porter, Jessica 199n15
postcolonialism 53–4, 177–8
postmodernism 29, 51, 98–102, 106

Poston, Ashley, *Geekerella* 83
power, representations of 24, 181–96
Prada 41
Pratchett, Terry 142
The Princess and the Frog (2009) 148–9
"The Princess and the Pea," stage/visual representations 7, *8*, 37
Princess Tutu (TV, 2002–3) 36
Propp, Vladimir 28–9
psychoanalysis 3, 51–2, 164–6, 173
Puella Magi Madoka Magica (TV, 2011) 36
Pullman, Philip, *His Dark Materials* 104, 141
Pushkin, Alexander 130

race, treatments of 24, 86–7, 148–9, 190–6
Rackham, Arthur 39, *40*
Radcliffe, Daniel 124
Ragan, Kathleen 72
Ramanathan, Rathna 198n9
Rank, Otto 51
Rao, Sirish, *The Old Animals' Forest Band* 63–5, *64*, *65*
Raven Tales (TV, 2004–10) 179
The Red Shoes (ballet) 37
Rego, Paula 39
   Little Red Riding Hood Suite 47
Reiniger, Lotte 1, 45
Reppion, John *see* Moore, Leah
Revolutionary Girl Utena (TV, 1997) 36
Revolve8 (computer game) 41
Richardson, Greg 170
Rodgers, Richard 35
Rogof, Barbara 180
Rossetti, Christina 188
The Routledge Companion to Media and Fairy-Tale Cultures 44
Rowe, Karen 78
Rowling, J. K., *Harry Potter* series 141
Rudy, Jill Terry 44
Rushdie, Salman 6, 25, 80, 98
   Haroun and the Sea of Stories 103–4, 105
Russell, Karen 107–10
   "Reeling for the Empire" 107–8, 109–10
   Vampires in the Lemon Grove 107

Said, Edward 16
Sam the Sham and the Pharaohs 38
Sanders, Rupert 34
Sarandon, Susan 35
Sasami: Magical Girls Club (TV, 2006–7) 36
Schacker, Jennifer 42, 218n2
  National Dreams 167
Schade, Michael 58
Schlegel, Friedrich 156
Schmiesing, Ann, *Disability, Deformity, and Disease in the Grimms' Fairy Tales* 62
Schwabe, Claudia 145
Seaton, Kit and Cat, *Norroway Book 1: The Black Bull of Norroway* 33
Second World War 4
Seifert, Lewis C., *Fairy Tales, Sexuality, and Gender in France, 1690–1715* 53
Seohyun, Ahn 126, *127*
Sexton, Anne 189
  Transformations 32, 50, 83
sexuality *see* gender/sexuality
Sfé R. Monster 42
Shannon, Michael 119
The Shape of Water (2006) 7, 34, 77, 119, *120*
Shelley, Mary, *Frankenstein; or, The Modern Prometheus* 118
Sherman, Cindy 48
Short, Sue 34
Shrek (2001) 29, 34, 46, 118–19, 124
Simonds, Isobel *149*
Simsolo, Noël 97
Singh, Tarsem 34
"Sleeping Beauty" (tale/theme)
  film versions 1, 34, 45, 172
  literary reworkings 2, 16, 32, 50–1, 157–8
  visual adaptations 44–5, 47–8
The Sleeping Beauty (1922 film) 1
Sleeping Beauty (1959 film) 34, 75–6, 77, 159
Sleeping Beauty: A Gothic Romance (ballet) 37
Smith, Kiki 39
  Born 47, 110
  Companions 47

  Daughters 47
  Gang of Girls and Pack of Wolves 47
  Rapture 47, 110
"Snow White" (tale/theme)
  artistic depictions 7, *8*
  film versions 33, 34, 83–4
  literary reworkings 29, 30, 50, 53–4, 82, 85–6, 139, 190–6
Snow White: A Tale of Terror (TV, 1997) 35
Snow White and the Huntsman (2012) 34, 46, 83–4
Snow White and the Seven Dwarfs (1937) 33, 45, 75, 159, 164
  merchandising/spin-offs 45–6, 169
  use of forest animals 94, 95, 96–7
Snow White with the Red Hair (TV, 2015–16) 36
Snyder, Louis 5
society/socialization 23–4, 159–80
  cognitive-affective approaches 173–7
  and feminism 166–9
  intergenerational relations 159–61
  and psychoanalysis 164–6, 173
  role in fairy-tale narratives 161–2
  through marketed content 169–73
  in traditional cultures 160–1, 162–4, 177–80
Sodomka, Andrea 66
Soja, Edward 143
Sondheim, Stephen 37
"The Sorcerer's Apprentice" (episode from *Fantasia*, 1940) 174
space, treatments of 23, 137–58, 193
  folk tale *vs.* fairy tale 140
  and socio-political context 147–50
  "third space" 143–7, 152
  and time 150–2
  and timelessness 152–7
  use of familiar landmarks 141 *see also* magical realism
Spanish Civil War (1936–9) 4
Steig, William, *Shrek!* 46, 124
Stephanou, Aspasia 199n13
Stone, Kay 71
'Storybrooke' (fictional location) 153–4
The Storyteller (TV, 1987) 35, 162, *163*
Straparola, Giovanni Francesco, *Le piacevoli notti (The Pleasant Nights)* 183, 198n2, 198n4

Studio Ghibli 46, 54, 110
subcreation 142–3, 148, 150
Suddath, Claire 198*n*5
Super Mario Bros (computer game) 41
SurLaLune Fairy Tales (online database) 41
surrealist movement 6–16, 21, 97
    Afro-Caribbean applications 13–15
    gender bias 9–11
Švankmajer, Jan 7
Swinton, Tilda 126

Taggart, James 79
Tale of Tales (2015) 34
The Tale of the Princess Kaguya (2013) 46, 110
Tan, Shaun 39
Tangled (2010) 76, 96
Tanning, Dorothea 11–12, 16
    Birthday 9–10, *10*
    Pour Gustave l'adoré 11, 11–13
Tasty Tales (computer game) 41
Tatar, Maria 17, 162, 166, 172
    Enchanted Hunters 168
    The Hard Facts of the Grimms' Fairy Tales 53
Tchombe, Therese Mungah Shalo 178, 180
technology, developments in 20–1
Tedeschi, Victoria 41
television 35–6
Tell Me a Story (TV, 2018–) 140
Tennant, Andy 34
Teverson, Andrew 106, 164, 177
Thackeray Ritchie, Anne 188
theatre 37 *see also* musicals
Thomas, Dominique 115
Thompson, Stith 186–7, 188 *see also* Aarne-Thompson-Uther (ATU) Tale Type Index
Thornton, Gypsy 42
Timberlake, Justin 125
time lag 150–2
Todrick Hall 42
Tolkien, J. R. R. 25, 142–3, 148, 158
    The Hobbit 142
    The Lord of the Rings 142
    The Silmarillion 142
    "Time and Tide" 142
    theoretical writings 142–3, 148, 156
Traister, Rebecca 76

transformation (magical)
    as defining element 188
transgender identities 71, 86–8
Trapino, Shaina 169–70
trolls, comic/infantilised depictions 124–5
Trolls (2016) 125

Ungerer, Tomi, *Zeralda's Ogre* 115
Uther, Hans-Jörg 186–7 *see also* Aarne-Thompson-Uther (ATU) Tale Type Index

Valente, Catherynne M. 189
    Deathless 30
verse, tales retold in 32–3, 50–1
Vess, Charles 39
Viehmann, Dorothea 52
Vikander, Alicia 117
Villiers, Pierre de, abbé 184–5, 198*n*5
violence, in retellings of fairy tales 83–4
Virgil (P. Vergilius Maro), *Aeneid* 19–20
visual arts 39–41
Vygotsky, Lev 180

Walker, Tom 41
Walckenaer, C. A. 199*n*7
Warner, Marina 17, 19, 95–6, 100, 145–6, 172, 188
    From the Beast to the Blonde: On Fairy Tales and Their Tellers 53
    Fly Away Home: Stories 19–20
Warren, Lesley Ann 35
Watson, Emma 124
Weaver, Sigourney 35
Weems, Carrie Mae 47, 54
Wells, H. G., *The Time Machine* 150
Whatman, Emma 41
Whitley, David 96
Wicked (stage musical) 37
Wild, Dortchen/Marie Elisabeth 50
Wilde, Oscar, *The Happy Prince and Other Stories* 3
Willett, Jennine 37
Williams, Robin 35
Willingham, Bill 189
    Fables 33, 41
Wilson, Rawdon 146, 152
Windling, Terri 42 *see also* Datlow, Ellen
Wirkola, Tommy 34

The Wolf Among Us (computer game) 41
Wolfe, Navah *see* Parisien, Dominik
Wood, Lucy
  "Beachcombing" 144
  Diving Belles 144, 146, 151, 157
Woolf, Virginia 1–2, 3
  Mrs Dalloway 2

Xandria 38

Yanagi, Miwa 47, 54
Yasunari, Kawabata, *Nemureru Bijo* (*House of the Sleeping Beauties*) 157–8
Yolen, Jane, *Briar Rose* 30
young adult literature 179–80

Yūko, Matsumoto, *Tsumibukai hime no otogibanashi (Fairy Tales of Sinful Princesses)* 84
Yumiko, Kurahashi, *Cruel Fairy Tales for Adults* 84–5

Zamora, Lois Parkinson 152
Ziolkowski, Jan M. 62
Zipes, Jack 5–6, 23, 25, 33, 72, 75, 77, 121, 188
  "Breaking the Disney Spell" 169
  Don't Bet on the Prince: Contemporary Feminist Fairy Tales of North America (ed.) 53, 101
  on social indoctrination 161–2, 166, 167–8, 169, 170, 172